IMAGES
of America

MUHLENBERG COUNTY

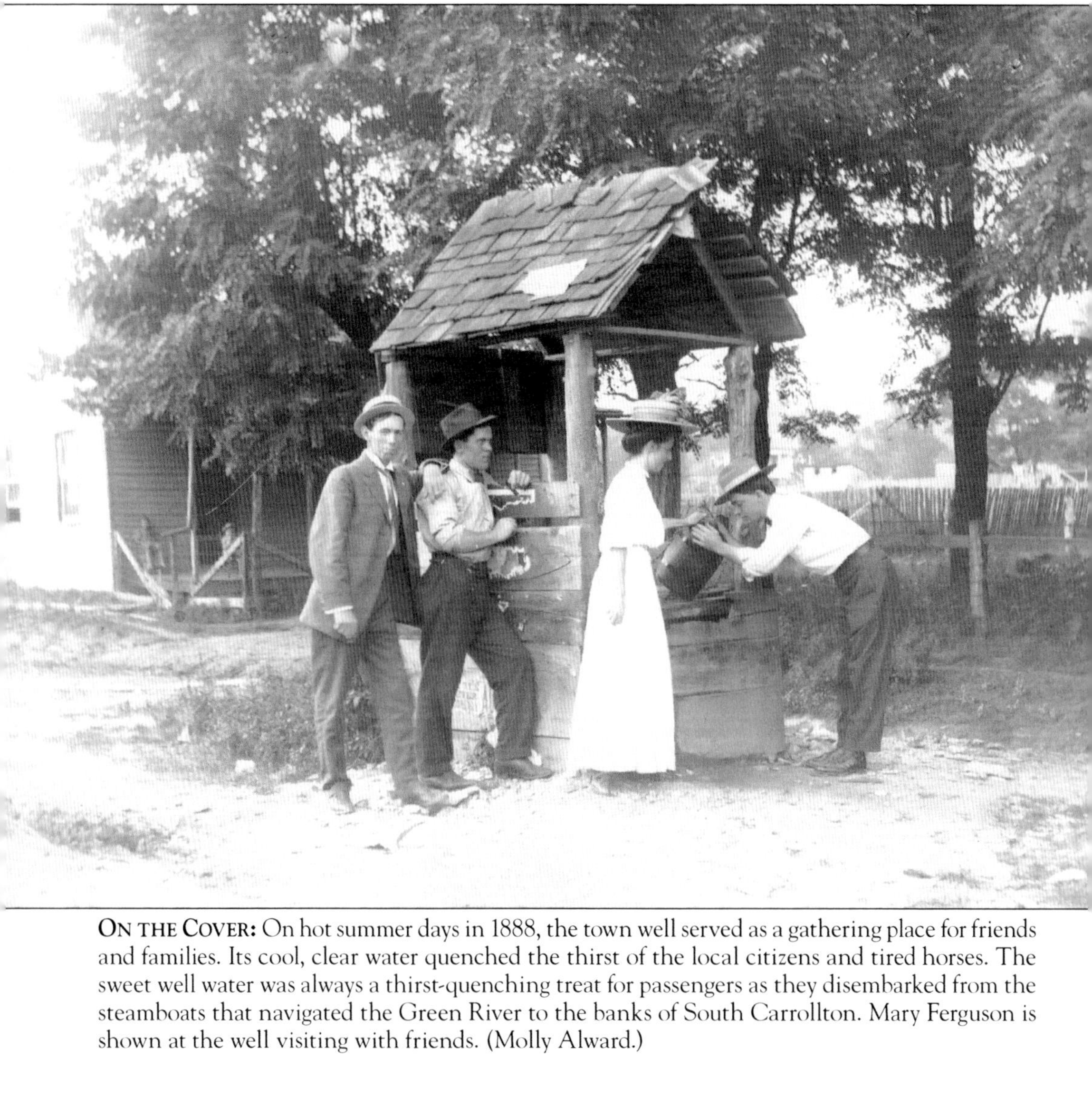

On the Cover: On hot summer days in 1888, the town well served as a gathering place for friends and families. Its cool, clear water quenched the thirst of the local citizens and tired horses. The sweet well water was always a thirst-quenching treat for passengers as they disembarked from the steamboats that navigated the Green River to the banks of South Carrollton. Mary Ferguson is shown at the well visiting with friends. (Molly Alward.)

IMAGES
of America

MUHLENBERG COUNTY

Cleo Roberson and Jan Anderson

ARCADIA
PUBLISHING

ISBN 978-0-7385-6728-0

Published by Arcadia Publishing
Charleston, South Carolina

Printed in the United States of America

Library of Congress Catalog Card Number: 2008926848

For all general information contact Arcadia Publishing at:
Telephone 843-853-2070
Fax 843-853-0044
E-mail sales@arcadiapublishing.com
For customer service and orders:
Toll-Free 1-888-313-2665

Visit us on the Internet at www.arcadiapublishing.com

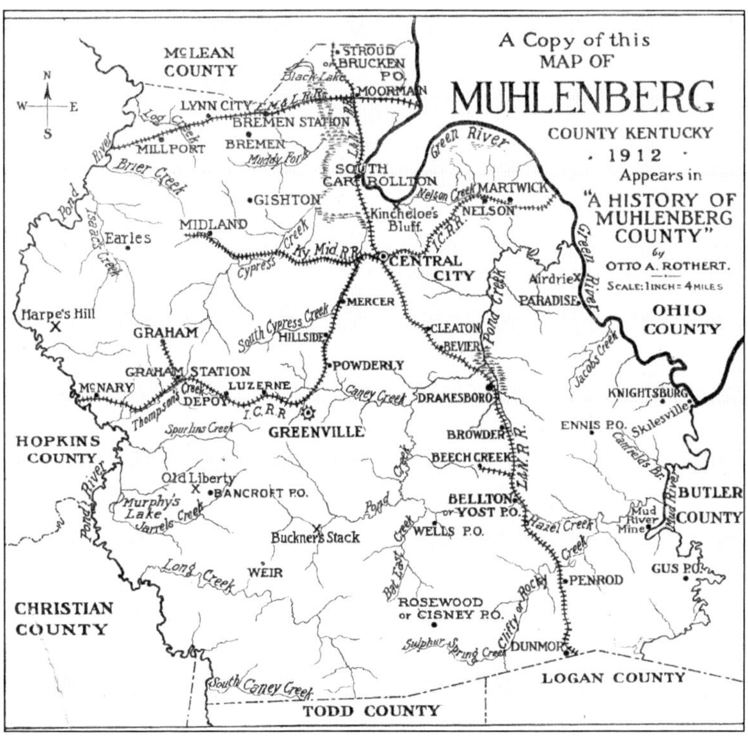

This 1912
map shows
Muhlenberg County.
(Christine Hinsey.)

Contents

Acknowledgments		6
Introduction		7
1.	Muhlenberg in the Beginning	9
2.	Business Ventures	27
3.	Faith and Education	51
4.	Medical Moments	67
5.	Public Service and Energy	75
6.	Military Matters	87
7.	Sorrow and Hardships	97
8.	Coal Mines and Miners	105
9.	Arts, Music, and Entertainment	119

ACKNOWLEDGMENTS

Special thanks go to our husbands for tolerating our absences; and to our children, grandchildren, and friends, who encouraged us by kind words, good deeds, prayers, and smiles. A heartfelt bow goes to our editor, Luke Cunningham, who plied us with inspiration, regaled us with tales, patiently tracked our progress, and gave us words of encouragement (and danced on his desk) as we neared the finish line—on time. And a million thanks to the people who said, "Sure, I can help!" and did help in so many ways with pictures, facts, dates, mementos, articles, reference books, names of people and places, and with sharing their time and their pieces of history with us: Anise Williams; Bobby Anderson; Carol McClure; Christine Hinsey for the Gayle Carver Collection; Diane Stringer; Don Roberson; Duncan Center and museum staff Peggy Gossett and Shara Snodgrass; H. L. Anderson Jr.; Georgiana Dotson; Irvin W. Gary; Jan Dempsey; Jim Walker; Joe Ben Tucker; Ken and Virginia Cummins; Larry and Venita Ray; *Leader-News* staff and Jowanna Bandy; Loretta and Jimmy Grace; Lyda Newman; Mollie Alward; Muhlenberg Community Hospital staff; Muhlenberg County Central City Library staff; Greenville Harbin Memorial Library staff; Wayne Crist; Richard Devers; Eddie Page; Patti Pryor; Robert Lawton; Patsy and Bobby Dunn; June and Leslie Scott; Thomas Brizendine; *Times Argus* staff and Mark Stone; W. L. Raymer; JoAnna Fox; Lin Cisney; Charles Cohen; and Jerry Solzman.

INTRODUCTION

"There is a time for war and a time for peace!" thundered the preacher. "And now is the time for war!" As those words hung in the air of the small church in Woodstock, Virginia, on January 21, 1776, legend has it that Rev. John Peter Gabriel Muhlenberg stepped down from the pulpit and removed his clerical robes to reveal his colonel's uniform beneath. He never wore his clerical robes again.

The next day, Colonel Muhlenberg led 300 men out of the county to begin the formation of the 8th Virginia Regiment of the Continental Army at the personal request of his friend Gen. George Washington. He and his men distinguished themselves as soldiers and patriots while forming friendships that would last a lifetime. At the end of the Revolutionary War, Colonel Muhlenberg was promoted to major general and settled in Pennsylvania. He served in Congress and in the U.S. Senate. He served as vice president of Pennsylvania during the presidency of Benjamin Franklin and was later appointed as customs collector for Philadelphia and served in that capacity until his death in 1802. He died never setting foot in the county that carried his name.

According to *Rothert's History*, 76 Revolutionary War veterans were the first white settlers in Muhlenberg County. Among these first pioneer soldiers was Capt. Henry Rhodes, who had served under General Muhlenberg. Rhodes and his two brothers established Rhodesville (later named Calhoun) before moving to his half of a 7,000-acre land grant in Logan County. Part of Logan County became Muhlenberg County, and in 1793 Rhodes settled in what is now Browder.

In 1790, James Inman left the first Rhodesville settlement, moved 5 miles south, and built Pond Station. In 1795, Caney Station was established 1 mile north of Greenville on land granted to Col. William Campbell, his wife Tabitha, and Gen. William Russell following the Revolutionary War. General Russell had also been part of General Muhlenberg's brigade.

In 1798, some of the first pioneers in the area established a small store, farm, and boat landing on Green River called Stum's Landing. Leonard Stum and his sons, Jake and Henry, helped run the farm, store, and landing where mail and supplies were delivered. Mail brought into the county was delivered on horseback or by stagecoach. In 1798, while serving as the representative for Logan County, Rhodes had the new adjoining county named Muhlenberg in honor of his pastor, friend, comrade, and general of the Revolutionary War.

By 1800, the population of Muhlenberg County had grown to 1,443. One quarter of the county's residents were children of Revolutionary War veterans and their descendants from Pennsylvania, North Carolina, and Virginia. At the end of the War of 1812, the county began to fill with settlers, including the Irish and the English who felt the area was safer from Native Americans and marauders now with experienced soldiers living in the settlements.

In 1820, the first coal deposits were mined from the area around Stum's landing by Alney McLean, but the coal drew little attention until 1855, when dwindling iron reserves in Scotland forced Sir R. S. C. A. Alexander to look for other sources of iron. He became convinced the ore in Muhlenberg County would be a good substitute for Scotland's ore and bought 17,000 acres of land. He invested $300,000 in building a smelting furnace, a home for himself, and a village for his workers. He named the town Airdrie after his home in Scotland.

Like Buckner's Stack before him, the venture never paid off, and Alexander closed the furnace. He left the dream behind along with his Scottish stonemasons, carpenters, architects, miners, engineers, blacksmiths, and furnace tenders. On their own, the Scottish people continued to pump new blood, new skills, and excitement into the county. The town of Airdrie continued to survive without its fiery furnace and even provided a peaceful home and retreat for Gen. Don Carlos Buell following the Civil War. General Buell, who had saved Gen. Ulysses S. Grant from defeat at Shiloh, retired to Airdrie to write his articles and memoirs.

In 1861, the Civil War again called the men of the county to battle. Though the majority of the locals signed with the Union army, the Confederate army had its followers too, and heroes arose from both sides. Edward R. Weir Sr. was considered the leader of the Union men, while Simon Buckner was the most noted of the Confederate leaders. Following the war, the veterans' reunions held in the county had soldiers of both sides in attendance. Soldiers from Muhlenberg County would answer the call to serve in every war ever fought for their country.

By 1870, Ulysses S. Grant was president, railroad bonds had been issued for the county, and new businesses along with the new courthouse had changed the face of the county. The county's tobacco business peaked from 1892 through 1898, reaching its production height at around one million pounds a year, and the coal business began to rapidly expand with the introduction of the railroad. Now coal could be loaded directly at the mines and shipped across the country. The 26 county mines operating in 1911 produced a total of 2,225,662 tons with an average of 3,504 employees. Of these men, 3,067 worked underground, and 437 worked on the surface. By 1972, surface mines outnumbered underground mines, and county production had risen to 26,083,768 tons a year. The largest stripping shovel in the world and the development of continuous mining machines contributed to securing the vast coal stores for plants like the Tennessee Valley Authority's Paradise Plant, which was one the world's largest steam generating plants built in the county in the 1960s.

The mining business made the county famous at an industrial level, but it was the music industry that made it known to the world. In 1946, Merle Travis, a singer and songwriter, penned the song *Sixteen Tons* about his father's life as a coal miner. John Prine's *Paradise*, in 1971, reminded the world again that the demand for coal exacts a toll on the people and the area where coal is found. But all the music from the county was not sad, and in 1957, the Everly Brothers again put Muhlenberg County front and center with their first hit, *Bye, Bye Love*. Like Merle Travis, their father, Ike, had worked in the coal mines, but not for long. Attempting to safeguard his sons from the mining vocation of his youth, he taught them to harmonize and play the guitar. It paid off. Fifteen hit tunes followed for the brothers between 1957 and 1967. Other musicians, artists, and actors have made the county proud, and among them are James Best, Warren Oates, and Jim Walker, a world-renowned flutist. His flute can be heard on the sound tracks of *Monsters Inc.*, *Far and Away*, *Memoirs of a Geisha*, *Titanic*, and many others. As evidenced by its history, Muhlenberg County has been blessed with natural resources that have provided for an entire nation's needs. But the greatest resource of all that the county continues to offer to the world is the knowledge, diversity, strengths, and talents of her people. That's what makes Muhlenberg County so very special.

One

MUHLENBERG IN THE BEGINNING

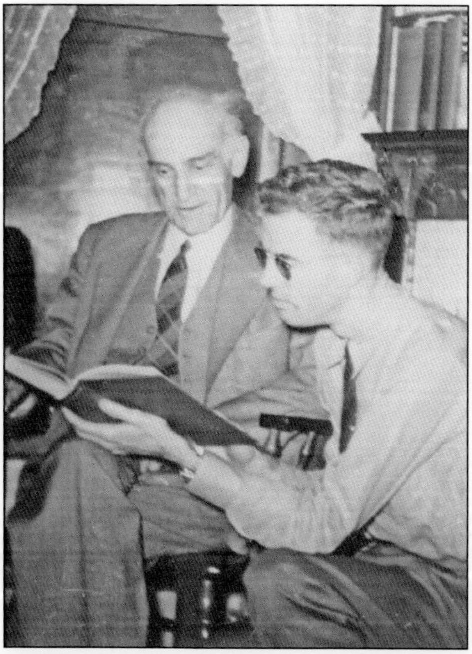

The history of Muhlenberg County lives on because of people like Otto Rothert (1871–1956) and Gayle Carver (1914–2006). These two men shared a common love for Muhlenberg County, its history, and its people. Rothert (left) published his extensive *History of Muhlenberg County* in 1913 detailing the lives of the early settlers as well as the lives of their descendants. He left no stone unturned in his quest for accuracy and validation. Gayle Carver returned to Greenville after serving 31 years as curator of the Kentucky Building at Western Kentucky University in 1971. He began volunteering at the Harbin Memorial Library, using his knowledge of the county's families to help people research their roots. His dedication was a factor in the establishment of the library annex dedicated to genealogical research. The pictures and the information compiled in this book would not have been available or possible without the hard work of these two men and other avid historians of our county, like Bobby Anderson, Paul Camplin, Agnes Harralson, and Leslie Shively Smith. (Christine Hinsey.)

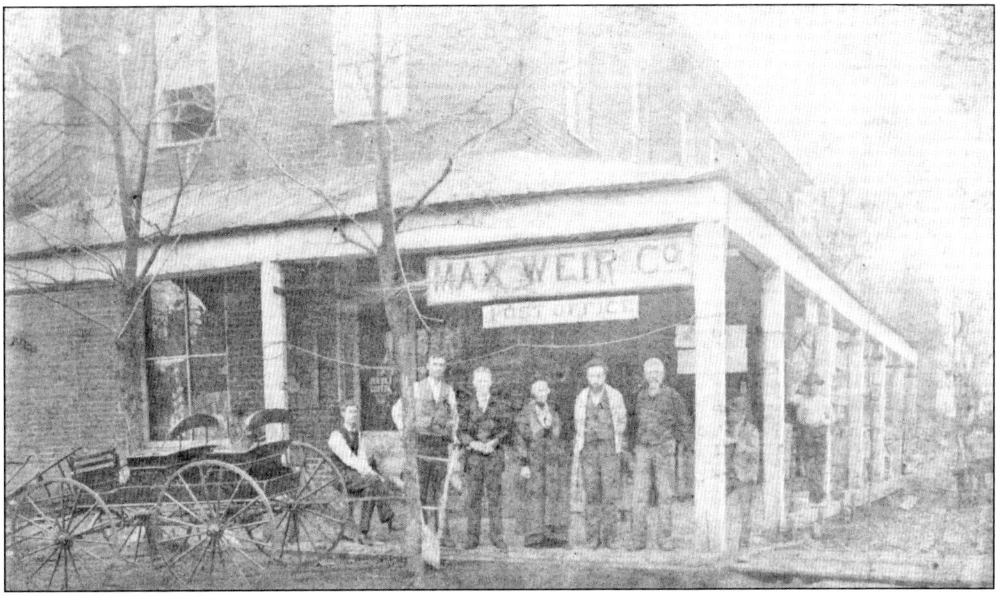

In 1812, the Max Weir store was the business hub on the corner of Main Street in Greenville. Max, the son of Edward and Harriet Weir, was known for being a handsome bachelor, a popular merchant, a devout Christian, secretary of the YMCA, and a writer. When Max died in 1904, he left $7,500 to the local YMCA for a new building. (Christine Hinsey.)

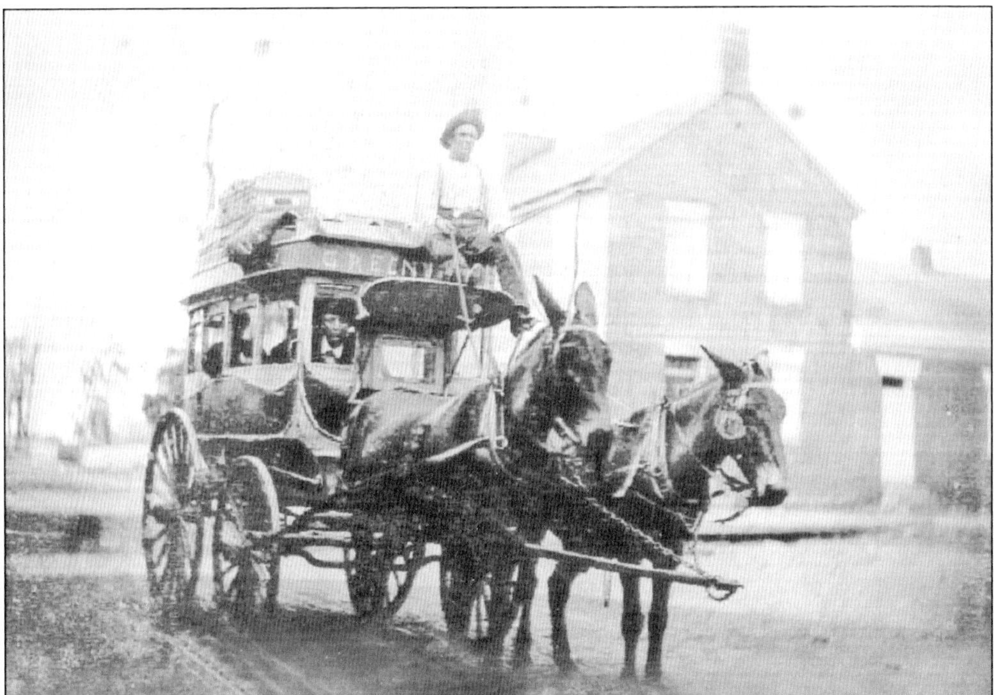

The mail coach made its runs through the county from Owensboro twice a week in the 1800s, carrying supplies and letters picked up from landings and post offices along the way. The coach also sometimes carried passengers, who arrived tired and dirty from their trips. Only the hardiest, most seasoned, or most exhausted passengers could sleep in the jolting confines of the coach. (Christine Hinsey.)

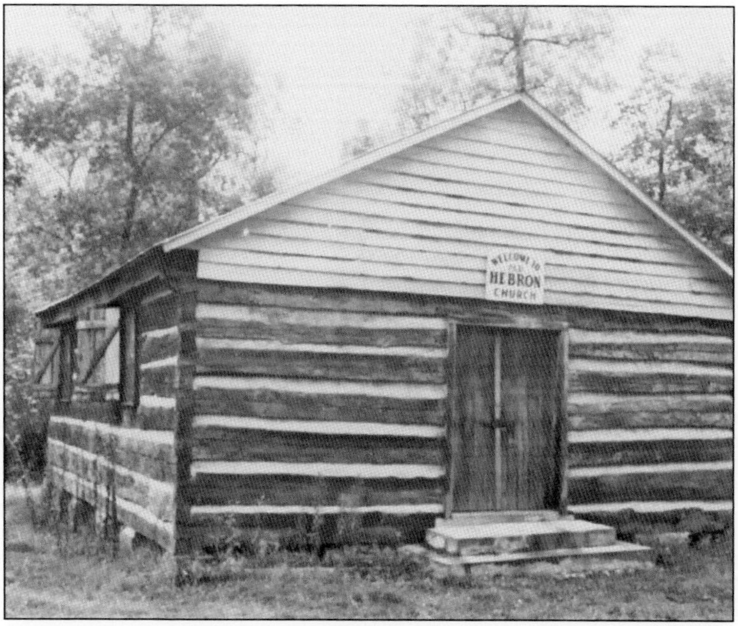

The Old Hebron Church, established in 1816, was the first log chapel in the Hunt Settlement, located near Penrod, Kentucky. John Hunt, a Revolutionary War soldier, received a large land grant for his war service and, along with his family, established the Hunt Settlement in the early 1800s. Daniel, his son, donated the land for the Old Hebron Church site and cemetery where his parents are buried. (Christine Hinsey.)

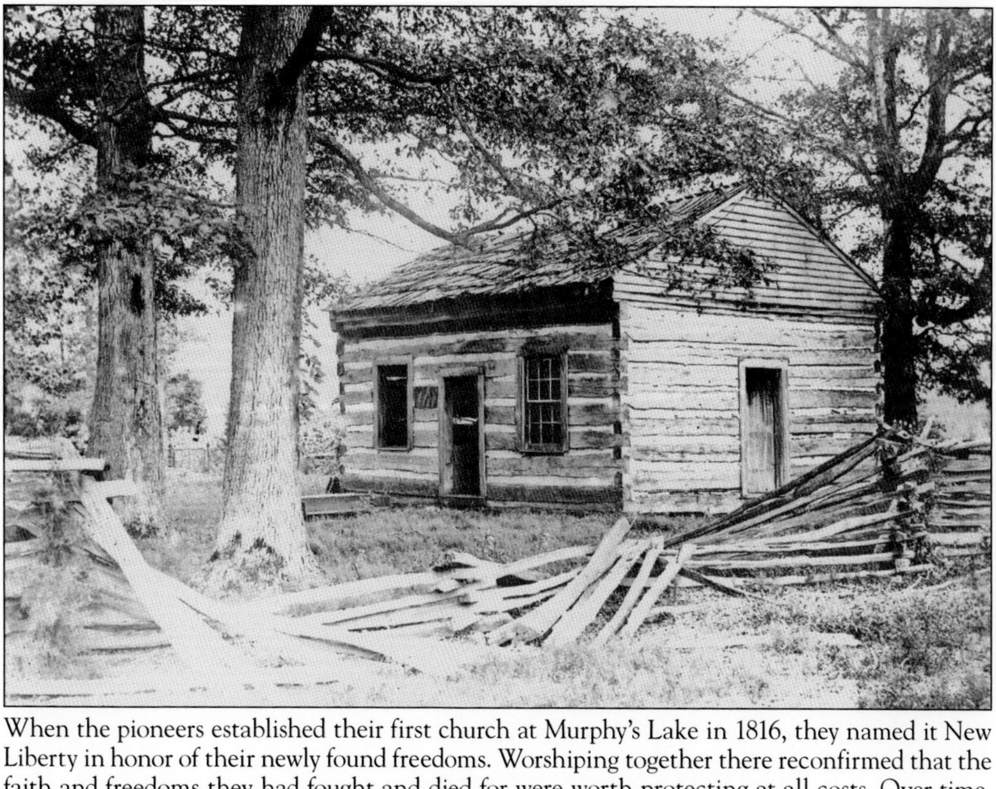

When the pioneers established their first church at Murphy's Lake in 1816, they named it New Liberty in honor of their newly found freedoms. Worshiping together there reconfirmed that the faith and freedoms they had fought and died for were worth protecting at all costs. Over time, the church and its grounds came to be called Old Liberty. (Christine Hinsey.)

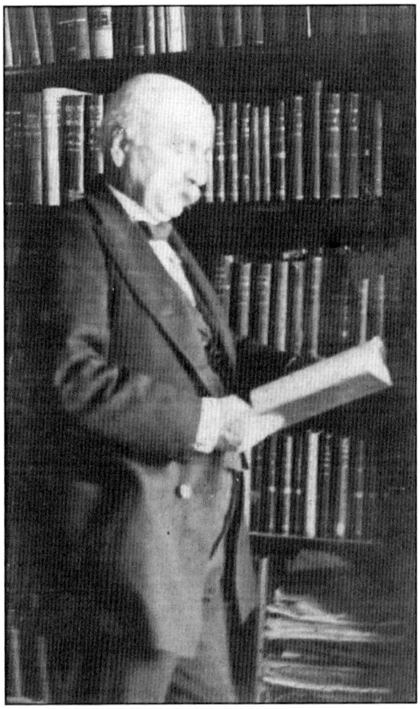

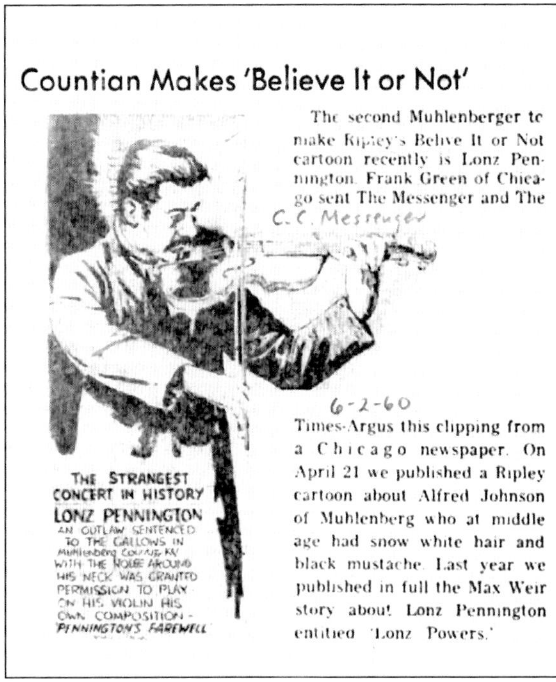

Countian Makes 'Believe It or Not'

The second Muhlenberger to make Ripley's Belive It or Not cartoon recently is Lonz Pennington. Frank Green of Chicago sent The Messenger and The Times-Argus this clipping from a Chicago newspaper. On April 21 we published a Ripley cartoon about Alfred Johnson of Muhlenberg who at middle age had snow white hair and black mustache. Last year we published in full the Max Weir story about Lonz Pennington entitled 'Lonz Powers.'

James Weir Jr., a banker, writer, and lawyer, wrote the book *Lonz Powers*, describing the capture of the leader of a band of cutthroats from Muhlenberg County who was hung in Christian County. Legend has it that Powers, also known as Pennington, maintained his innocence to the gallows, where he requested his violin to play one last song. This scene was featured in a *Ripley's Believe It or Not* strip in 1960. A comrade of Lonz's confessed to the murder on his death bed. (Christine Hinsey.)

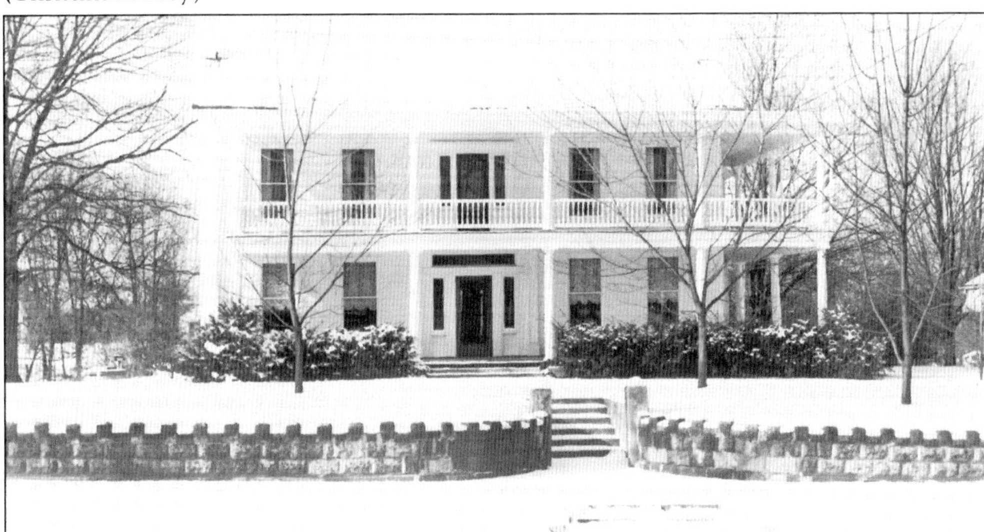

The George Short house at 151 Main Street in Greenville was built to woo Tabitha Brank into marriage. Rejected, George gave the house to his sister instead. The beautiful home that love built is still standing and belongs to Sue Walters. It has been placed on the Kentucky and National Register of Historic Places. (Tom Brizendine.)

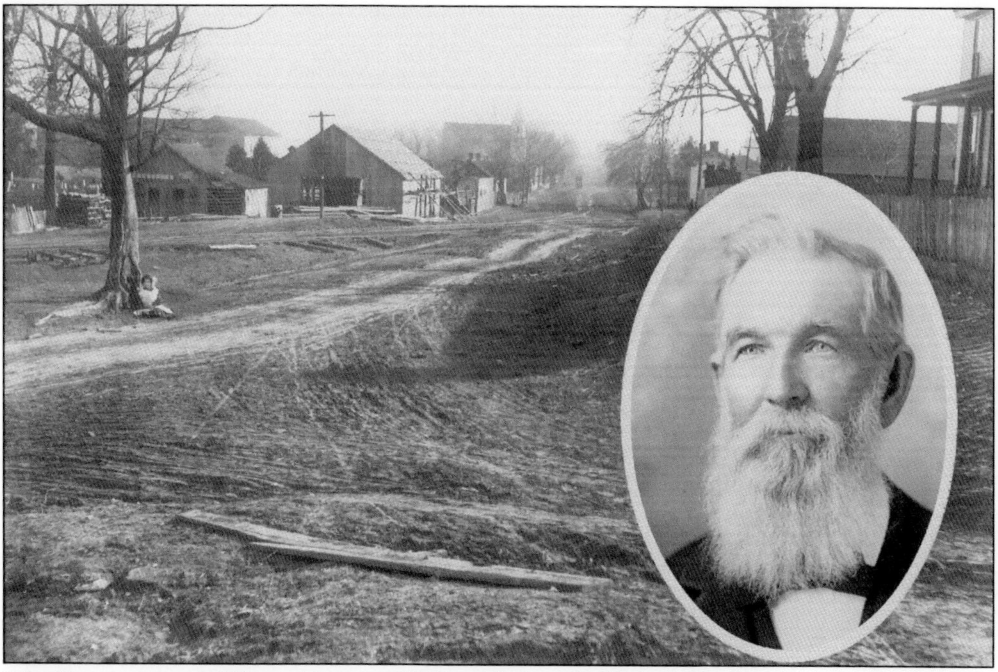

John Fentress married Elinor Dozer in 1805 and built a double log cabin on the bluff above Green River. He began a ferry operation on the river and in 1838 laid out the town of South Carrollton on what was formerly known as the Old Randolph Farm. He sold off lots to the town and it grew as a port of commerce for many years. (Molly Alward.)

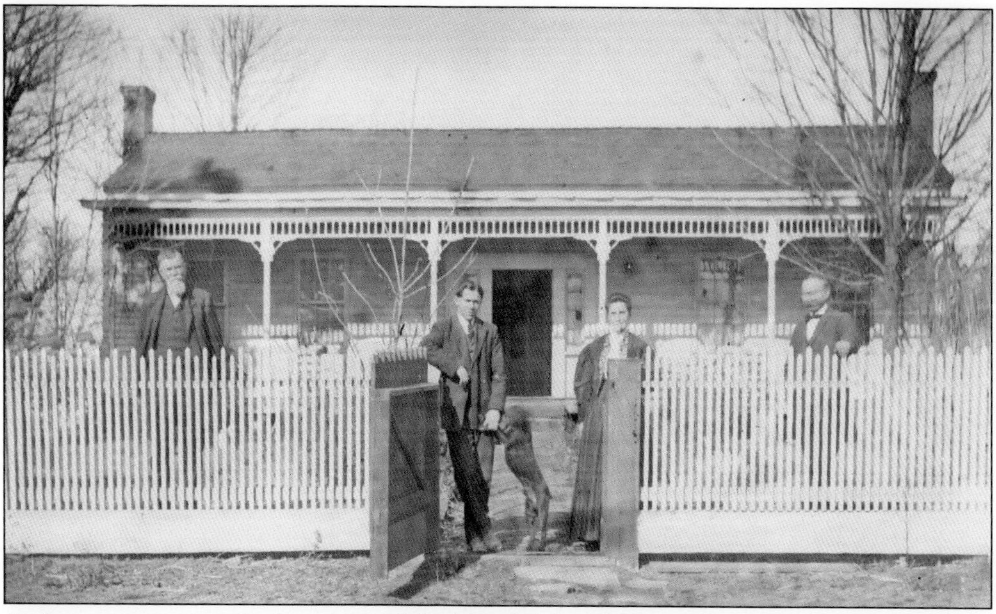

A glass negative reveals the image of the Marples' and Walstons' home in South Carrollton around 1900. The house was bought by Joe and McCowan Ferguson in 1906 and was part of the Ferguson farm until 1937. Virginia and Ken Cummins now own the home that has stood steadfast since the Civil War. From left to right are Warren Marple, Lee Walston, a loyal dog, aunt Sebe Walston, and Will Walston. (Virginia and Ken Cummins.)

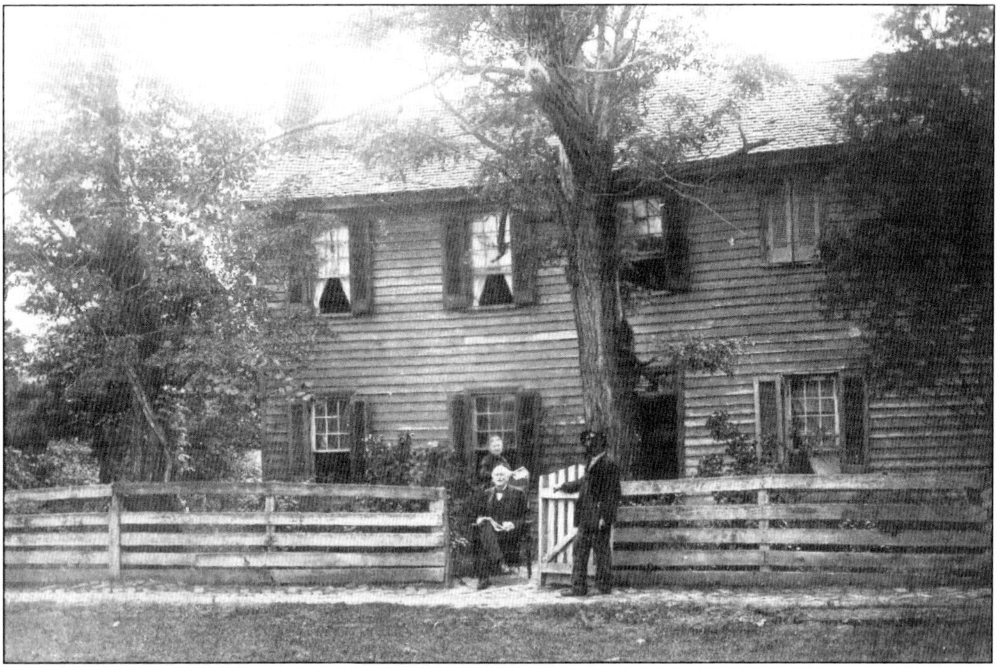

The Charles Fox Wing home, as it looked in 1891, was owned by a man revered for his intelligence and patriotism. He was a hero of the War of 1812 and served as county court clerk for over 50 years. He was passionate about his country and was buried in the American flag he had raised and lowered at the courthouse for the last 15 years of his life. (Christine Hinsey.)

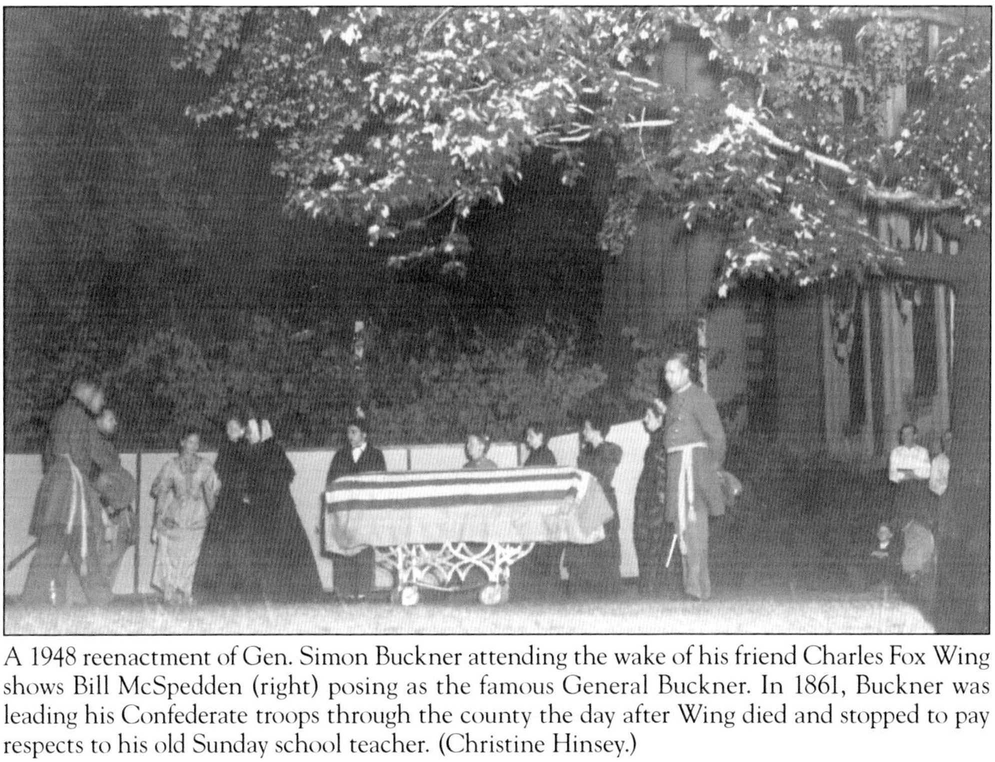

A 1948 reenactment of Gen. Simon Buckner attending the wake of his friend Charles Fox Wing shows Bill McSpedden (right) posing as the famous General Buckner. In 1861, Buckner was leading his Confederate troops through the county the day after Wing died and stopped to pay respects to his old Sunday school teacher. (Christine Hinsey.)

Alyette Buckner and Cadwalader Churchill built their iron smelting furnace in Muhlenberg County in 1838. The men had found ore deposits in the county sufficient to meet their needs for more than a century. After successfully operating their furnace for four years, the shipping costs became prohibitive, and they abandoned their furnace. Confederate general Simon Buckner was the son of Alyette Buckner. (Christine Hinsey.)

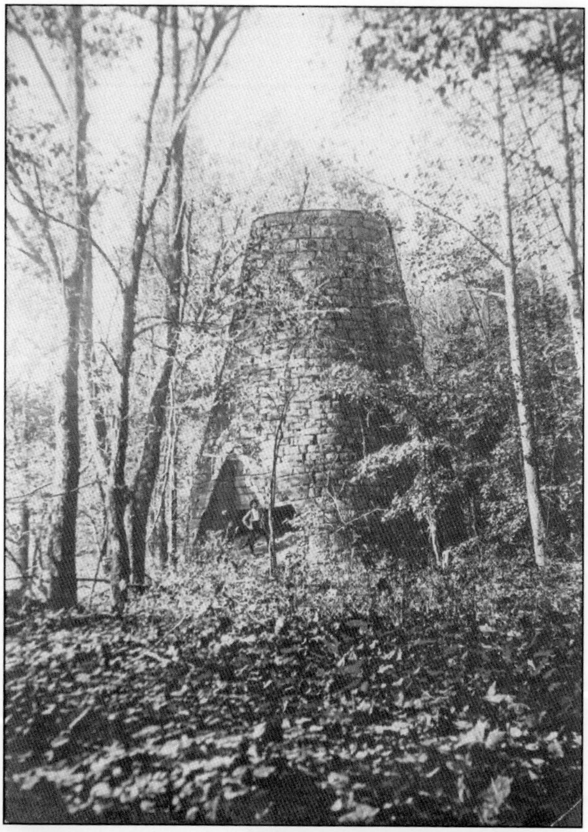

In 1965, state representative James Hahn admires the Buckner-Churchill Furnace historic marker No. 1389 in Drakesboro. This marker lists products made from the local pig iron, such as kettles, shovels, tongs, and andirons. The marker sites 1842 as the last blast from the furnace. Standing to the right of the marker are James Hahn (left) and Jim Wilcox. Others are unidentified. (Christine Hinsey.)

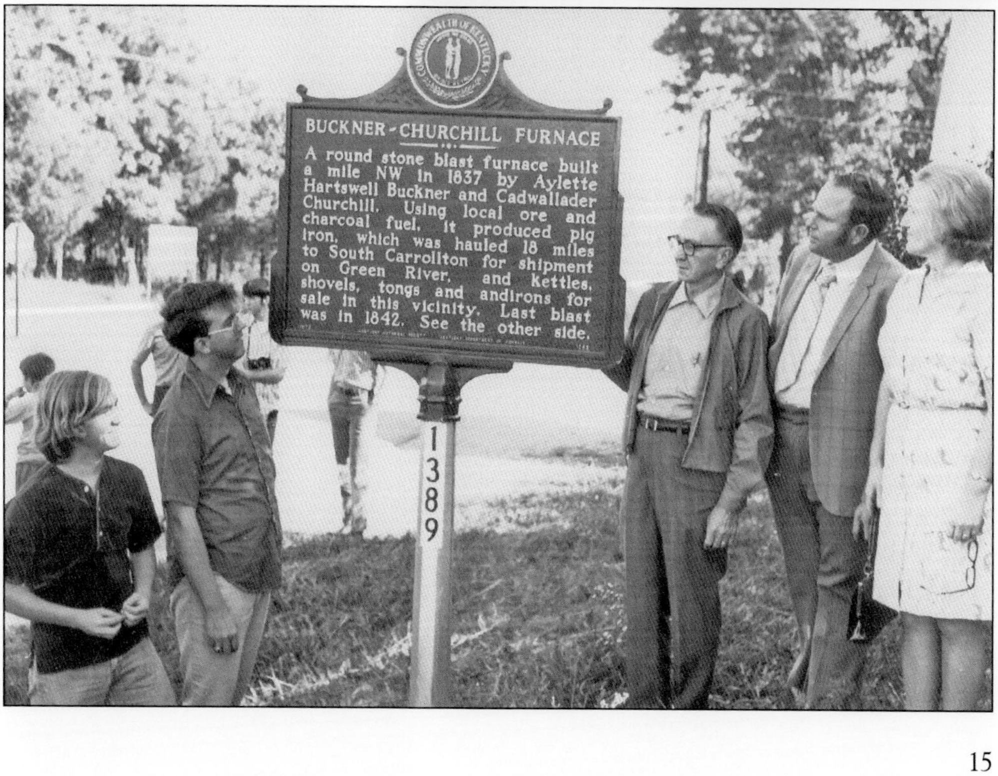

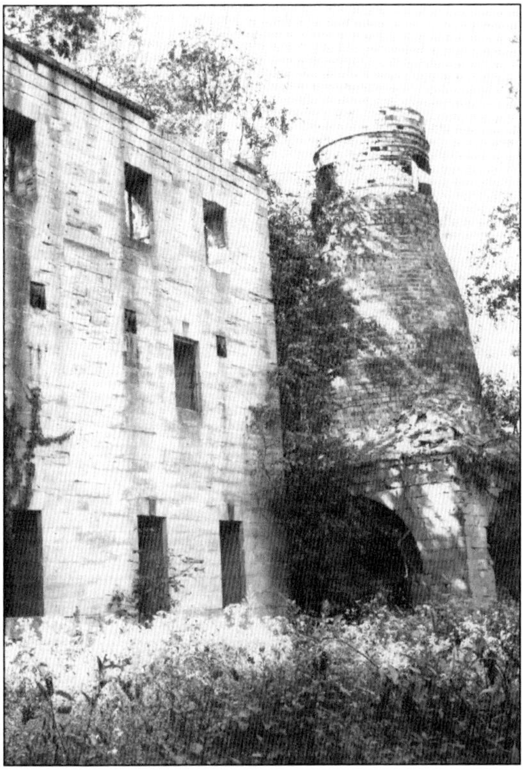

Whispers of a dream on a windswept hill end with the abrupt manifestation of a lonely icon to impatience. A ghostly furnace is all that remains of a once grand attempt by Sir Robert Alexander to produce pig iron in Muhlenberg County. In 1855, he bought 17,000 acres and spent over $300,000 to build a town named Airdrie, complete with a smelting furnace. He brought masons, carpenters, metal workers, miners, engineers, and furnace tenders from Scotland who were not familiar with the local ores. They experimented with methods to adapt their processes, but after two months, Sir Robert grew impatient, shut the furnace down, and left the area and all of his Scottish workers and families behind. (Christine Hinsey.)

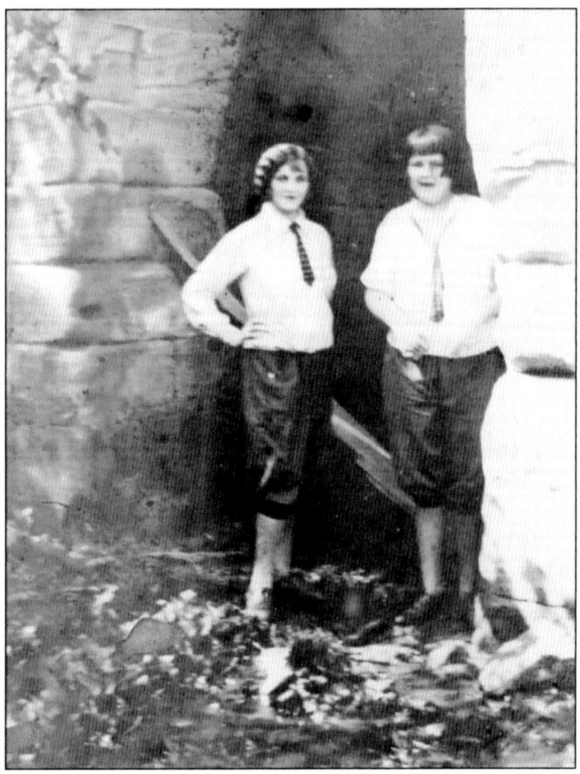

Enjoying a visit to Old Airdrie in 1928 are Lorraine Grable (left) and Margie Brownie Grable. (Don Roberson.)

The Ezekiel Rice Putnam family poses for a photograph in 1898. From left to right are (first row) Paul, father Ezekiel, baby brother Hugh, and mother Sarah Jane; (second row) siblings Edgar, Mary Jane, Claude, and Clyde. (Jan Anderson.)

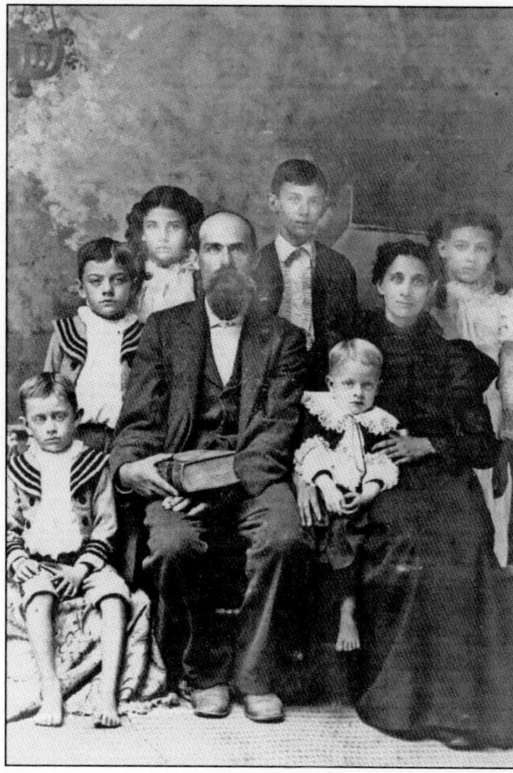

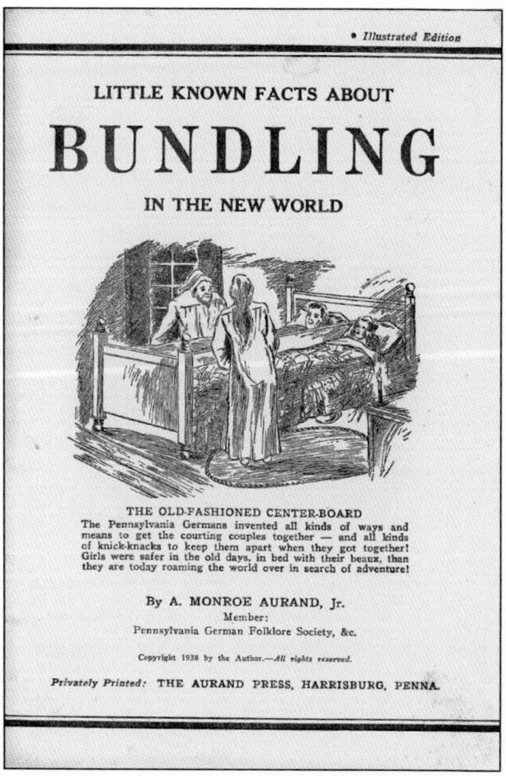

• *Illustrated Edition*

LITTLE KNOWN FACTS ABOUT

BUNDLING

IN THE NEW WORLD

THE OLD-FASHIONED CENTER-BOARD

The Pennsylvania Germans invented all kinds of ways and means to get the courting couples together — and all kinds of knick-knacks to keep them apart when they got together! Girls were safer in the old days, in bed with their beaux, than they are today roaming the world over in search of adventure!

By A. MONROE AURAND, Jr.
Member:
Pennsylvania German Folklore Society, &c.

Copyright 1938 by the Author.—*All rights reserved.*

Privately Printed: THE AURAND PRESS, HARRISBURG, PENNA.

A pamphlet available in the 1700s listed the pros and cons of "bundling." When a shortage of beds existed, parents placed members of the opposite sex in blankets or in long pillowcase-type sackings secured with drawstrings at the top. Using this method, supposedly, members of the opposite sex could share a bed without becoming intimate. Sometimes a "bundling board" was placed between the parties instead. Unfortunately, in some cases, pregnancies were known to have occurred even with the bundling techniques in place. (Molly Alward.)

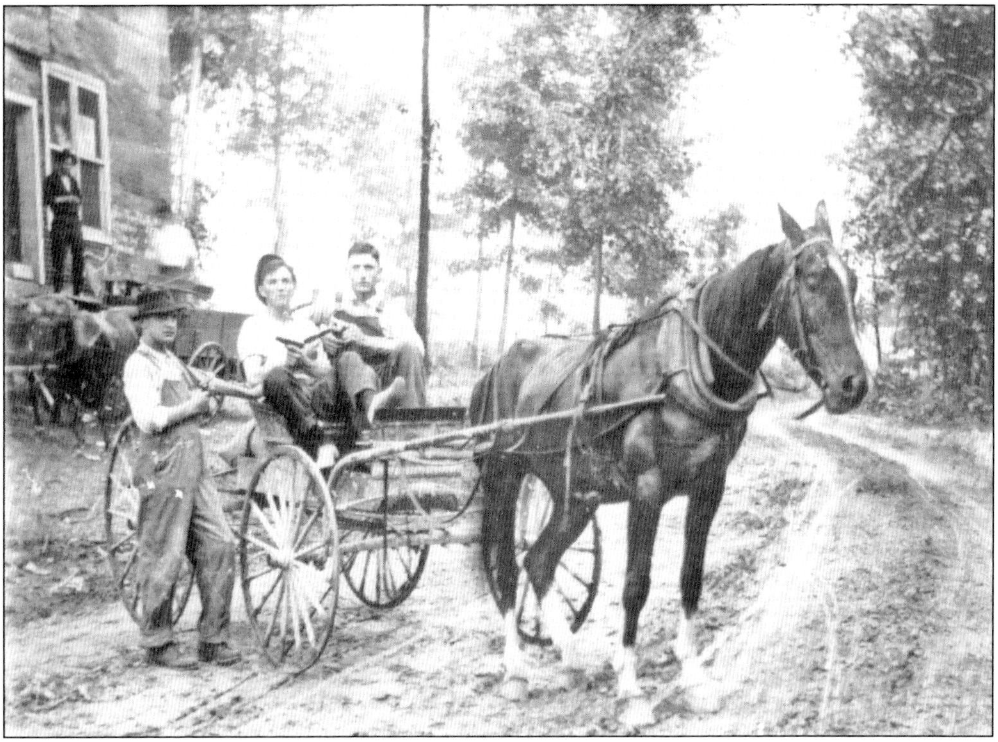

Around 1898, three unidentified men wait in a buggy outside the general store on Main Street in Paradise, Kentucky. The town of Paradise, established in 1798, completely disappeared in 1967, as the town's last residents left their homes behind to make way for the Tennessee Valley Authority to build the world's largest steam generating plant on the Green River. (Christine Hinsey.)

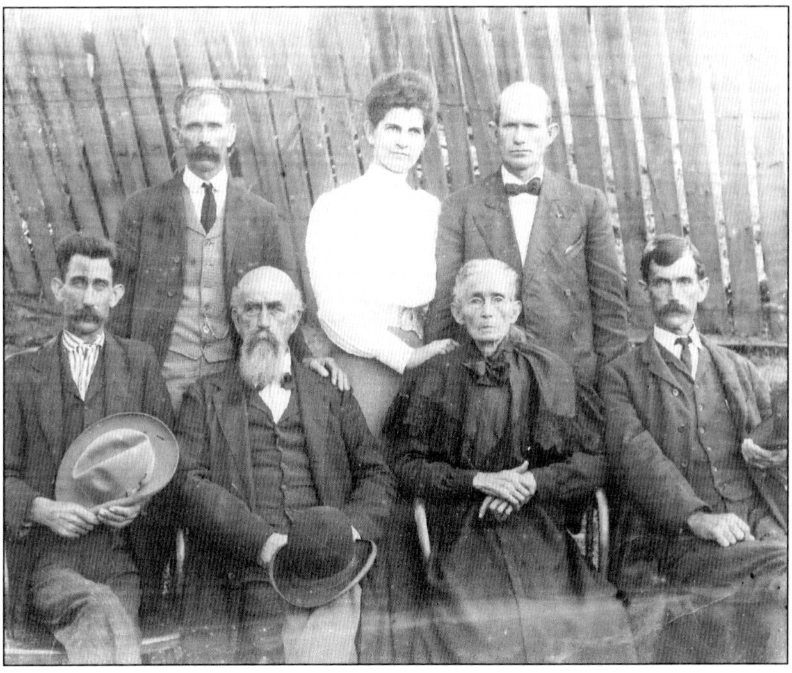

Rev. George Jeffries's family is pictured around 1880 in South Carrollton. From left to right are (first row) Jackson Jeffries, Rev. George Jeffries, Margaret Jeffries, and Willie Jeffries; (second row) Dotson Jeffries, Bettie Jeffries Blackwell, and Johnny Jeffries. (Molly Alward.)

A 1860s locomotive represents the rail system's introduction to Muhlenberg County. Prior to the railroad's appearance, goods were shipped on the Green River, which was expensive and inconvenient. The first railroads in the county renewed the opportunity for industrial growth, as coal mines opened along it, farmers and traders began to ship on it, property values rose, and more settlers found their way into the county. (Christine Hinsey.)

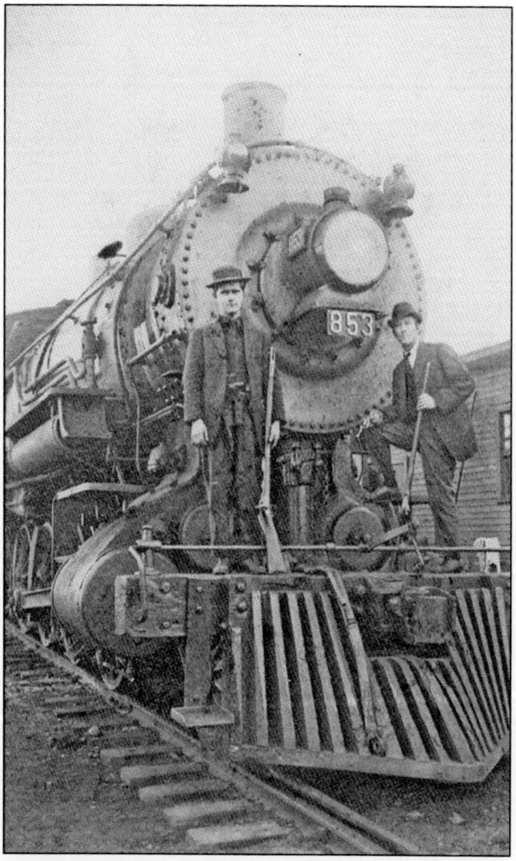

Capt. William H. H. Sandusky opened the Sandusky Hotel in 1878 along the line of the Illinois Central Railroad in downtown Central City. It was a popular haven for travelers until it burned in 1909. Geneva Sandusky, the beautiful daughter of the captain, was reported to have been a congenial and gracious hostess to all the travelers who visited there. (Christine Hinsey.)

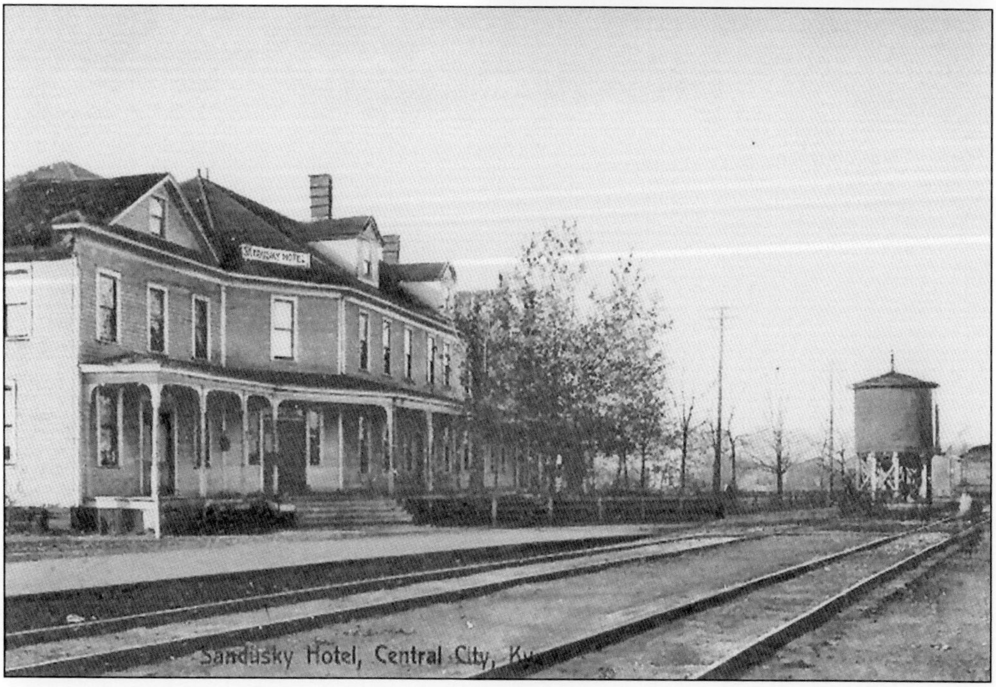

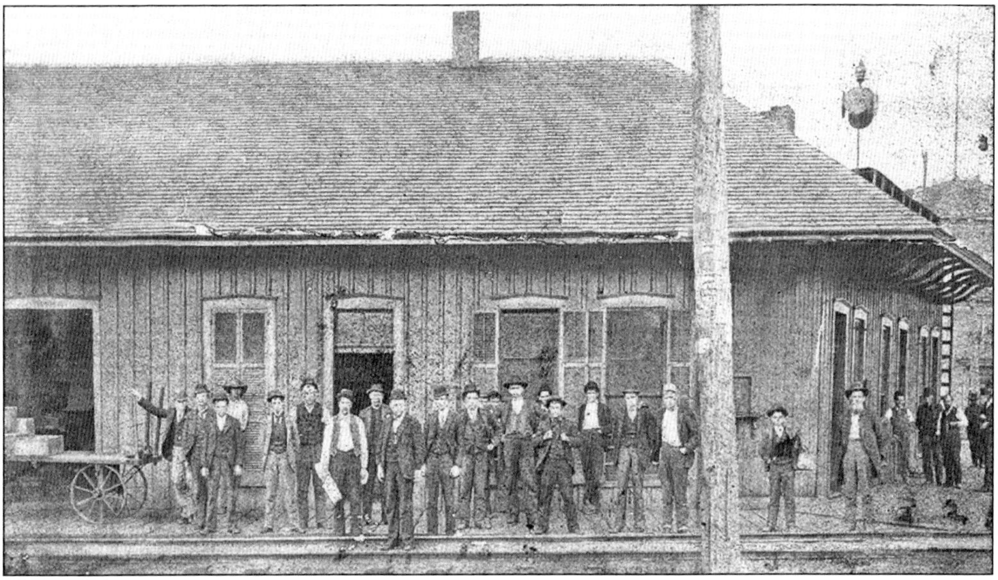

Union Station in Central City, pictured around 1890, was a bustling place as people gathered to catch their trains or to meet newly arrived passengers. On any given day, train depots in the county were animated with activity as people congregated on the platforms to watch the comings and goings of others and to participate in the excitement of the newest mode of travel at their disposal. (Christine Hinsey.)

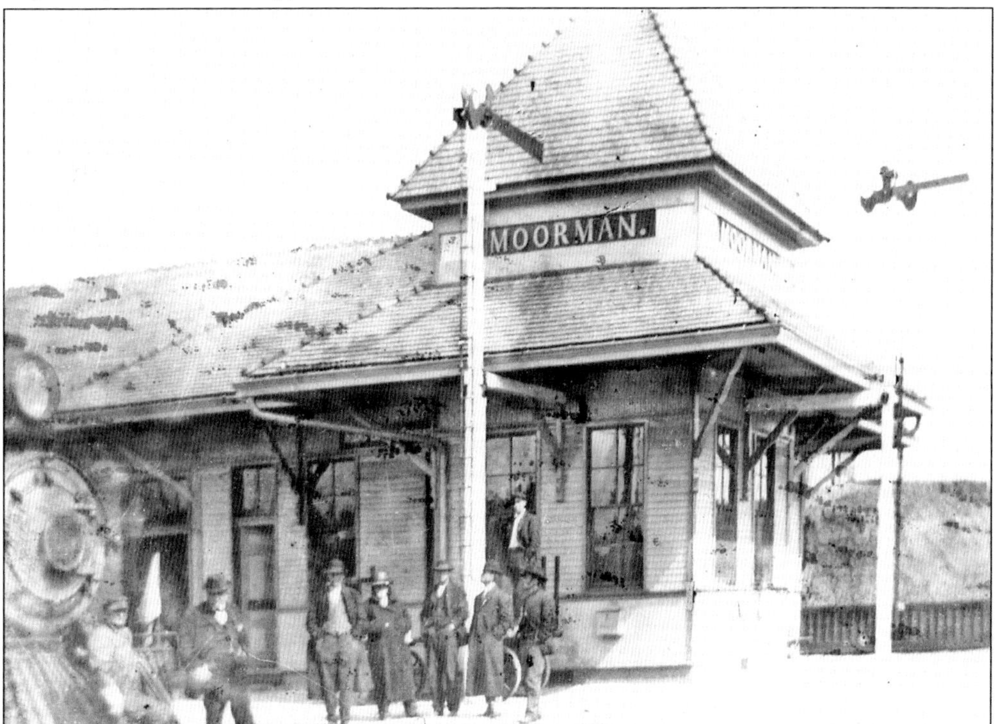

People gather at the Moorman train station north of South Carrollton to await the arrival of their train around 1860. (Christine Hinsey.)

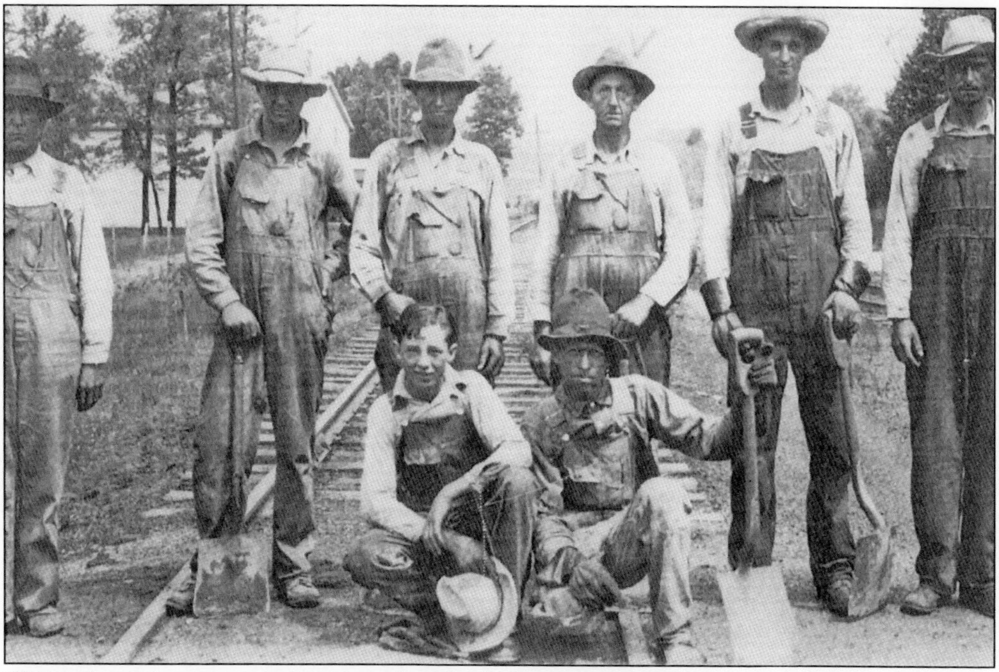

The railroad section crew is pictured at the Belton crossing around 1920. Seven of the men identified are, in no particular order, Irwin Mallory, Vernon McPherson, C. T. Mallory, Marman Mallory, Melvin Mallory, Dock Blake, and Daffie L. Mefford. (Christine Hinsey.)

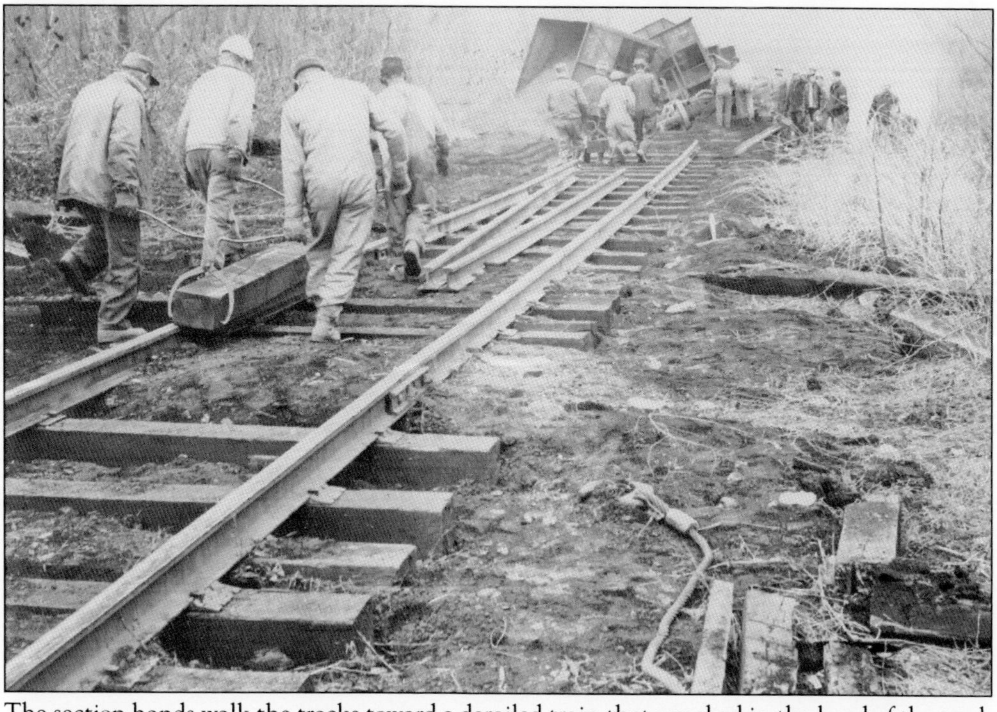

The section hands walk the tracks toward a derailed train that wrecked in the bend of the track earlier in the day around 1920. The section crews were responsible for repairing and maintaining all the tracks to keep trains running safely and on schedule. (Christine Hinsey.)

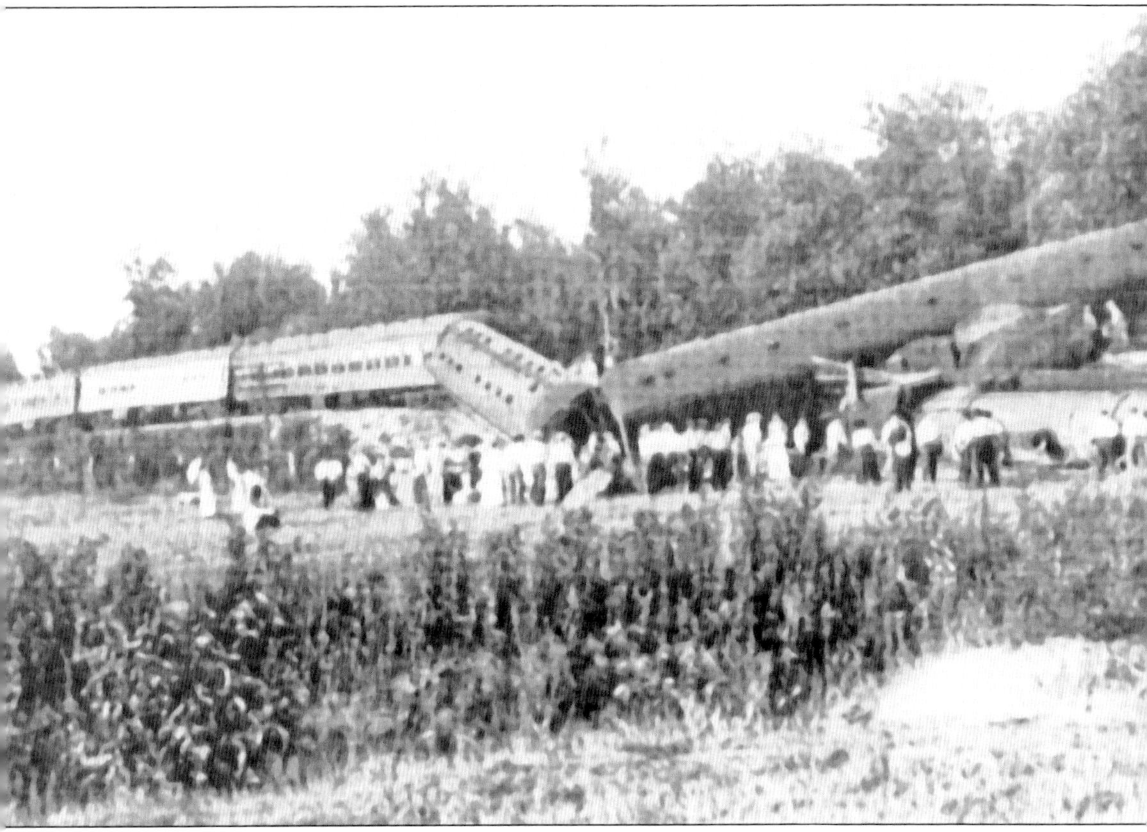

Engineer William Curley realized something was wrong as he slowed Train 101 to 30 miles per hour going into the curve headed into Baxter Crossing. He applied the emergency brakes, but the train continued on for 200 feet before becoming airborne and plummeting down the 12-foot embankment. In the investigation that followed, it was determined that the July 20, 1913, train wreck was caused by 14-year-old Benjamin Avery, who placed a spike on the rail at the crossing of Baxter's farm. The spike resulted in the derailment of the train near Brownie Mine, causing serious injuries to several passengers. In the final judgment of the investigational body, it was determined that Avery "had not acted maliciously, but ignorantly, unaware of the consequences." Over 5,000 people poured into the area to view the Illinois Central wreckage site. (Christine Hinsey.)

The Twin Tunnels were carved through a hillside by the Louisville and Nashville Railroad around 1880 to establish a connection between Belton and Penrod. One tunnel collapsed in 1901, and today only one tunnel remains. The train made four daily runs and cost a dime to ride. Harry Anderson Sr., who rode the train as a boy to visit his grandfather Hackett Anderson, still had a 6-mile hike after disembarking. (Christine Hinsey.)

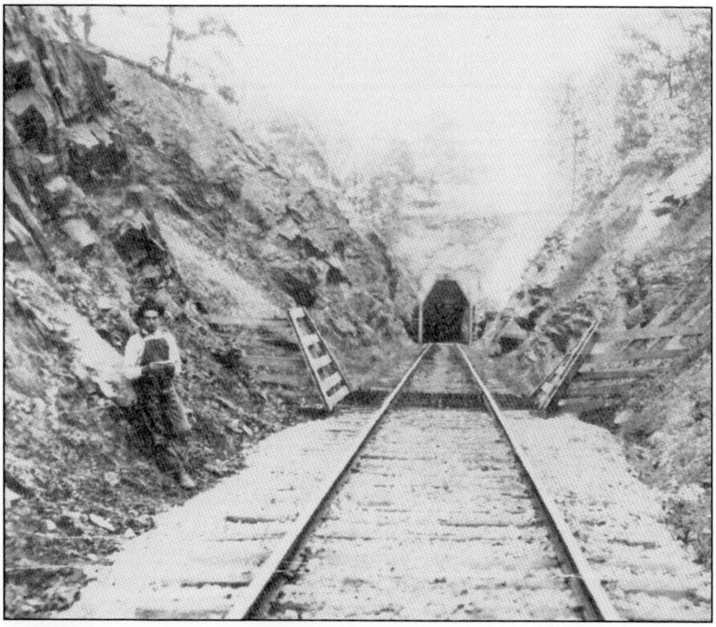

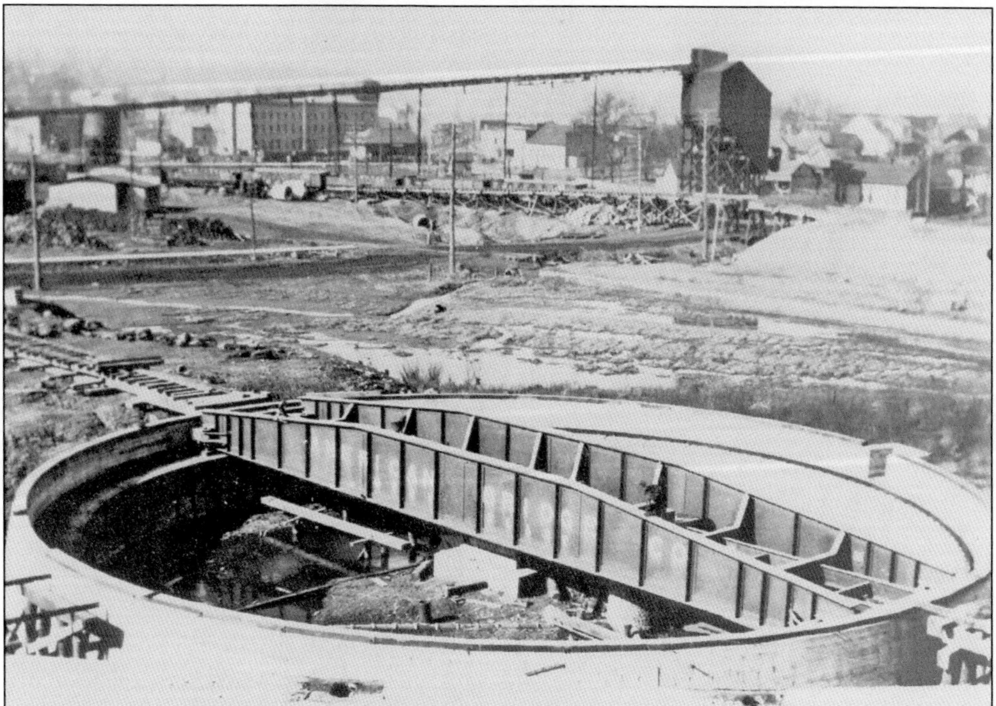

As the maintenance, storage, and repair facility for steam engines between 1920 and 1940, the Central City roundhouse (pictured around 1930) was built to be a hub of activity. Since many of the first steam locomotives only traveled forward, the turntable allowed a locomotive to be turned around for its return journey. The advent of diesel engines in the 1940s and 1950s contributed to the demise of the roundhouses. (Christine Hinsey.)

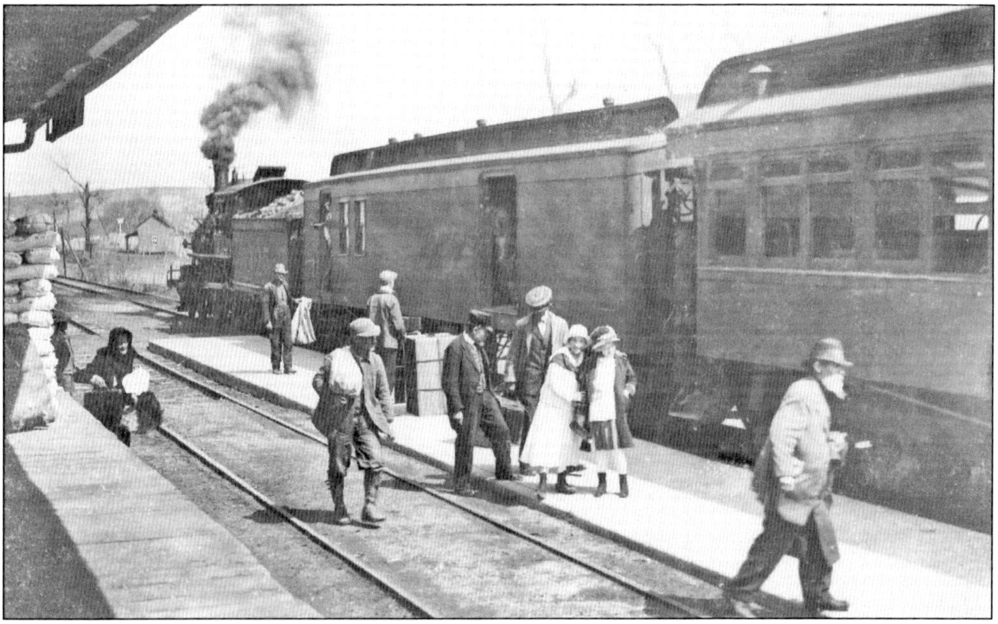

Pictured above is the South Carrollton train station with Mr. Liter on the right preparing to board. Below around 1940, the Illinois Central railroad depot was located 1 mile from the county courthouse in Greenville. Four passenger trains made daily runs through the county and connected Greenville with Louisville and Paducah. (Muhlenberg County Library Archives.)

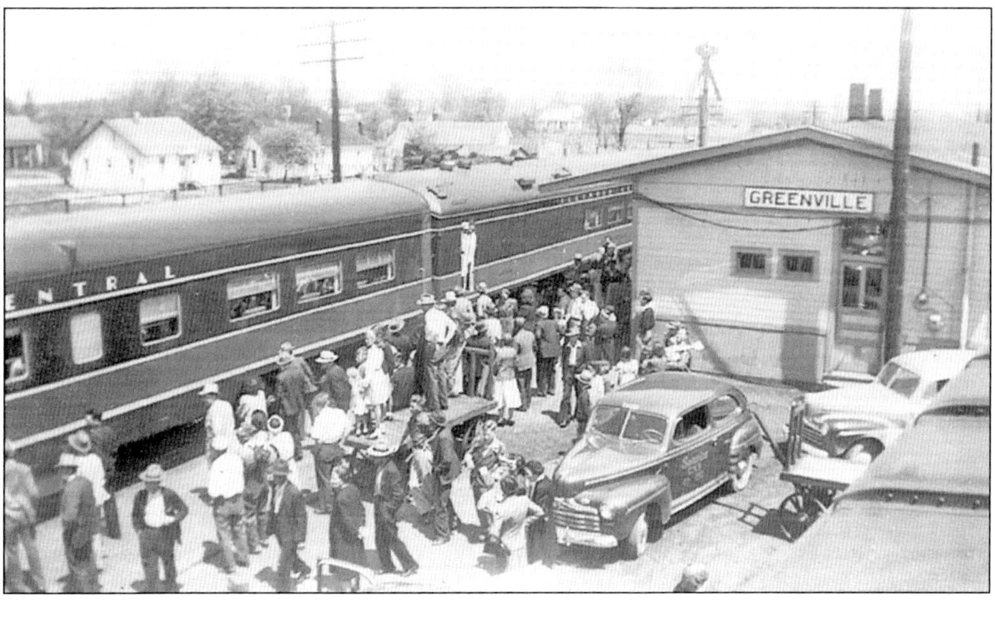

An unidentified South Carrollton family around 1890 gathers on the front porch of their home dressed in their Sunday best. Full-length dresses, high-button shoes, full bodices, and large hats contributed to episodes of the "vapors" for many fashionable women. In the summer, men were uncomfortable too in hats, ties, long-sleeved shirts, jackets, and heavy pants. (Molly Alward)

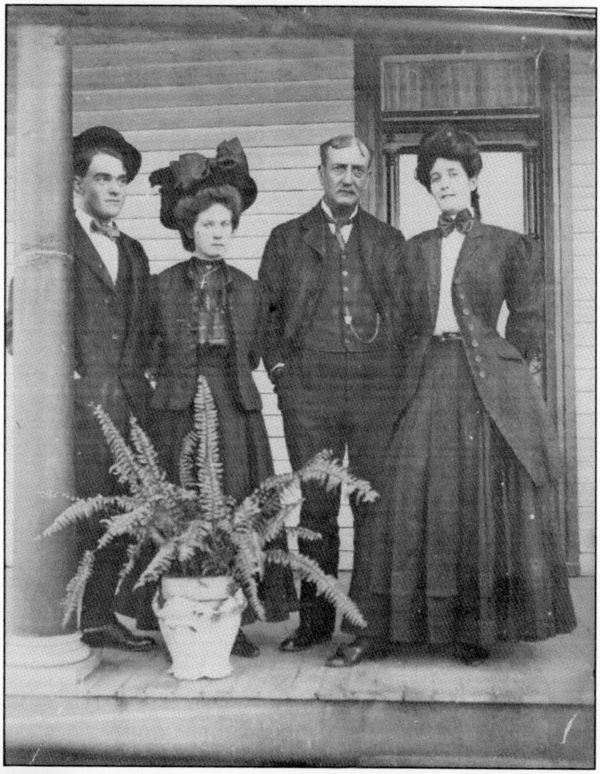

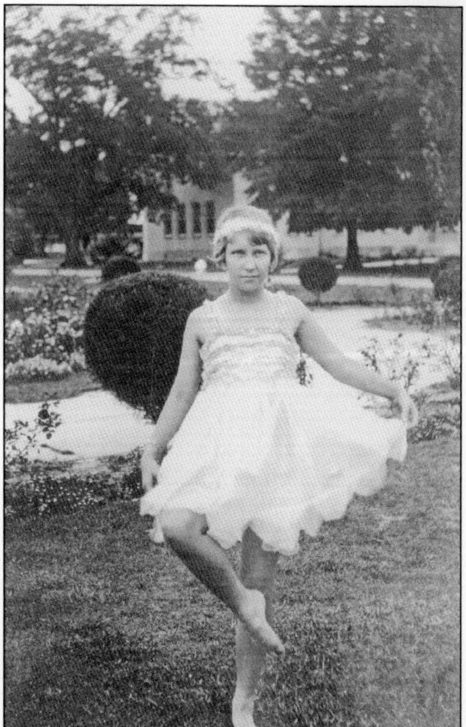

Mary Ellen (Ferguson) Hunter, a tomboy and reluctant ballerina, shows her poise, grace, and style at age 10 around 1930. A longtime resident of South Carrollton, Mary Ellen taught at South Carrollton Elementary School and in Central City. She also served on the Muhlenberg Community Hospital board. Her brother Jo Ferguson is a former attorney general of Kentucky living in Louisville. (Molly Alward.)

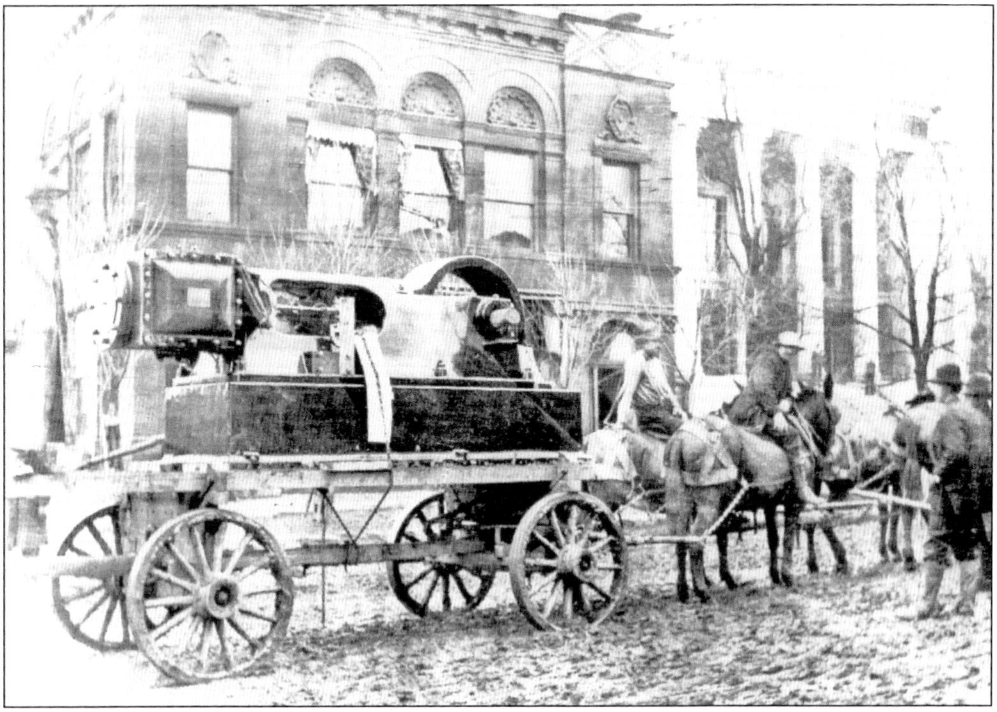

A traveling salesman navigates the dirt roads through Greenville with his wagon and mule team around 1920. The current chamber of commerce building and courthouse are seen in the background. (Carol McClure.)

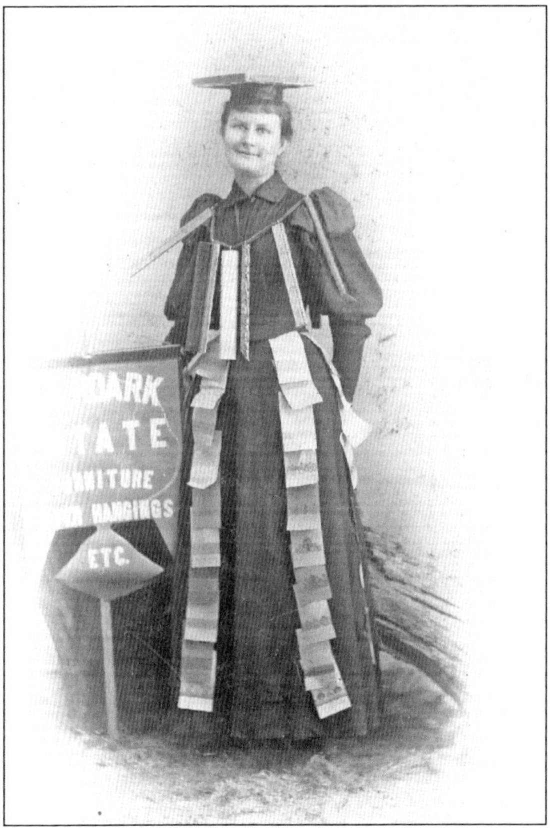

Lucy Carolyn Roark became a unique mobile display board to educate the public about the many fine wallpaper samples available at the Roark's store around 1879. (Carol McClure.)

Two

BUSINESS VENTURES

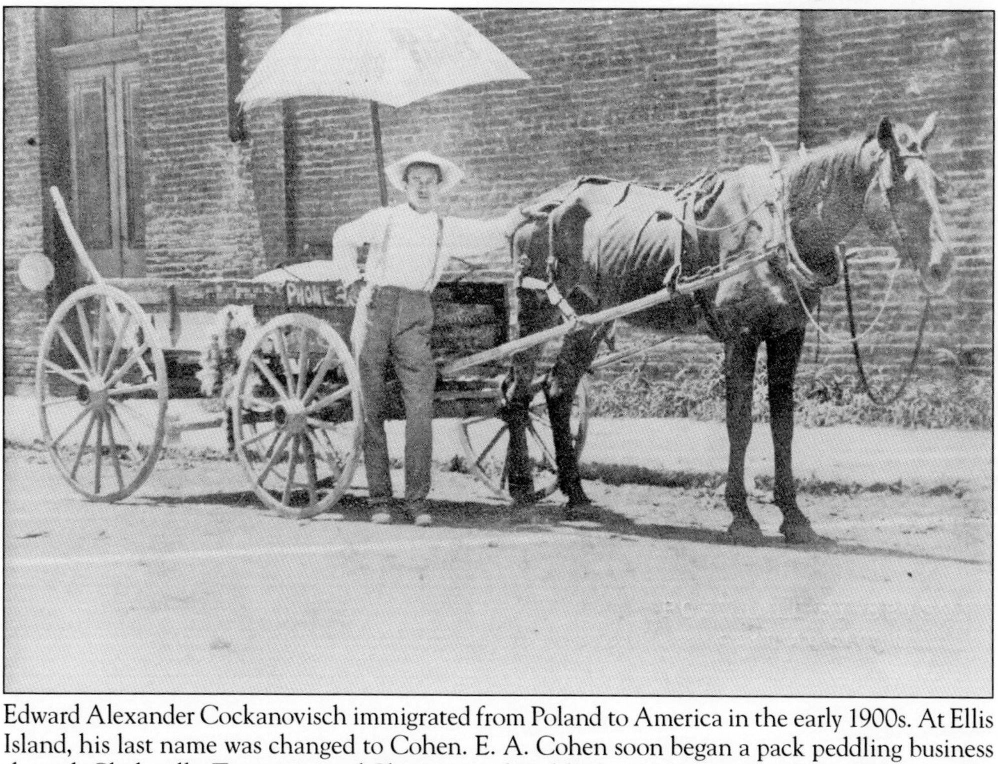

Edward Alexander Cockanovisch immigrated from Poland to America in the early 1900s. At Ellis Island, his last name was changed to Cohen. E. A. Cohen soon began a pack peddling business through Clarksville, Tennessee, and Christian and Muhlenberg Counties, Kentucky. He eventually settled in Greenville and saved enough money to buy his horse and wagon. In 1908, he and his brother Louis opened a store called the E. A. and L. Cohen Store. Alex enjoyed being settled, but Louis did not, and he soon left Alex behind. The store had several names during its life: Cohen and Solzman, E. A. Cohen, and then finally E. A. Cohen and Son. With the help of his family, the store on Main Street remained in business for 90 years. Over the years, the well-known store motto became "If Cohen's doesn't have it, you don't need it." (Christine Hinsey.)

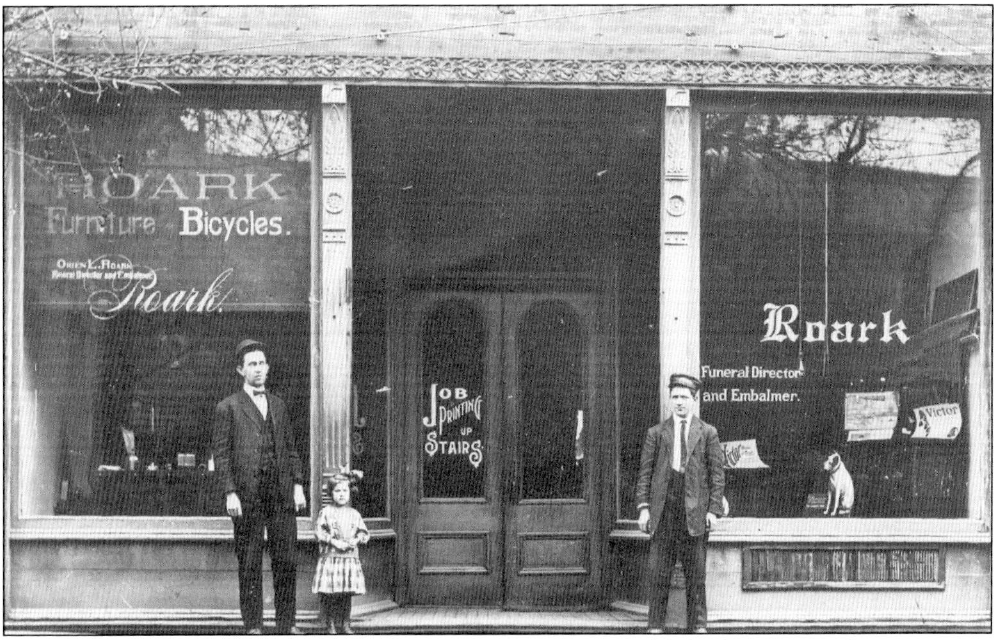

The Roarks' business on Main Street in Greenville was established in 1879. The owner was Orien Roark, and the store advertised the availability of everything from bicycles to coffins. (Carol McClure.)

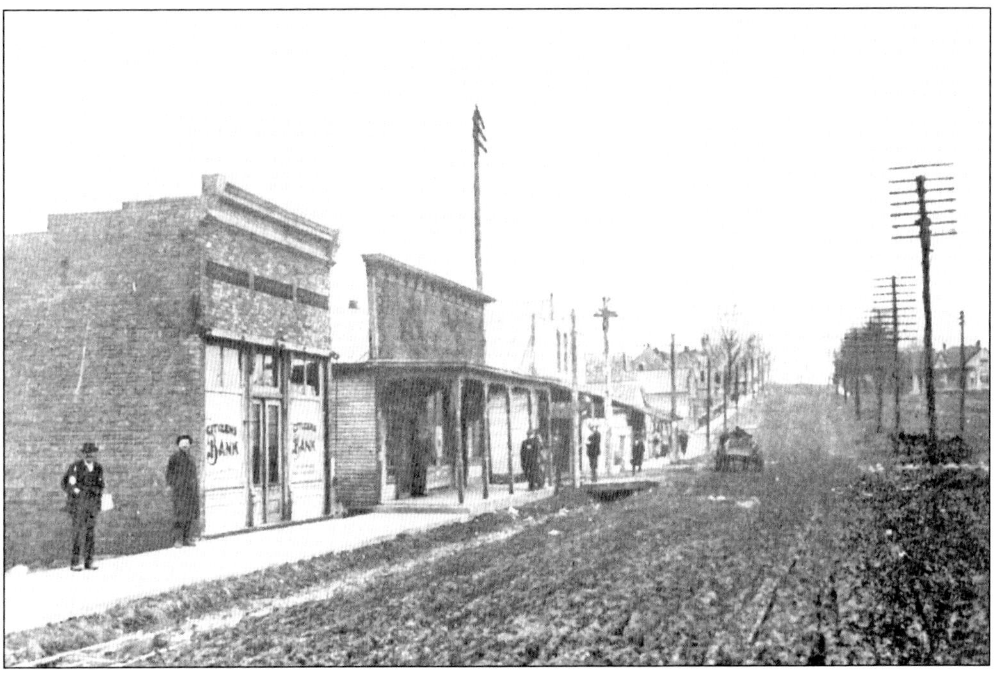

A dirt road paves early Main Street in Drakesboro around 1886. In the early days of the settlement, Drakesboro was known for its abundance of hardwood timber but eventually became even more famous for its coal mines and for being the hometown of thumb-picking guitar legends Kennedy Jones, Mose Rager, Ike Everly, and Merle Travis. (Muhlenberg County Library Archives.)

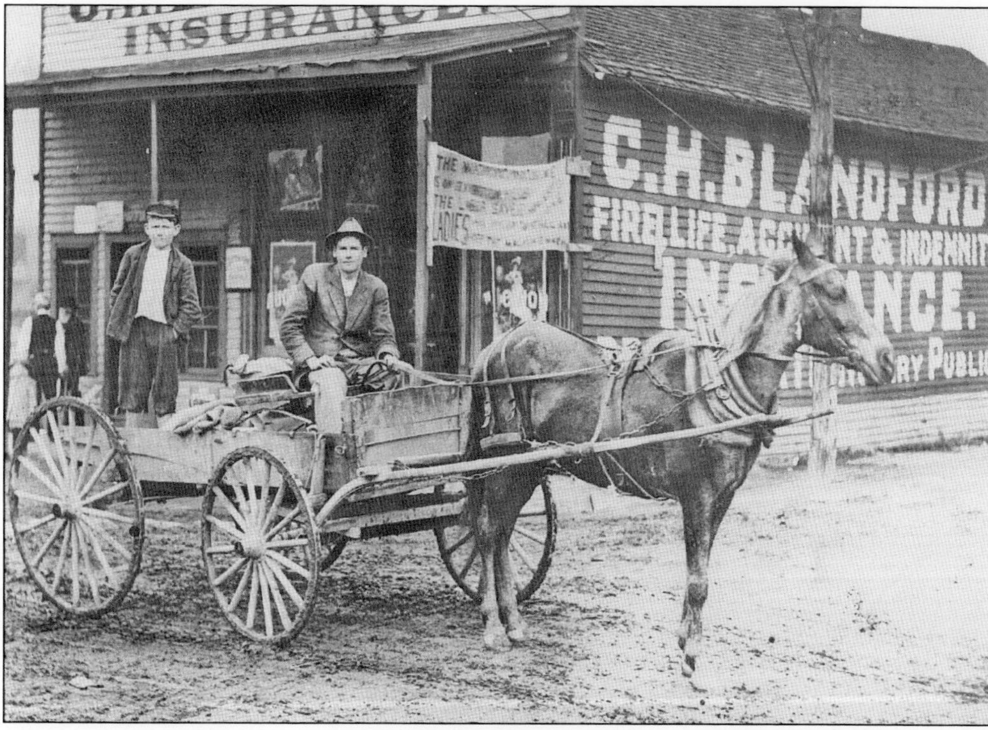

Customers wait in their horse and buggy outside the C. H. Blandford Insurance Company in Central City in the early 1900s. James Bryant Lawton and Robert A. Lawton bought the insurance company from Mrs. Blandford in 1947. (Christine Hinsey.)

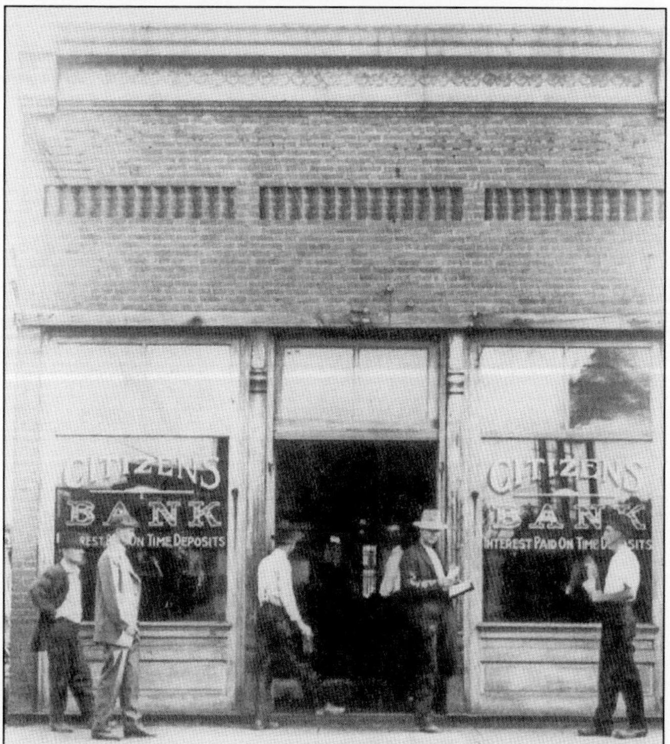

The Citizens Bank of Drakesboro opened in 1907. The officers of the bank were W. W. Bridges, president; Dr. J. D. Cundiff, vice president; and U. W. Jenkins, cashier. The directors were W. W. Bridges, E. Howard Boggess, John Kittinger, and Felix Kelley. The bank was a successful enterprise until the Great Depression and finally closed in 1932. (Christine Hinsey.)

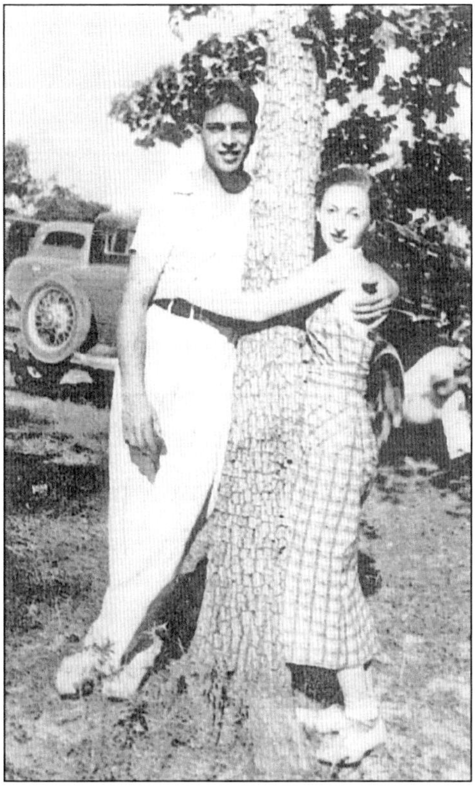

Julius Cohen (left), 19, and his fiancée Rose Silverman, 18, share a smile in this 1935 photograph. As a boy, Julius worked with his father and mother in their family store. As a man, he worked there with his wife, Rose, and their four children, Dolores, Charles, Marcia, and Beverly. Julius cared about people and was known to open his store late on holidays or during emergencies to help someone in crisis. He gave generously of his time and money to county, military, and civic organizations. He imparted to his children the importance of charity and responsibility toward their fellow man. And like extraordinary people before him, Julius has left his mark on the pages of Muhlenberg County history. Below, Julius poses with the original peddler's cart used by his father, E. A. Cohen, in the early 1900s. (Marcia Storch.)

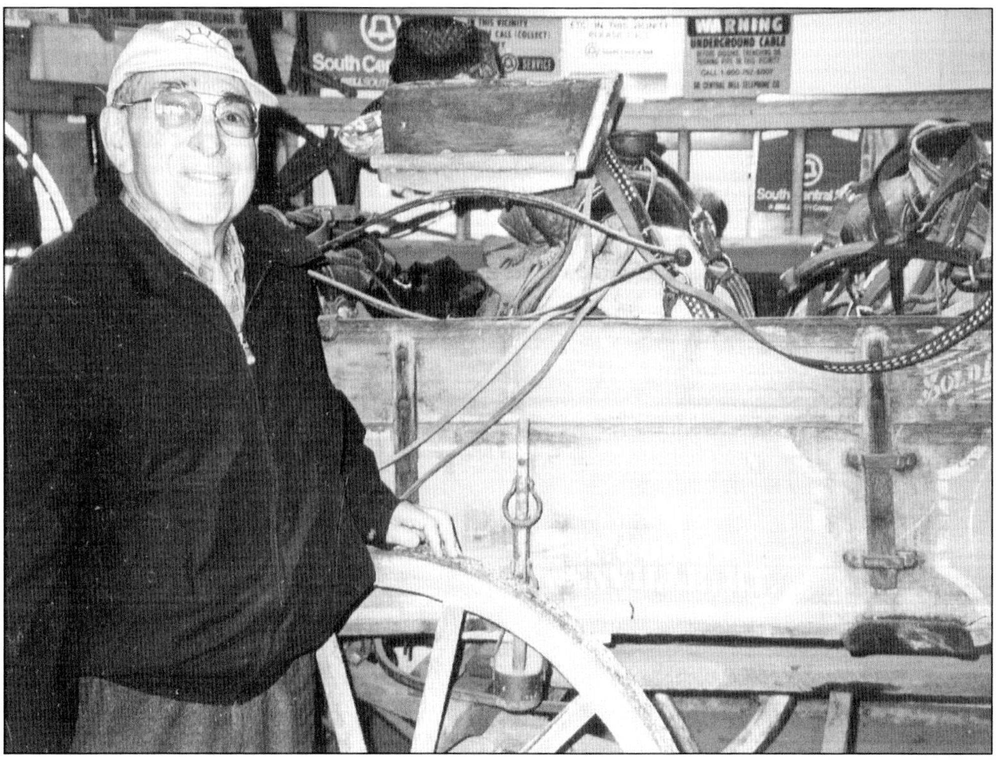

The E. A. Cohen family gathers in the county for an afternoon's visit around 1930. The family members are, from left to right, Dave Cohen, Agnes Cohen Abroms, Dora Cohen, Louis Cohen, and Sam Brenner. Pictured in the inset are, from left to right, Jettie Cohen, Sam Brenner, and E. A. Cohen holding baby Louise. (Muhlenberg County Library Archives.)

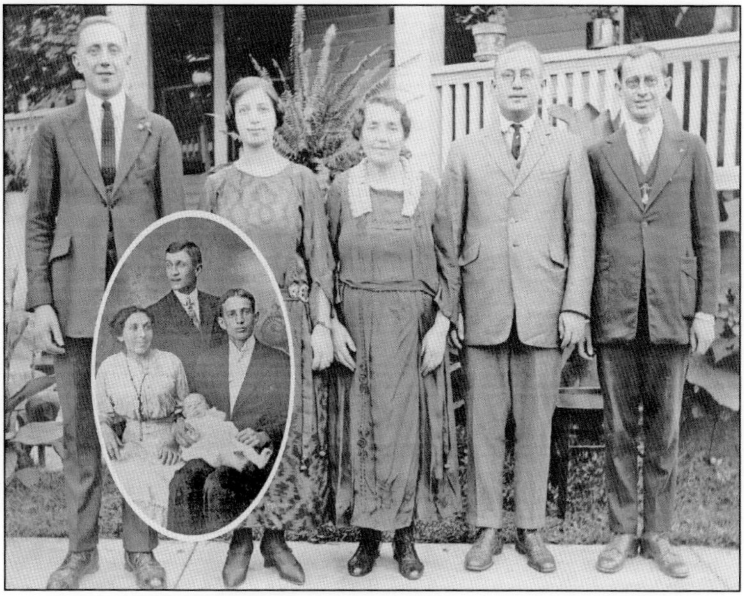

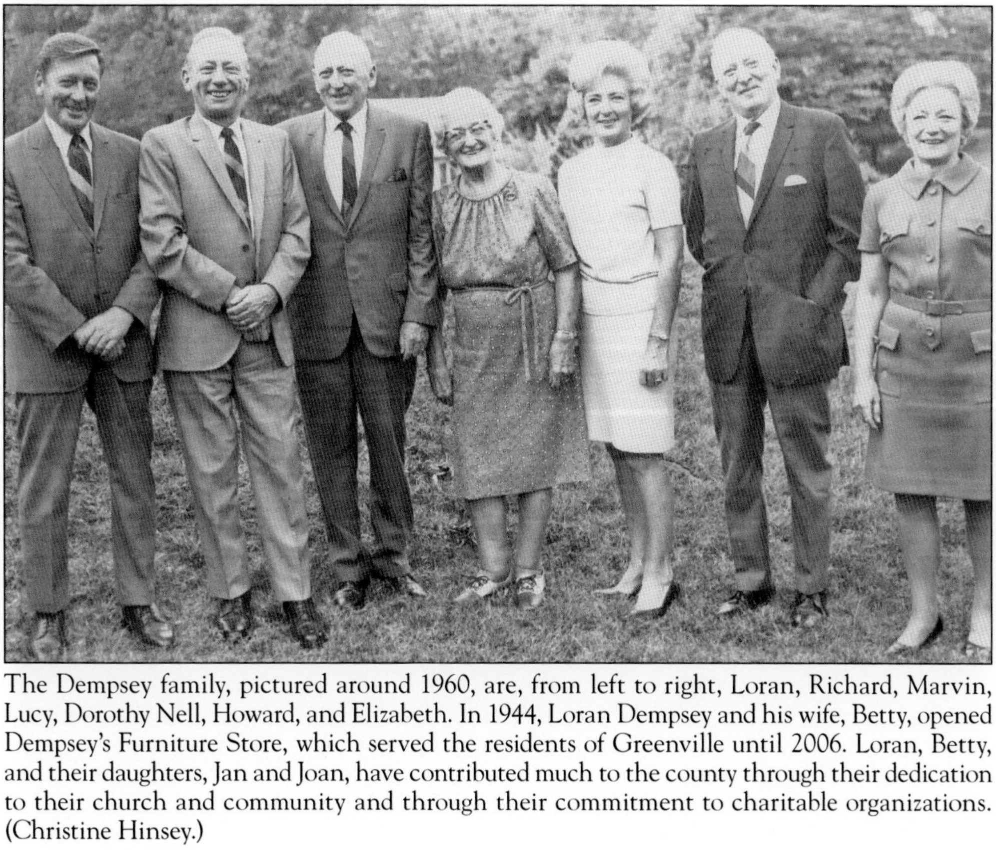

The Dempsey family, pictured around 1960, are, from left to right, Loran, Richard, Marvin, Lucy, Dorothy Nell, Howard, and Elizabeth. In 1944, Loran Dempsey and his wife, Betty, opened Dempsey's Furniture Store, which served the residents of Greenville until 2006. Loran, Betty, and their daughters, Jan and Joan, have contributed much to the county through their dedication to their church and community and through their commitment to charitable organizations. (Christine Hinsey.)

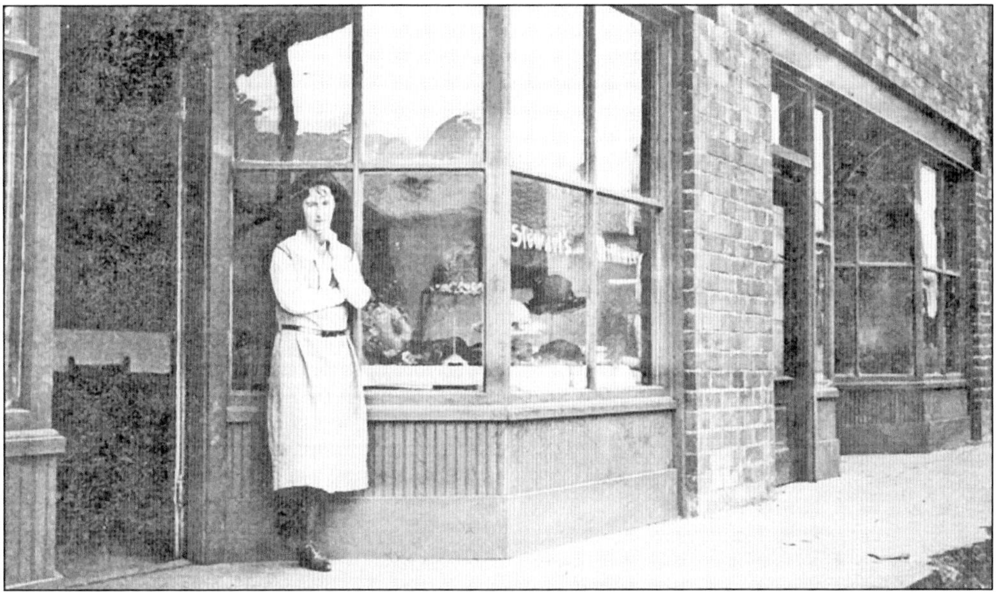

An unidentified clerk takes a break outside of Stewert's Millinery on Main Street in Central City around 1900. Hats were a very important accessory in the 1900s, and milliners were in great demand. (Carol McClure.)

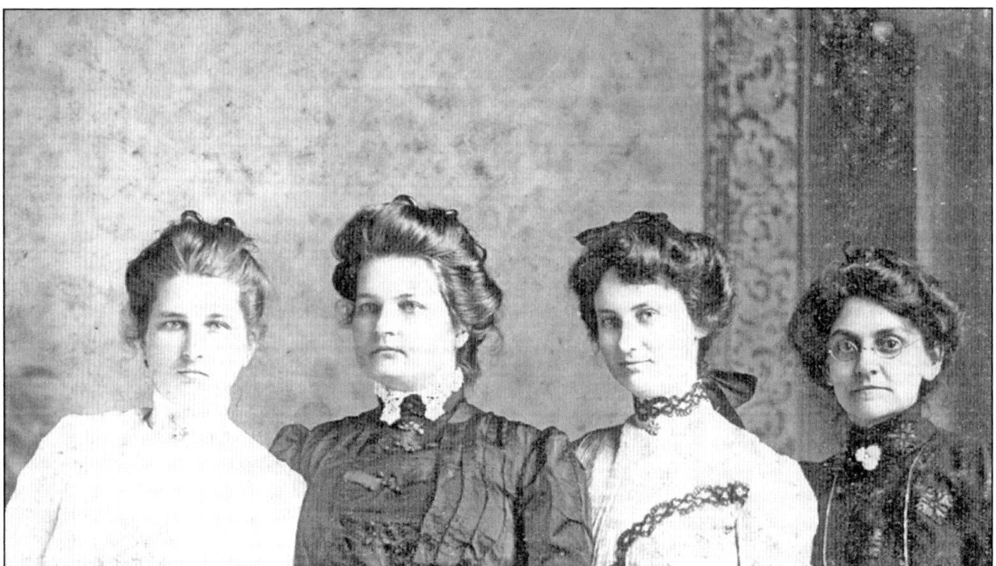

Four sophisticated ladies of the Morgan Millinery in Central City pose for this photograph in 1900. In the late 19th century, hat creations using exotic bird feathers and one-of-a-kind designs created a demand for skilled milliners, but by the early 1900s, mass production of lower priced hats caused many craftswomen to lose their businesses. (Christine Hinsey.)

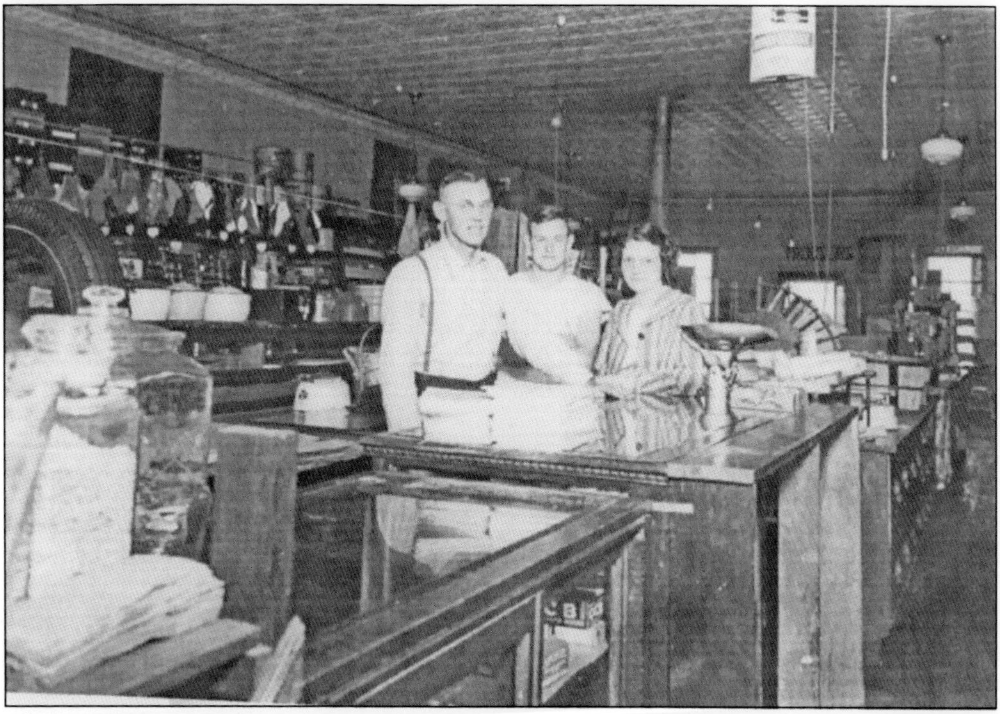

Clerks at their stations await customers inside the Fox store in Drakesboro in 1932. (Muhlenberg County Library Archives.)

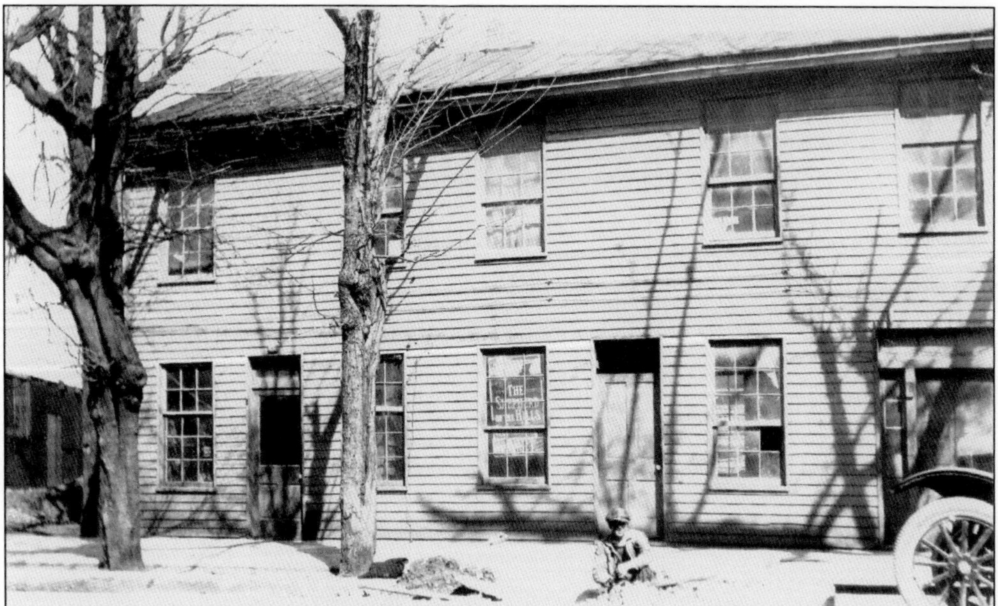

The first Greenville Hotel was built on East Main Street in 1855 and became known as a war hotel during the Civil War. It was the meeting place of the secessionists and the Confederate sympathizers. After the war, it became the headquarters for the Democratic Party, where their political strategies were put into action. The Reno house was the federal headquarters of the county and burned in 1903. (Christine Hinsey.)

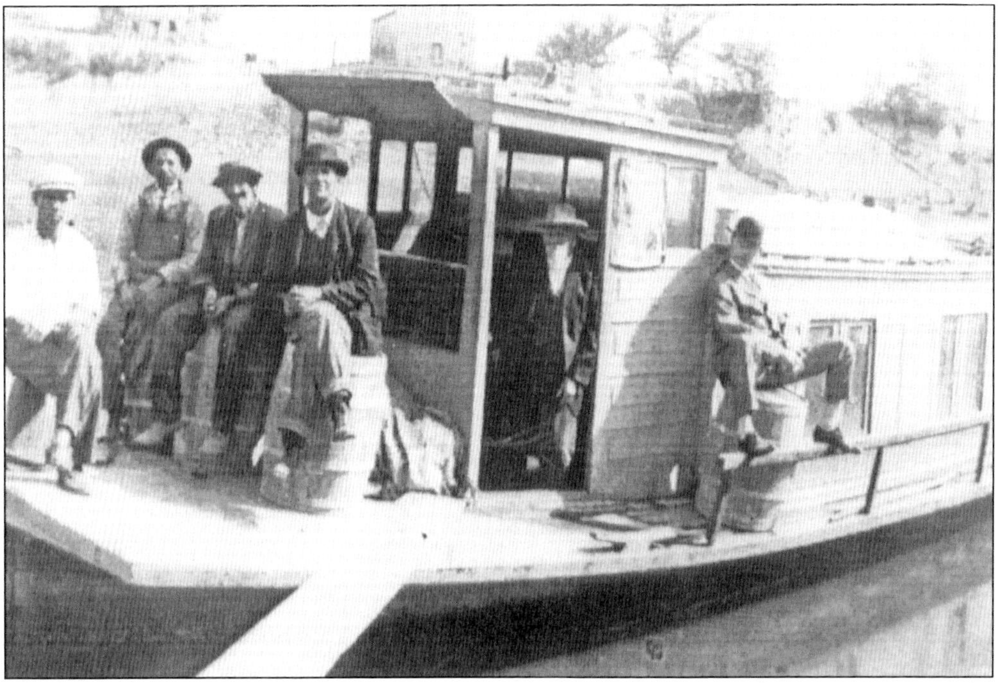

A mail boat delivers the mail at Paradise, formally known as Stum's Landing, around 1890. The mail boat arrived two to three times weekly for pickup and delivery of the mail. Ras Schull, standing in the doorway of the boat, was a Civil War veteran. (Christine Hinsey.)

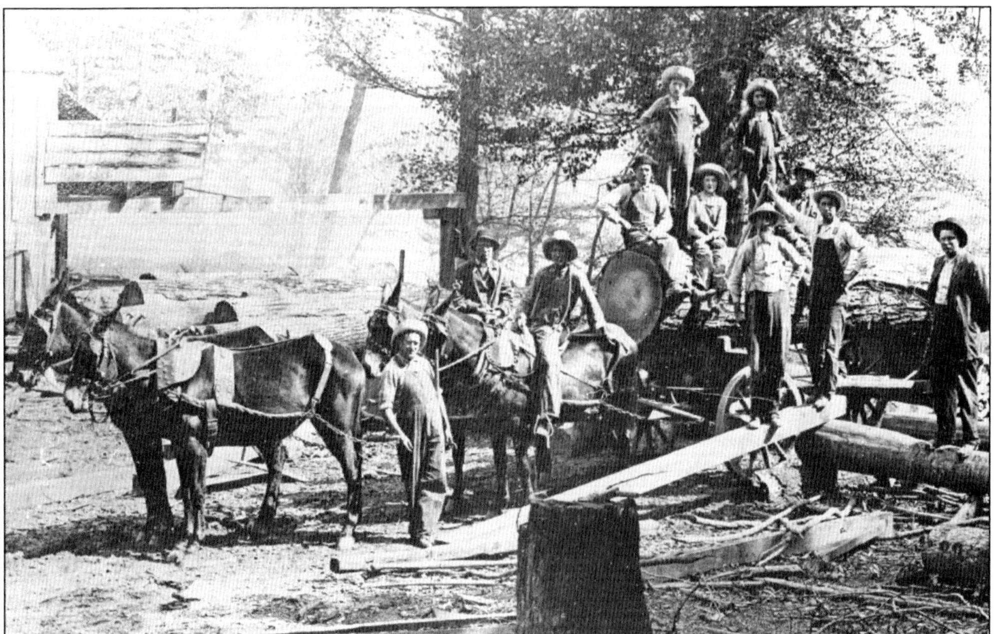

Workers at the Vincent sawmill near Bremen in 1900 are shown hauling huge trees out of the woods. One of the natural resources attractive to the first pioneers of the county was the amount of hardwoods found in the dense forests. These forests became the foundation for the forts and homes built in the new frontier as well as fuel for their fires and their first industries. (Christine Hinsey.)

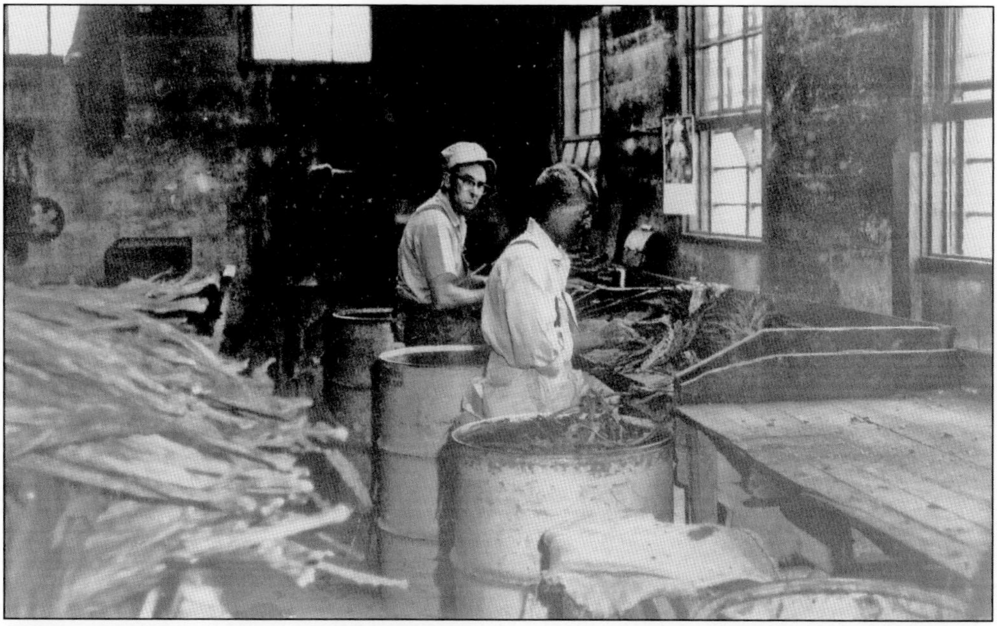

Tobacco was first cultivated in Muhlenberg County in 1802. William Martin, who arrived in the county around 1805, pioneered the plug tobacco business in 1835 in the Old Liberty neighborhood. In 1840, Dabney and Ellington Martin, grandsons of William Martin, began to make a sweetened and flavored brand of plug tobacco known as Greenville tobacco. This plug was manufactured for more than half a century and became a favorite throughout the South. During the Civil War, the Martins' tobacco was confiscated, their slaves were set free, and they became unable to collect on their southern accounts; this was disastrous for their business, and they sold their holdings. Other tobacco companies in the county continued to grow. From 1892 to 1898, five tobacco companies in the county produced approximately one million pounds of tobacco per year. Unidentified workers at the Rice Tobacco Warehouse separate tobacco leaves from stems around 1892. Below, John Barkley (right) and a friend stand in Barkley's tobacco patch in 1914. (Christine Hinsey.)

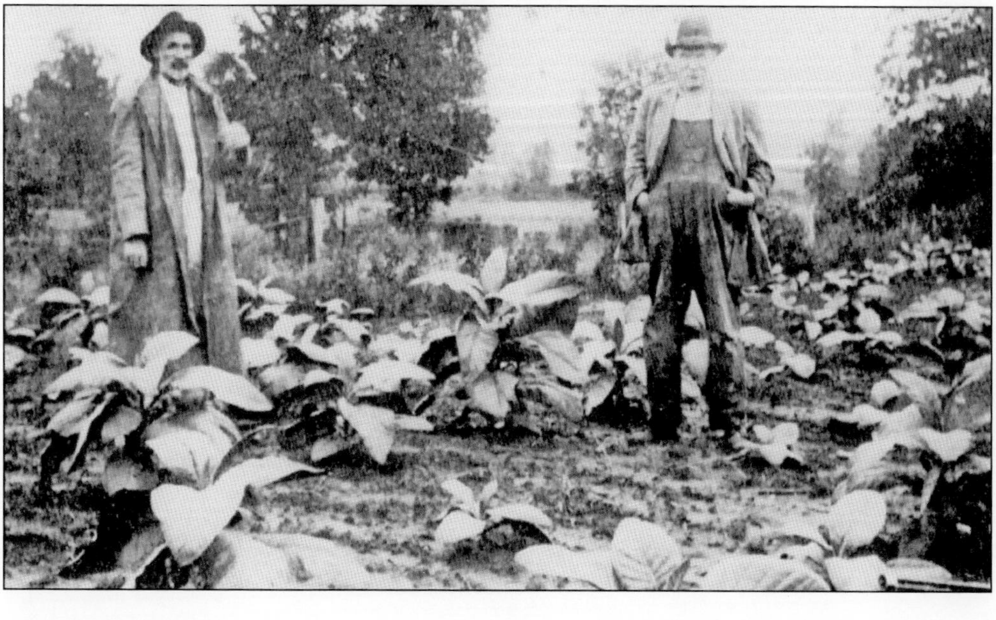

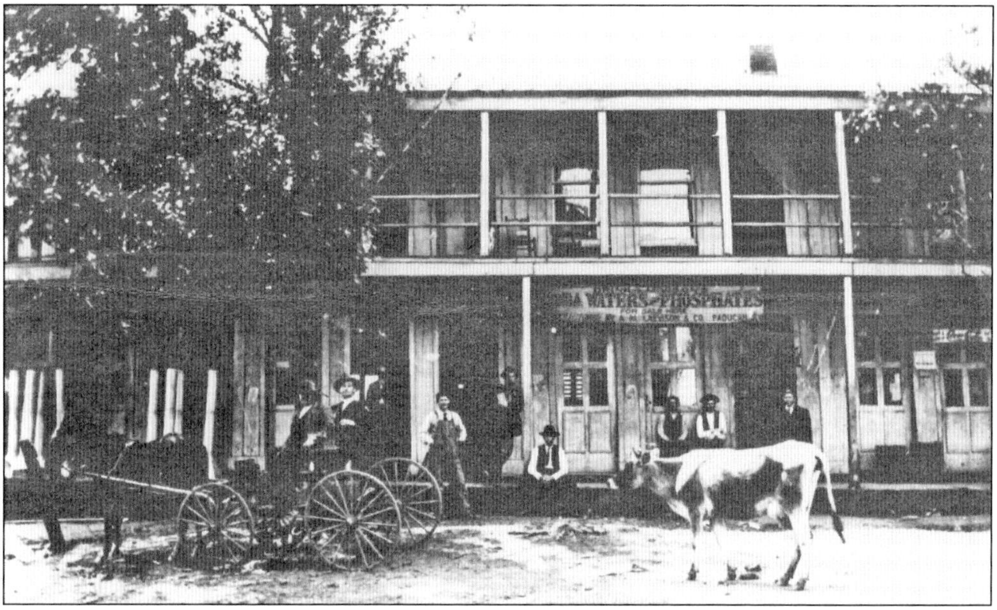

A solitary cow wanders across Court Row in Greenville while the store in the background prominently advertises "Waters and Phosphates for sale from Paducah, Kentucky." Customers relax on the porch, enjoying the shade and the refreshment offered by the establishment in the early 1900s. (Christine Hinsey.)

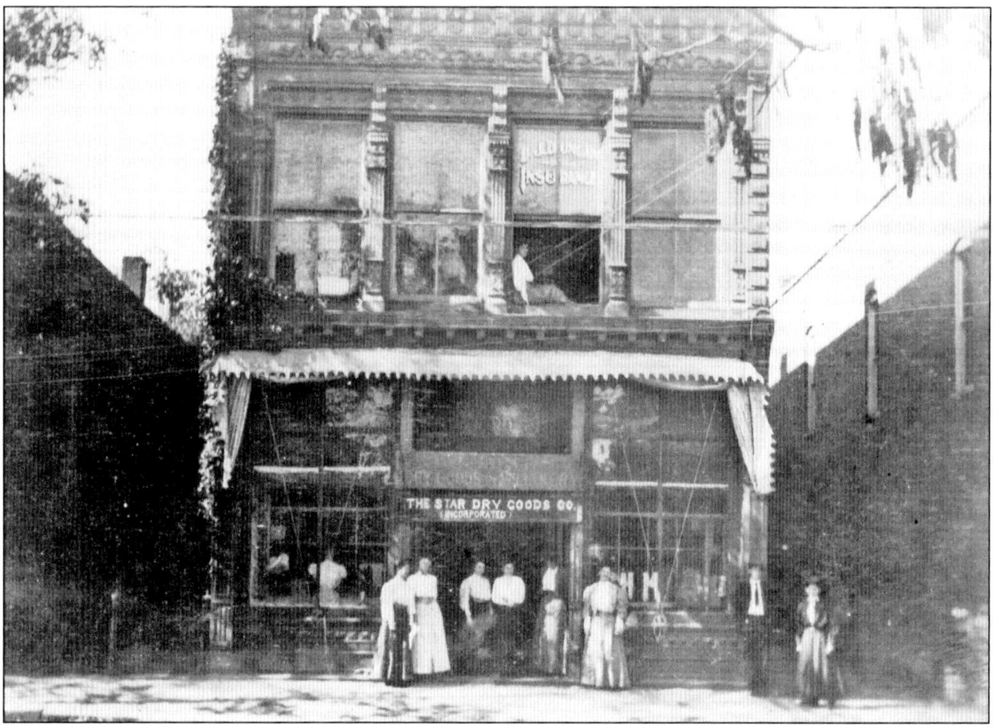

Unidentified customers pose in front of the Star Dry Good Company on Main Street in Greenville while a young lady takes a break from the summer's heat in the upstairs window of the D. J. Duncan Insurance Company around 1910. (Christine Hinsey.)

Jailer "Uncle Rip" Jenkins is pictured with some friends, a jug of moonshine, and a confiscated still in 1929. Backwoods distilleries flourished during Prohibition, and the homemade product was sometimes extremely dangerous and deadly, containing ingredients such as lead, lye, and rubbing alcohol. From left to right are (first row) Uncle Rip Jenkins; (second row) unidentified, Raymond Jenkins, Melbourne Jenkins, and unidentified. (Christine Hinsey.)

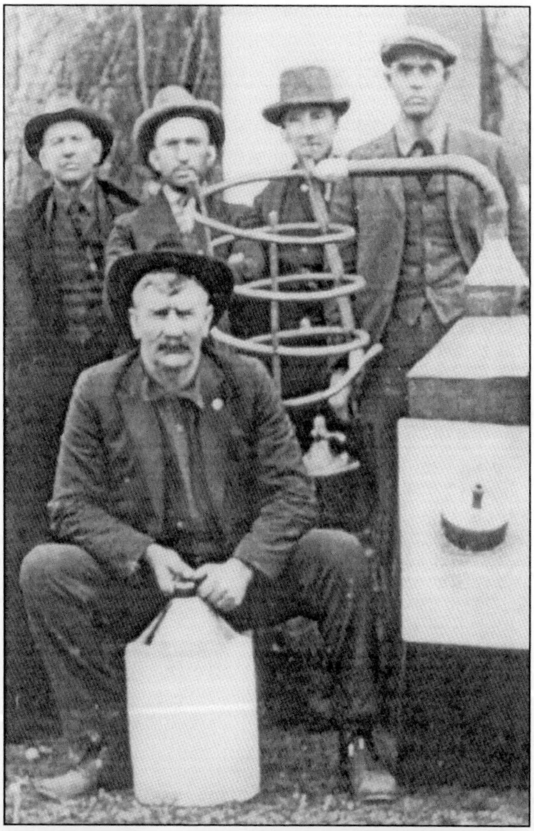

Members of the county's Women's Temperance Movement gather to celebrate Greenville voting dry in 1910. Jennie (Morgan) Roark in the front row offers tea to guests as the groups' recommended alternative refreshment. (Carol McClure.)

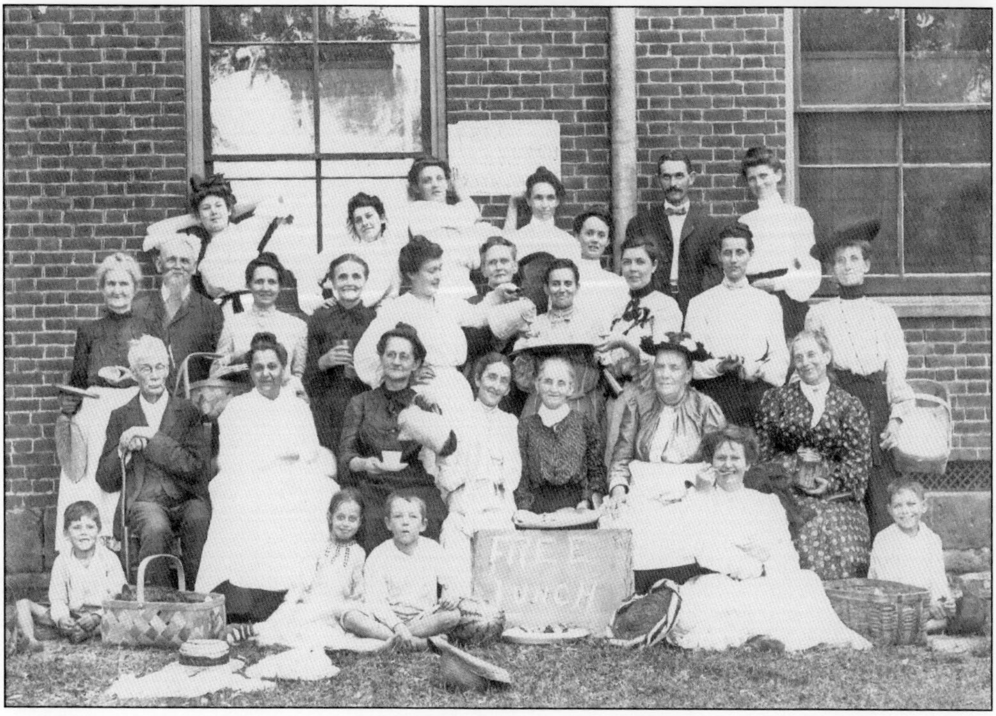

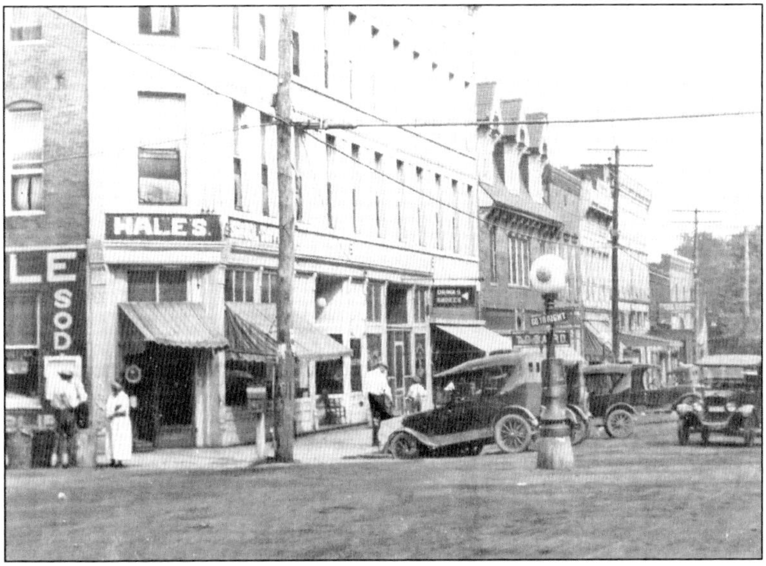

The 1920s street sign directs traffic along Main Street in front of Hale's Corner. Hale's was a popular gathering place for drinks and sandwiches complete with a modern soda fountain. In the 1960s, the store was known as Camera Corner, but it still had its soda fountain. (Christine Hinsey.)

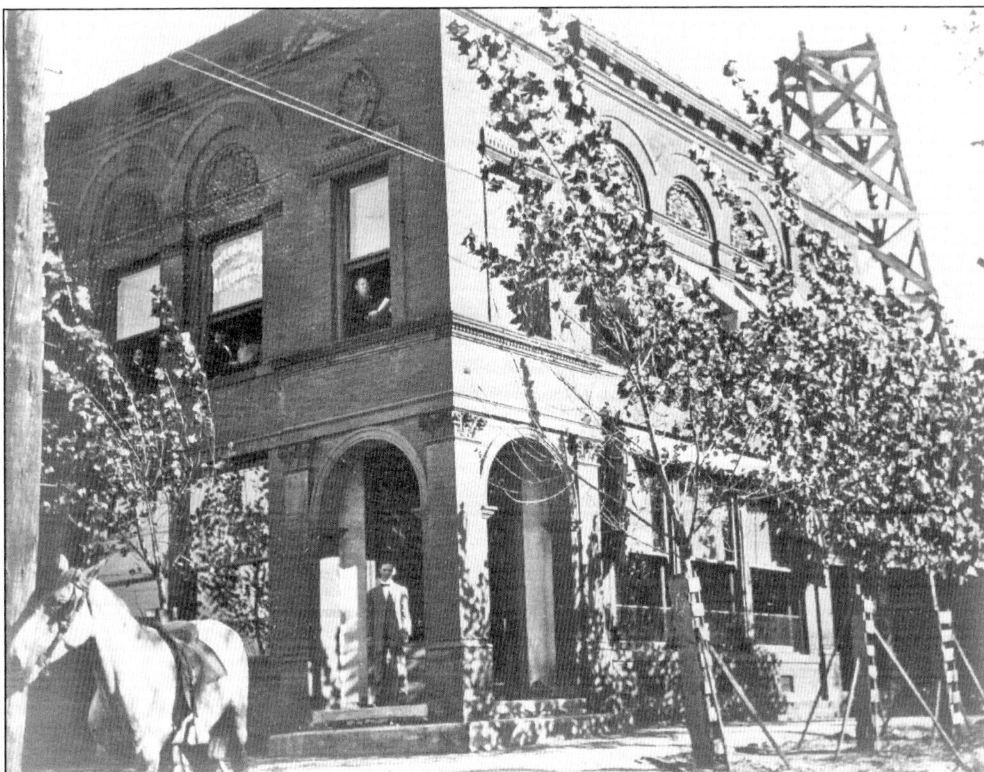

In 1819, the northwest corner of the courthouse lot was sold to the Bank of Greenville, which erected a two-story brick building there. In 1894, the building was demolished, and the First National Bank occupied the new structure on the site until 1907, when the building was sold to the Greenville Coal Company. Since then, the building has been home to various offices and is currently home to the Muhlenberg County Chamber of Commerce and Red Cross offices. Courthouse construction is underway in the background. (Christine Hinsey.)

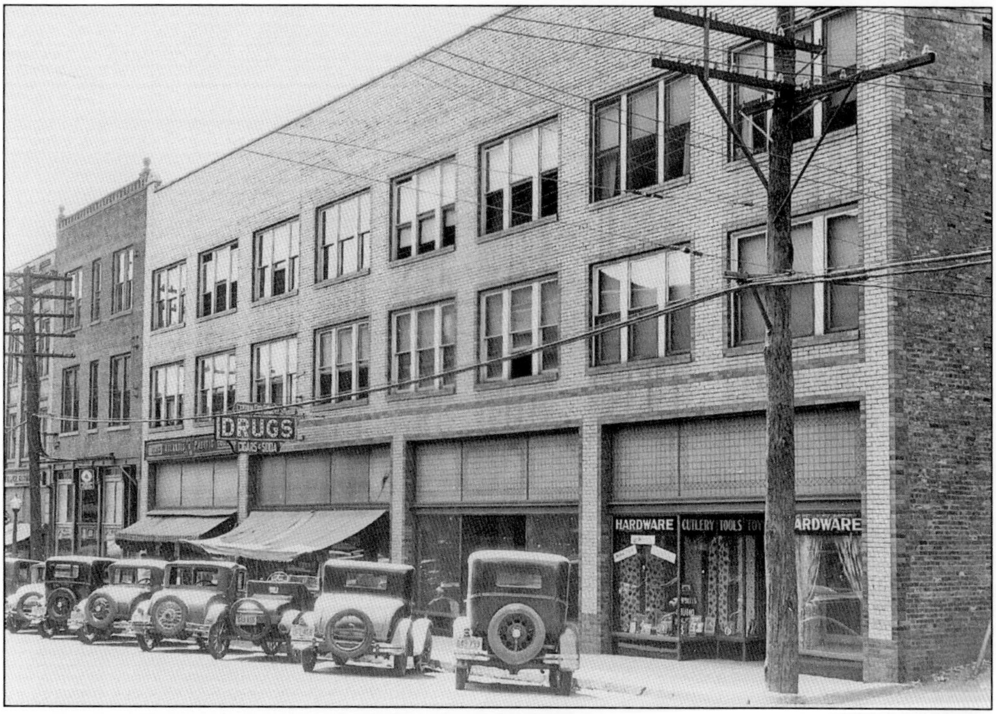

In 1930, the Gish Apartments sit atop the Great Atlantic and Pacific building (also known as the A&P store) in downtown Central City. The drugstore next door advertises cigars and sodas, while the hardware store promotes cutlery, tools, and toys. Campbell's framed photography is displayed in the downstairs window of the hardware store. (Muhlenberg County Library Archives.)

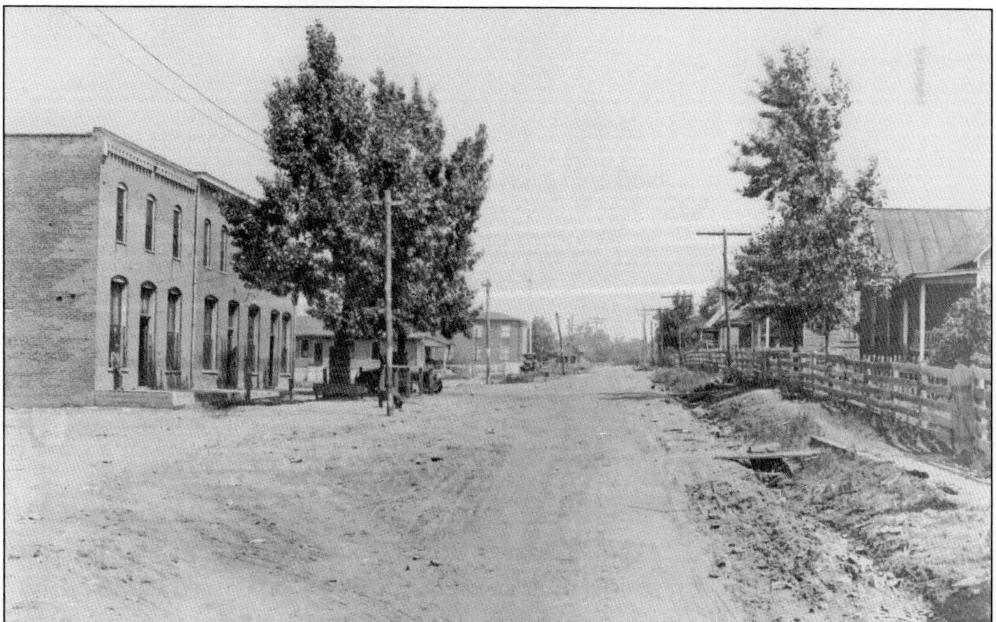

Quiet buildings line the dusty Main Street thoroughfare in Graham after business hours around 1899. (Christine Hinsey.)

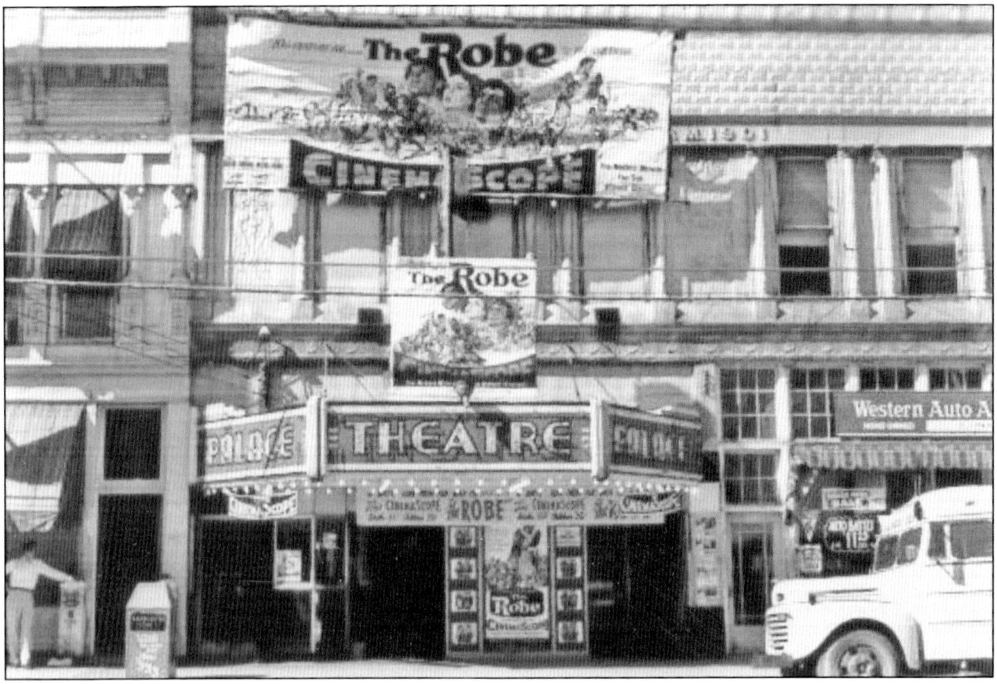

Bill McSpedden went all out to advertise the showing of *The Robe* in 1953 at the Palace Theatre in Greenville. The theater boasted cinemascope and had busloads of children waiting to see the show. The building still stands, purchased and renovated for live performances by the popular Muhlenberg County Theatre, Inc. The building has been added to the National Register of Historic Places. (Christine Hinsey.)

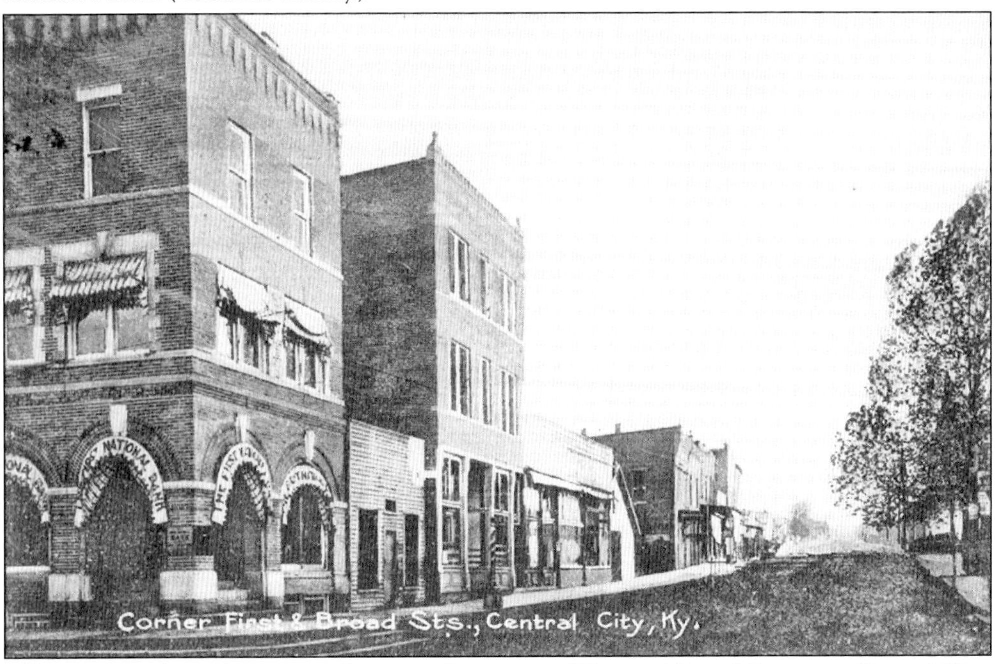

All is quiet in the early morning hours at the corner of First and Broad Streets in Central City. In 1910, a dirt road was still the conduit to the downtown business district. (Christine Hinsey.)

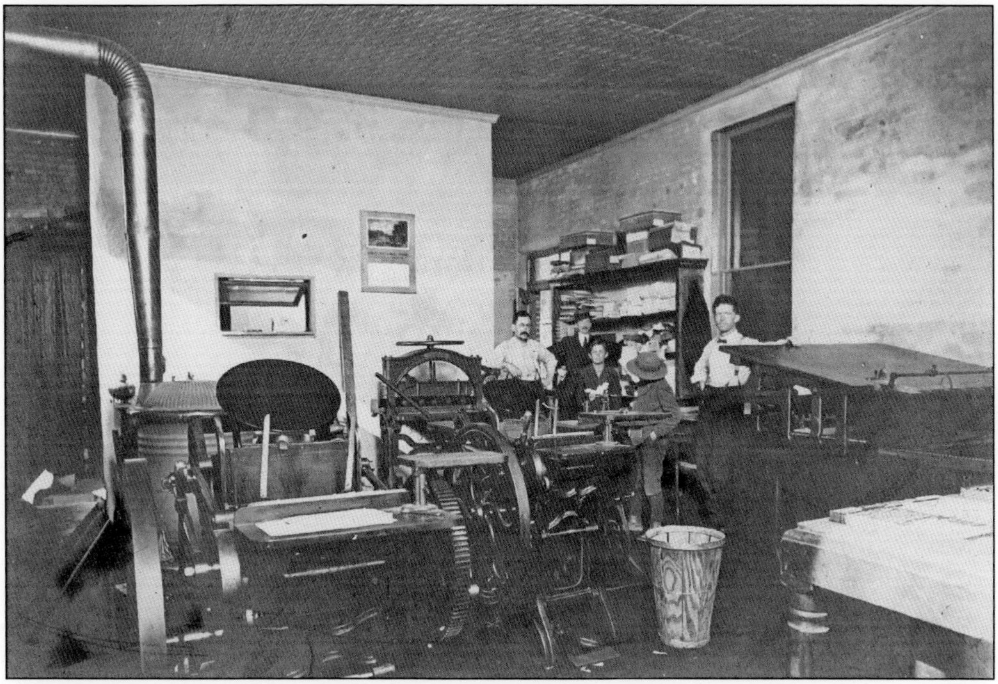

Around 1903, Orien Roark is shown in the pressroom, where he printed a weekly paper first called the *Greenville Record*, begun in 1899. The paper's name was later changed to the *Record*. Two weekly papers remain in business in Muhlenberg County. The *Times Argus*, owned by Mark Stone, is located in Central City, and the *Leader-News*, owned by the Andy Anderson Corporation, is located on Everly Brothers Boulevard between Greenville and Central City. (Carol McClure.)

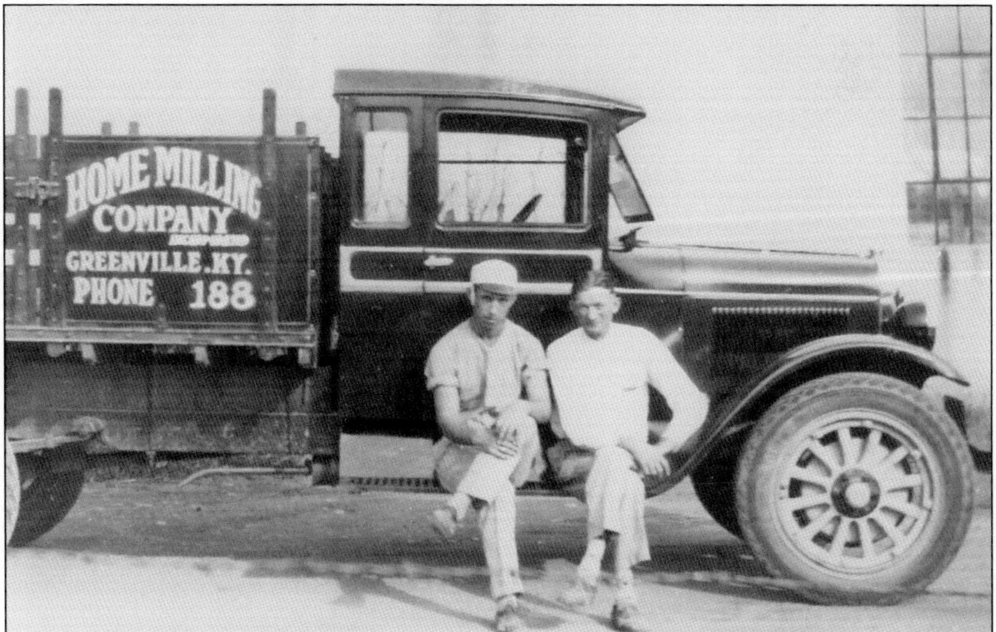

Two unidentified men take a break on the running board of the Home Milling Company truck in 1920. (Christine Hinsey.)

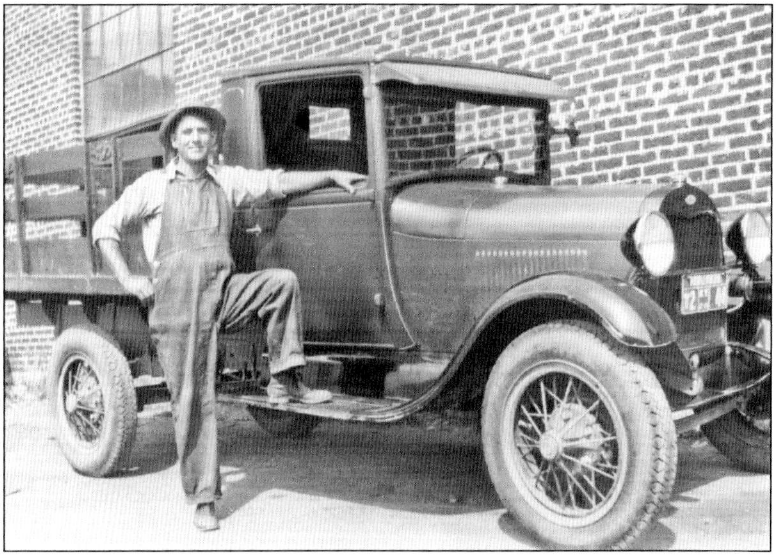

C. K. Sherrod, a Zinmeister employee, stands beside a new delivery truck purchased by the firm in 1928. (Tom Brizendine.)

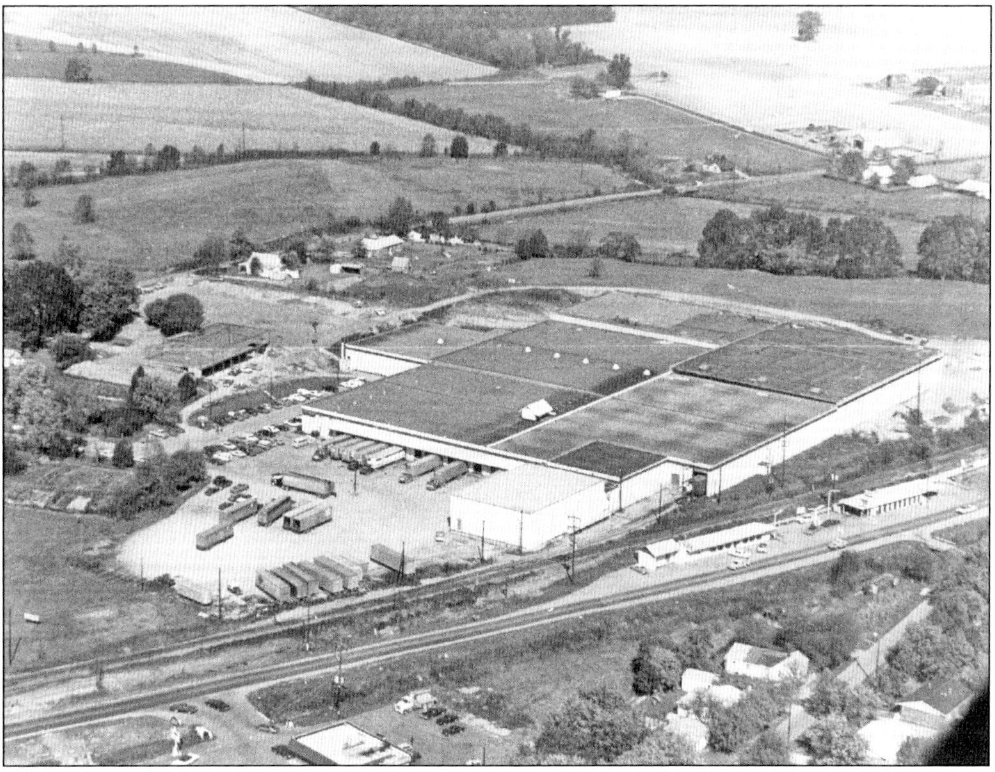

The Zinmeister plant, as seen from the air in 1973, demonstrates its considerable growth from humble beginnings in 1926, when John S. Brizendine, a salesman for J. Zinmeister and Sons in Louisville, opened his own wholesale business in Greenville. After his death in 1942, his widow, Josephine, and sons, John Jr. and Thomas, ran the successful business and sold it to Wetterau Food Services in 1973. (Tom Brizendine.)

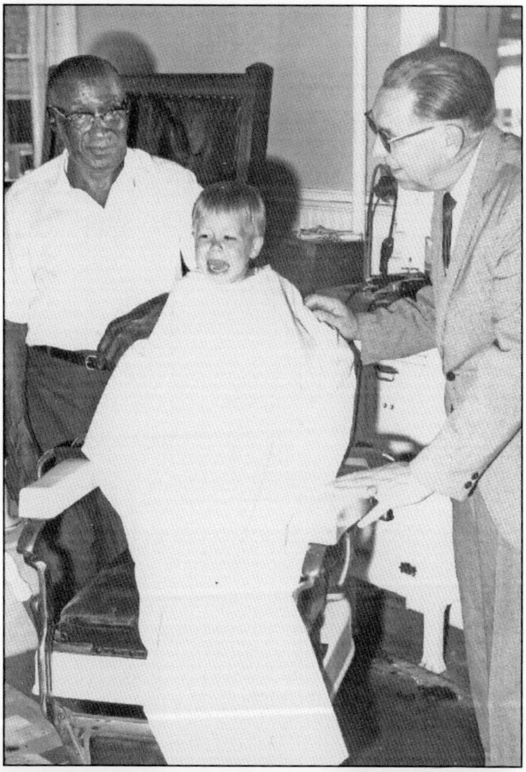

Barber Edgar T. "Trib" Reynolds looks on as Lilburn Nofsinger tries to calm unhappy grandson Bruce Nofsinger during a haircut in 1968. Trib, who worked his way up from shoeshine boy to barber in the Mathis Brothers barbershop, was also a member of the city council. He cut hair in Greenville for 55 years, from 1919 until his death in 1974. (Christine Hinsey.)

Around 1963, Wayne Cisney (left), president of L. B. Knight Motor Company, hands the keys to a new Chevrolet to Brad Nofsinger, 70, a retired rural mail carrier for the Graham post office. Nofsinger carried the mail for 37 years, starting in 1926. Each car he used was a Chevrolet from the L. B. Knight Company except his first car, which was a Model T Ford. (Christine Hinsey.)

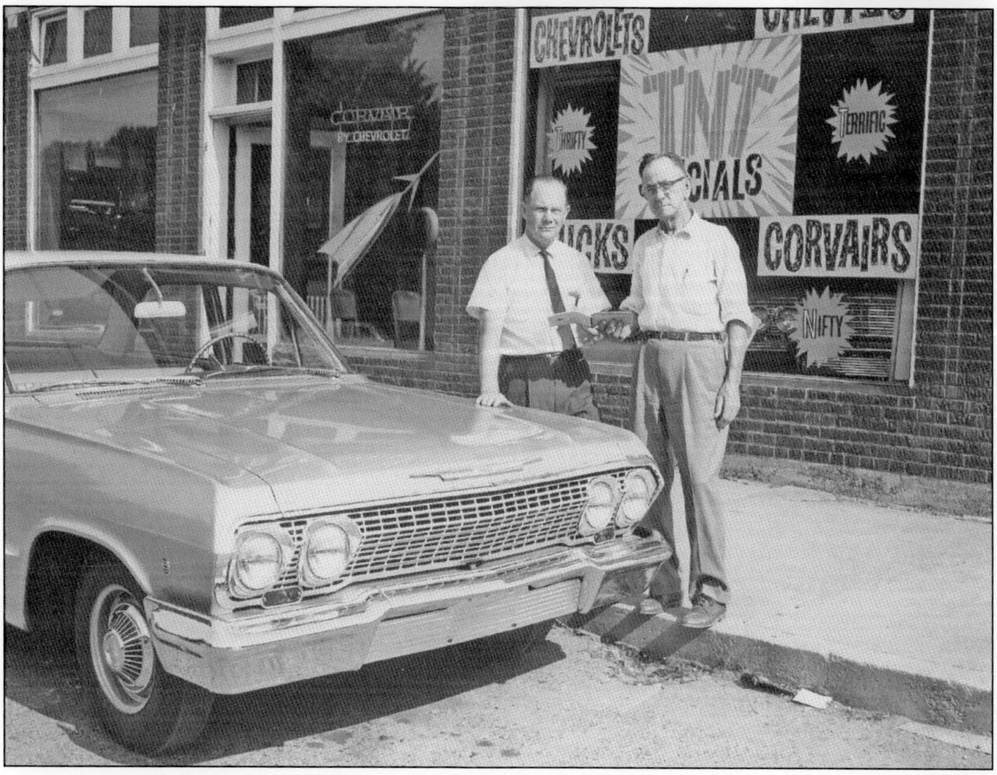

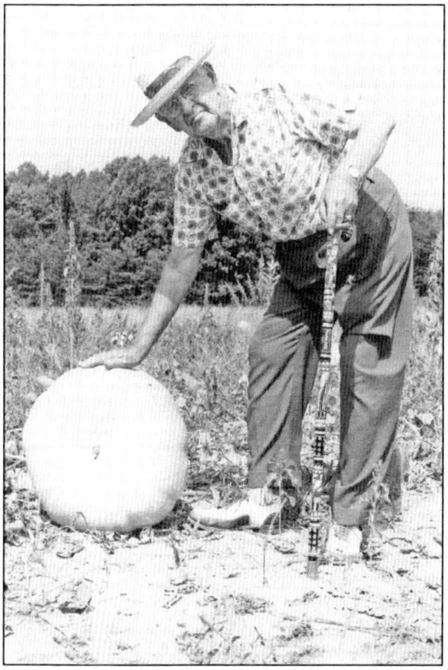

Wallace C. Malone taps a 35-pound pumpkin growing on his farm in 1962. Wallace and his wife, Edna, gave extensive acreage toward the development of Lake Malone along with 300 acres of land valued at $99,000 for the establishment of a state park that was later named in their honor. The total value of land donated by the Malones was estimated at $191,000. (Christine Hinsey.)

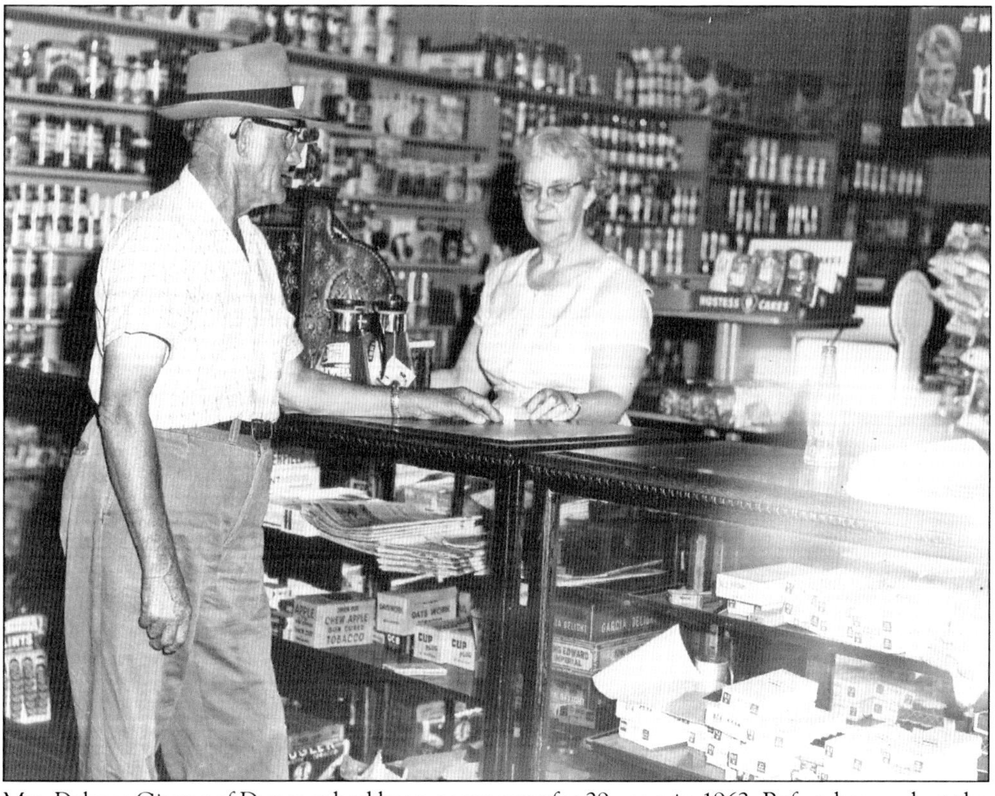

Mrs. Delmas Givens of Dunmor had been postmaster for 29 years in 1962. Before her work at the post office, she taught first grade at Browder for four years. She was the first postmaster appointed to office under Pres. F. D. Roosevelt. (*Times Argus.*)

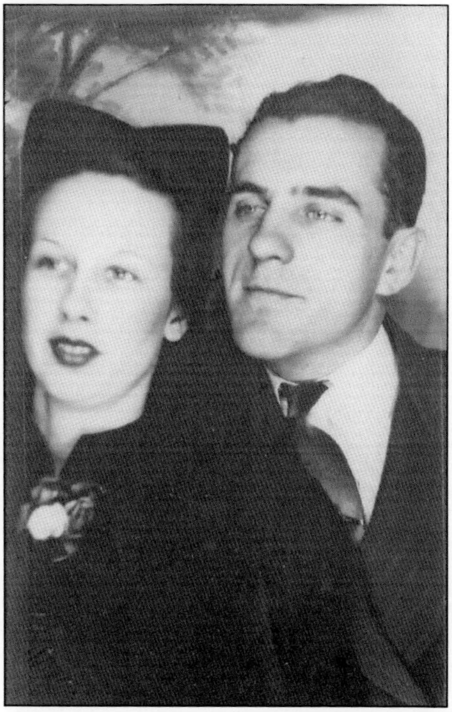

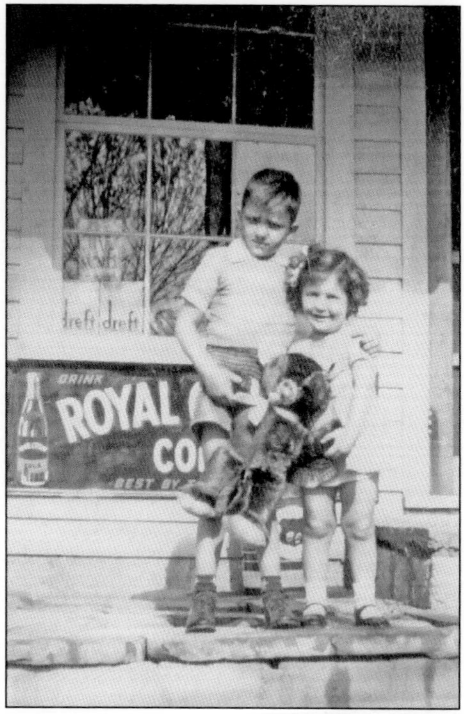

Marie (Putnam) Bivins and Ras Edward Bivins pose for a 1930s photograph. Their children, Ken and Jan, wait on the porch of the Bivins Service Station and Grocery in South Carrollton around 1947. In a 30-year span from 1930 through 1960, Ras Bivins, who was a Greenville native and a Central City businessman, helped spur the economic growth of the county. Ras and his wife, Marie, built, purchased, co-owned, or managed 10 different county businesses during this time. They were the Bivins Service Station; the Dan-Dee Motel; Bivins Service Station and Grocery; the R&M Florist; the Owensboro Concrete and Block Company; R&G Building Supply; the Rambler Rose Motel (below), which was the first motel in the county; the Royal Palm Restaurant; the A-Bo-K Florist; and the Sears Bowling Alley. (Jan Anderson.)

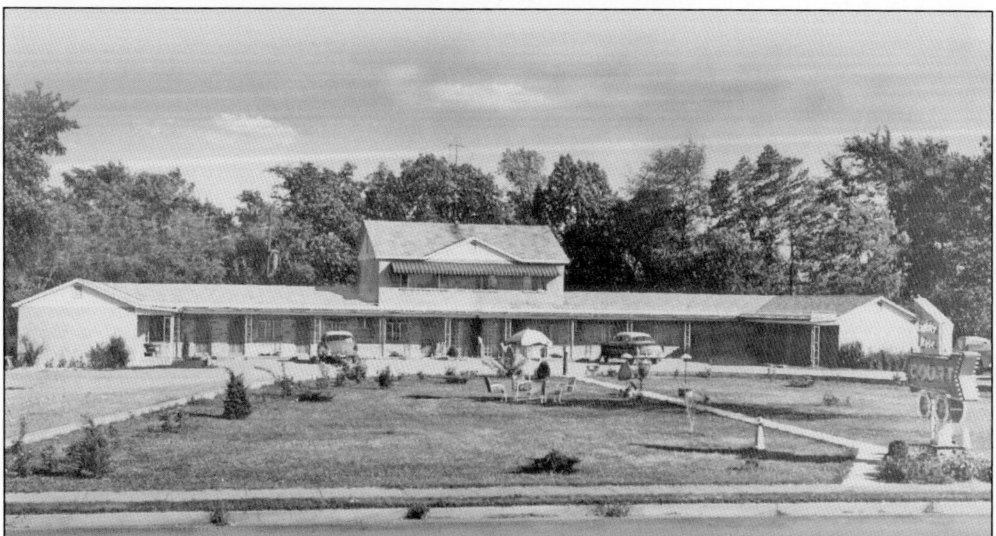

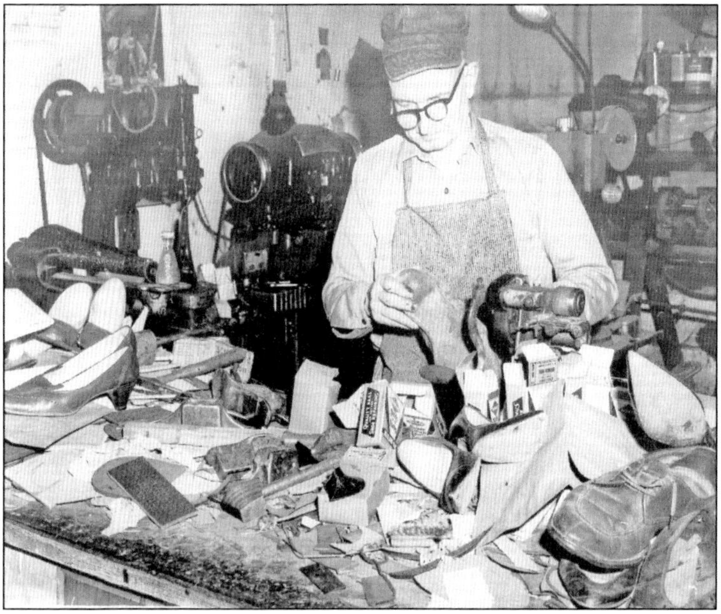

Homer Moore repairs shoes at the work counter in his shop in Greenville in 1964. Homer's knack for restoring lost soles was appreciated by the citizens of the county, who constantly needed heels or soles replaced and colors matched. Homer methodically went about his business day after day and could always successfully work his way through the mountains of shoes left in his care. (Muhlenberg County Library Archives.)

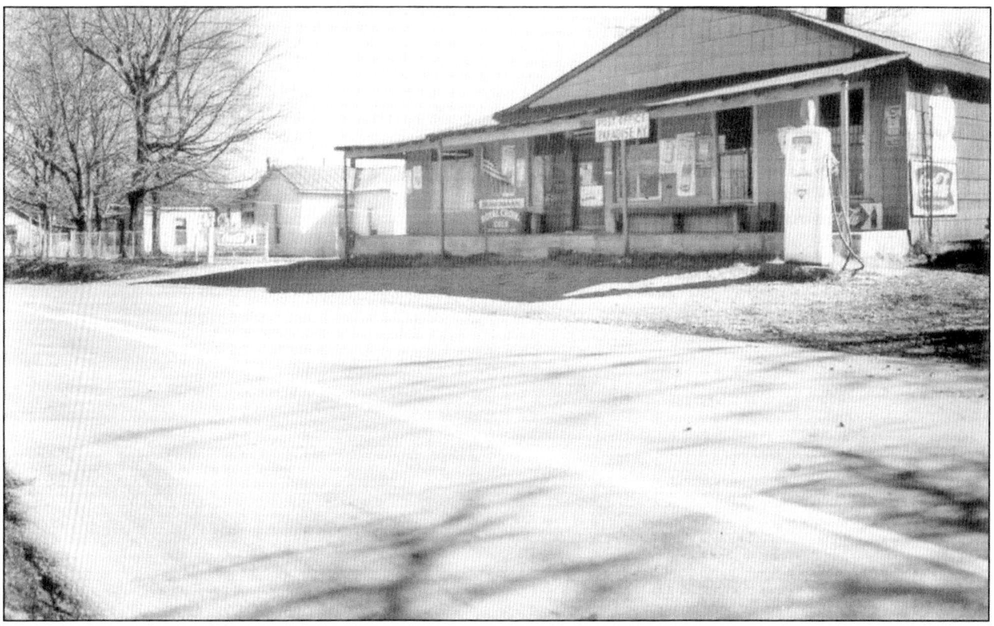

Buchanan's Grocery signs advertise RC Cola, Coca-Cola, and gasoline for sale. The grocery-and-post-office combination was located on Main Street in Paradise, Kentucky, in 1957 but was gone by 1967, like the rest of the town. All the citizens lost their "Paradise," as the Tennessee Valley Authority located the largest steam plant in the world on the Green River near their town. (Christine Hinsey.)

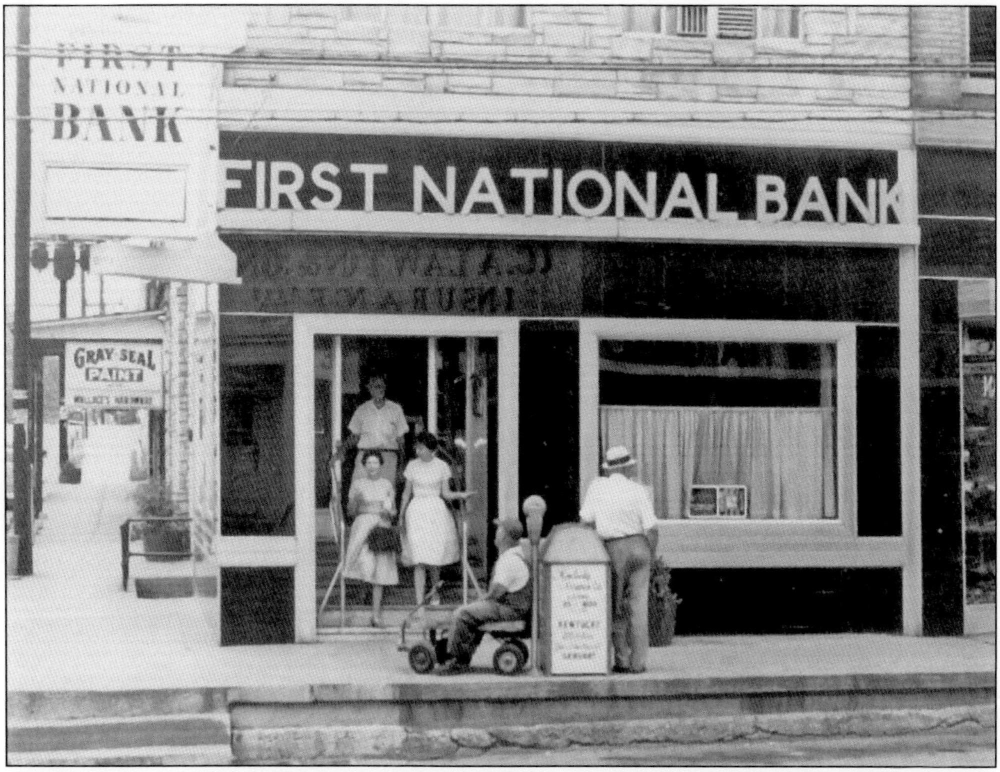

The First National Bank, located on Broad Street in Central City, was initially called the Home Deposit Bank in 1902 and had resources of only $36,409.83. By 1942, that figure had increased to over $1 million. In 1906, it changed its name to First National Bank and survived the financial crisis of the 1920s and 1930s. When this picture was taken in 1962, Cy Ross was bank president and Walter Creager in his wagon was a familiar town figure. (Muhlenberg County Library Archives.)

Members of the 1975 Central City Retail Merchant's Association participating in the ribbon-cutting ceremony dedicating the new car lot are, from left to right, Rodney Kirtley, John Kirtley, Orvil Brand, David Greenwood, Bill Greenwood, Ida Wheeldon, Tom Shewmaker, Charles Bennett Greenwood, and Sammy Gish. (Muhlenberg County Library Archives.)

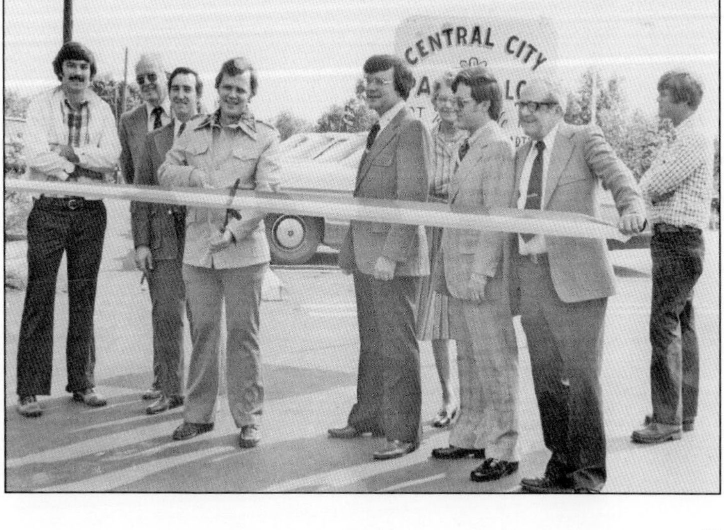

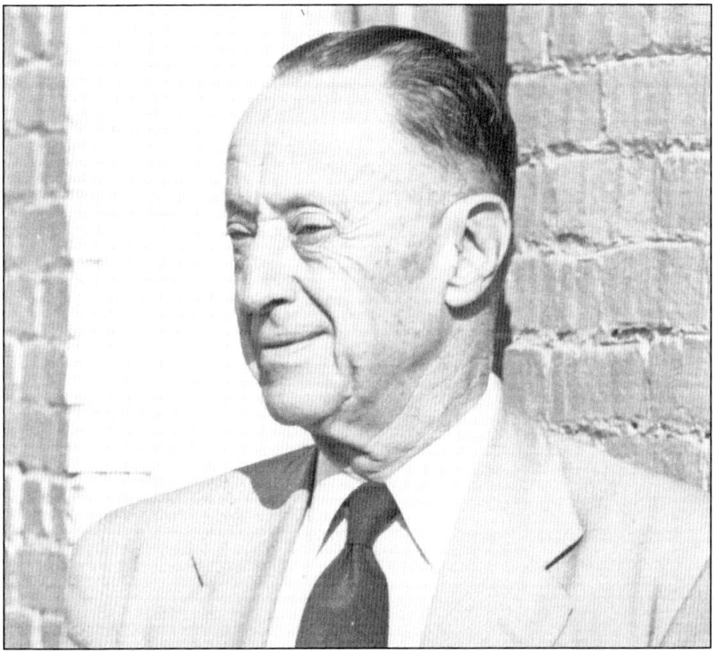

J. Pat Morgan, a successful businessman, generously divided an estate valued at over $2 million among the libraries, schools, churches, hospital, and the town of Greenville. A city park complete with a swimming pool was built and named in his honor. Morgan and his sister Geneva left no heirs, but county residents continue to benefit from their generosity on a daily basis. This picture dates to around 1960. (Muhlenberg County Library Archives.)

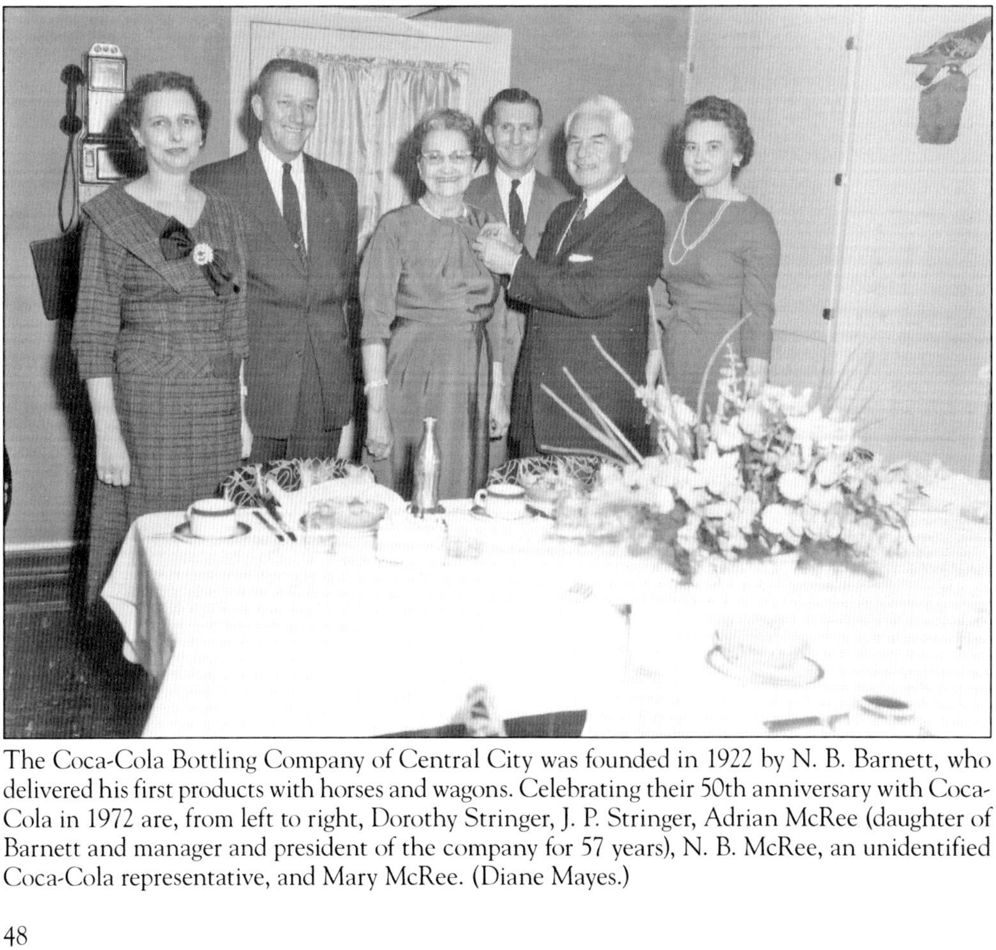

The Coca-Cola Bottling Company of Central City was founded in 1922 by N. B. Barnett, who delivered his first products with horses and wagons. Celebrating their 50th anniversary with Coca-Cola in 1972 are, from left to right, Dorothy Stringer, J. P. Stringer, Adrian McRee (daughter of Barnett and manager and president of the company for 57 years), N. B. McRee, an unidentified Coca-Cola representative, and Mary McRee. (Diane Mayes.)

Leslie Scott of Scott Hams in Greenville, Kentucky, washes salt off a ham in preparation for the smoking process. June and Leslie Scott prepare 5,000 hams a year using the same recipe their granddad used in the early 1900s to produce smoked hams, bacon, country sausage, and summer sausage. One of the Scotts' prize hams was auctioned at the Kentucky State Fair for $200,000. (June Scott.)

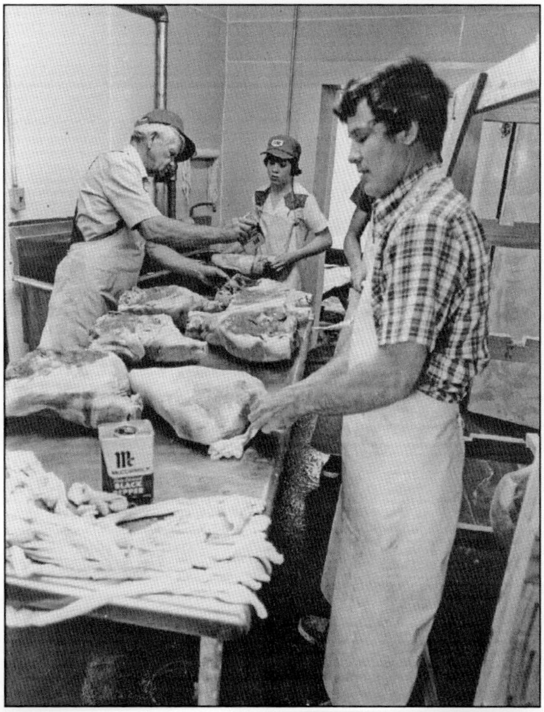

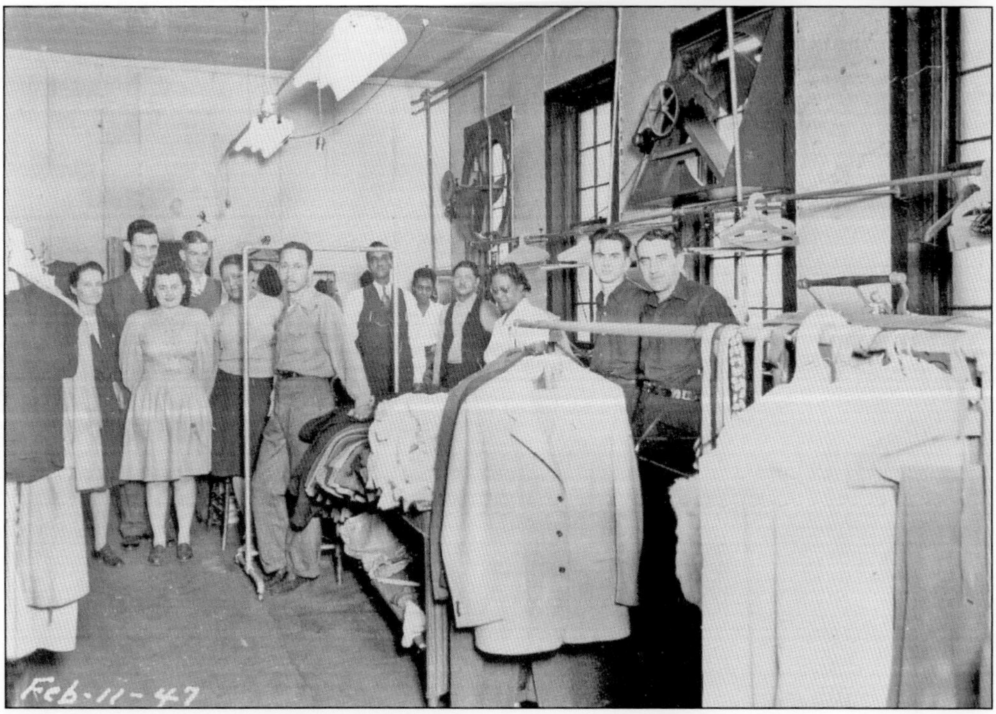

Employees of the Sanitary Cleaners in Central City pose for a group photograph in 1947. Standing from left to right are Eula Mae Bennett, Albert Harding, Mary Bryan, Leroy Griffin, Charlene Grace, Bill Venerable, Willis C. Grace, Anna Mae Bard, Bill Robinson, Willis C. Rorer, Alton Weatherford, and Gerald Sanford. (Muhlenberg County Library Archives.)

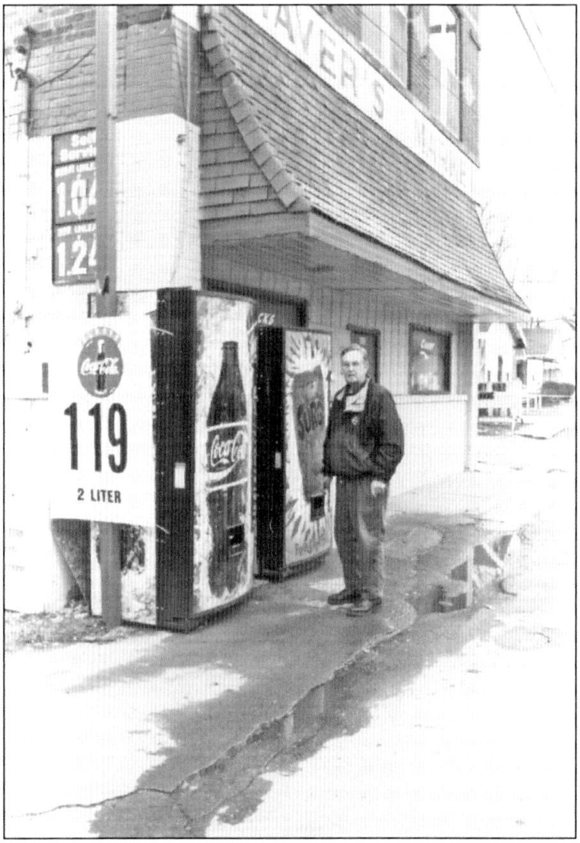

Roy Shaver stands in front of Shaver's Grocery in Bremen in 1972. He bought the store from his grandfather in 1948 after returning from World War II. "My dad thought the store would be a good thing for me," explained Roy. "And as usual he was right." The store was the town gathering place for discussing politics, weather, and world views. (Roy Shaver.)

Reba and Roy Shaver stand behind the counter at Shaver's Grocery in Bremen, Kentucky, around 1972. Roy and his wife, Reba, sold the store in 2000 after Roy had put in a total of 52 years serving his customers. Roy is still busy with his duties as mayor of Bremen and says, "My philosophy is to make my hometown a better place to live and work." (Reba Shaver.)

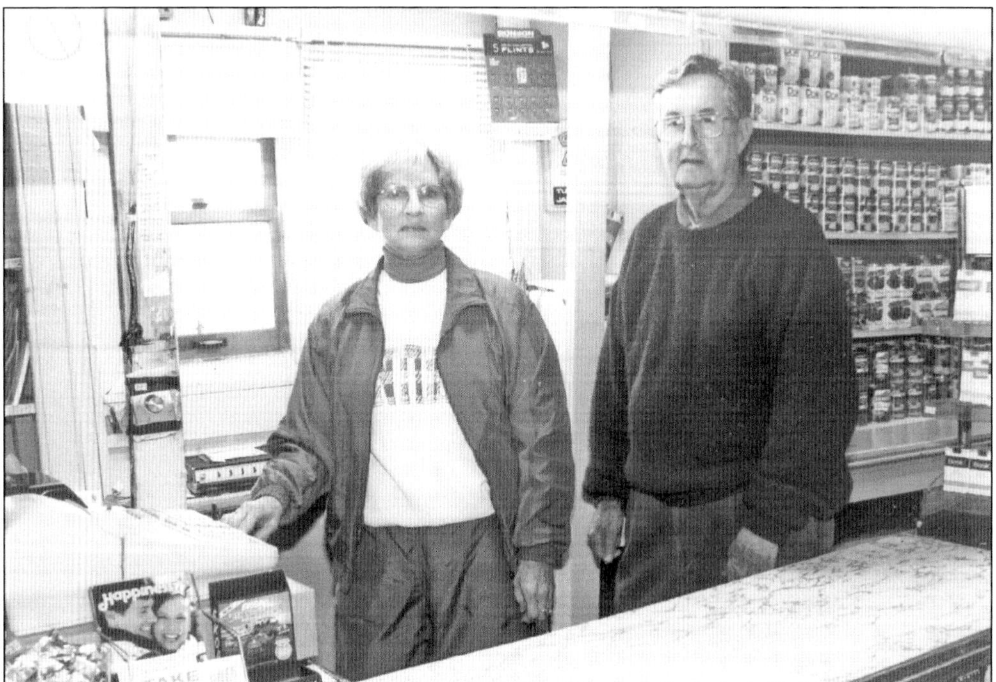

Three

FAITH AND EDUCATION

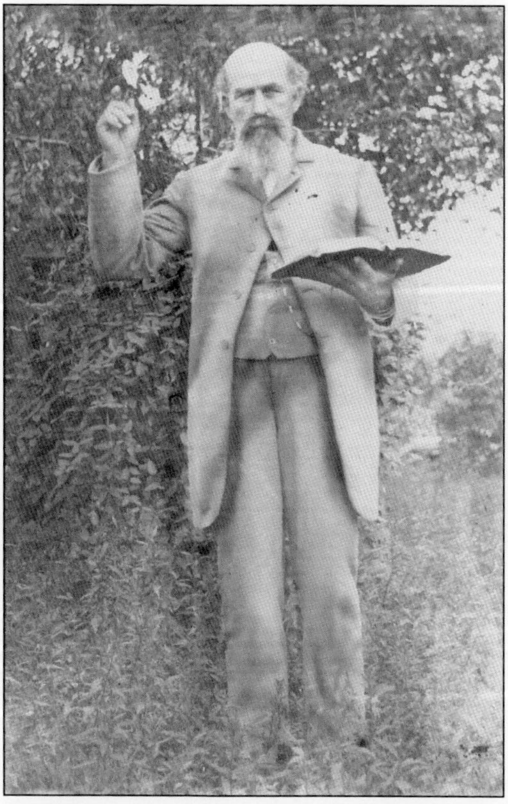

"I have heard preached all my life on the Trinity of the Father, Son and Holy Ghost but there is a trinity in right living and unless each is practiced proportionately life is bound to be a failure. This is the trinity of Learning, Labor and the Love of the Lord," said an anonymous source in 1900. Many of the pioneers were more interested in religion than any other subject, and many of the first religious meetings were held in individual homes until churches could be built. Attempting to strike a balance between learning and religion, the Greenville Academy was established by an act of the legislature on January 18, 1810, and served as the district schoolhouse until around 1890. None of the schools in Muhlenberg County went beyond primary work until about 1850, when post-primary classes were offered by Prof. William Lewis Green. While institutions of learning continued to increase, so did the number of churches and circuit preachers. Rev. George Jeffries (1823–1900) strikes an evangelical pose in South Carrollton around 1870. (Molly Alward.)

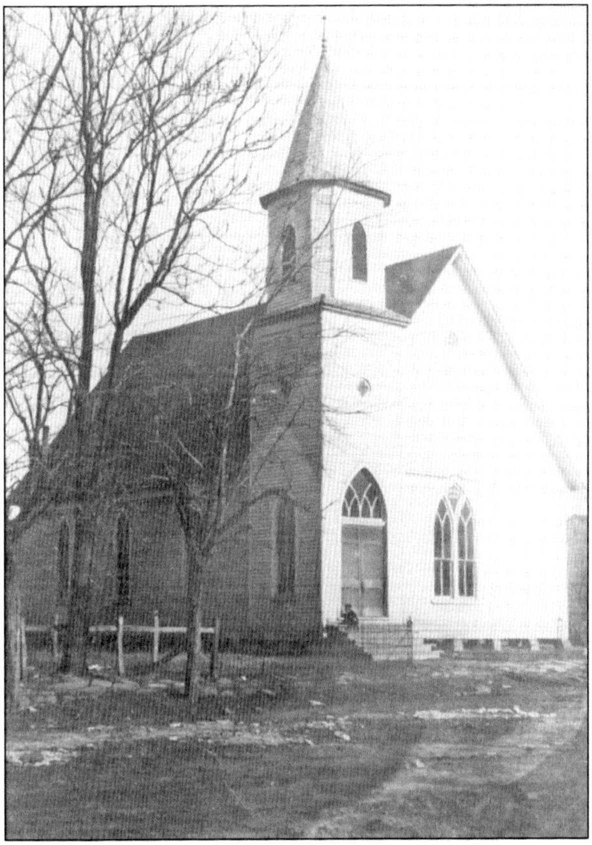

The Great Revival arrived in Logan County in 1799 under the ministry of John McGee of the Methodist church and his brother, William McGee, a Presbyterian. Their camp meetings resulted in many "bodily agitations" by those in attendance and soon spread over the state. Great additions were made to the Methodist churches during this time. The South Carrollton Methodist Church, pictured here around 1900, burned in 1964. (Molly Alward.)

A full congregation gathers at the river in 1900 to take part in a Mormon baptism in Bremen. (Peggy Gossett.)

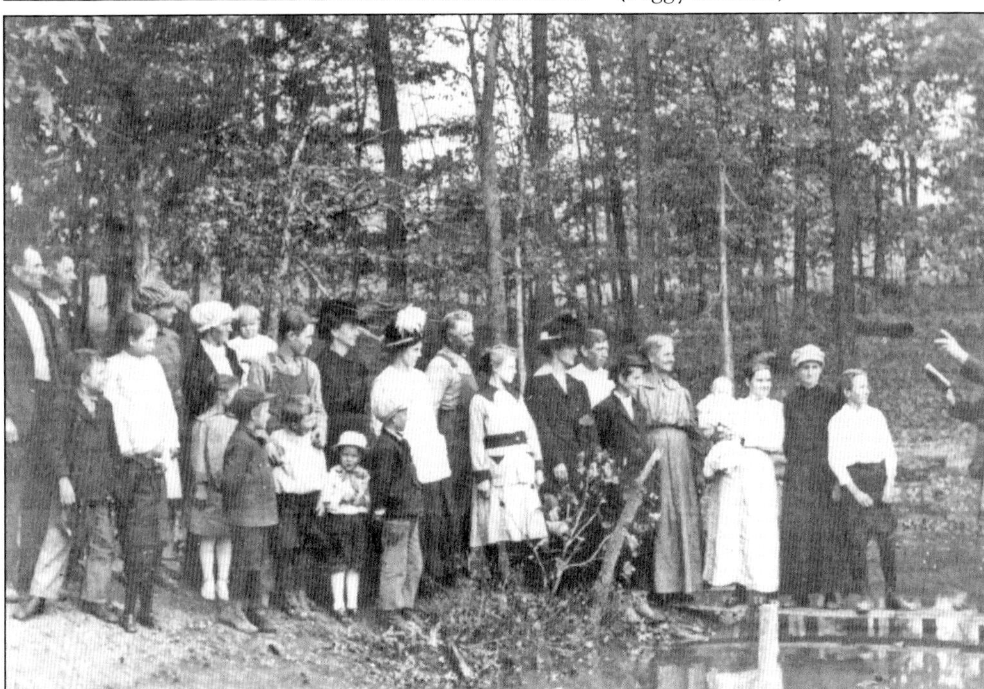

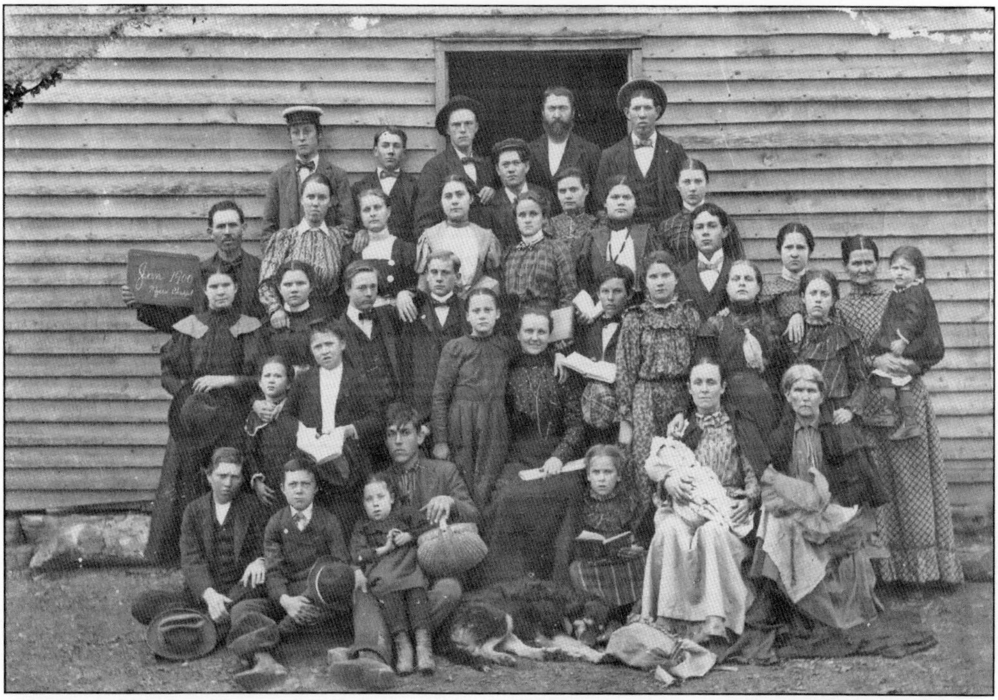

In January 1900, the Myers Chapel members congregate on the church steps for a group picture. The church was built in 1880 and was also used as a grange hall. It was abandoned in 1855. Lying in front of the group is a good dog also enjoying the Sabbath's rest. (Christine Hinsey.)

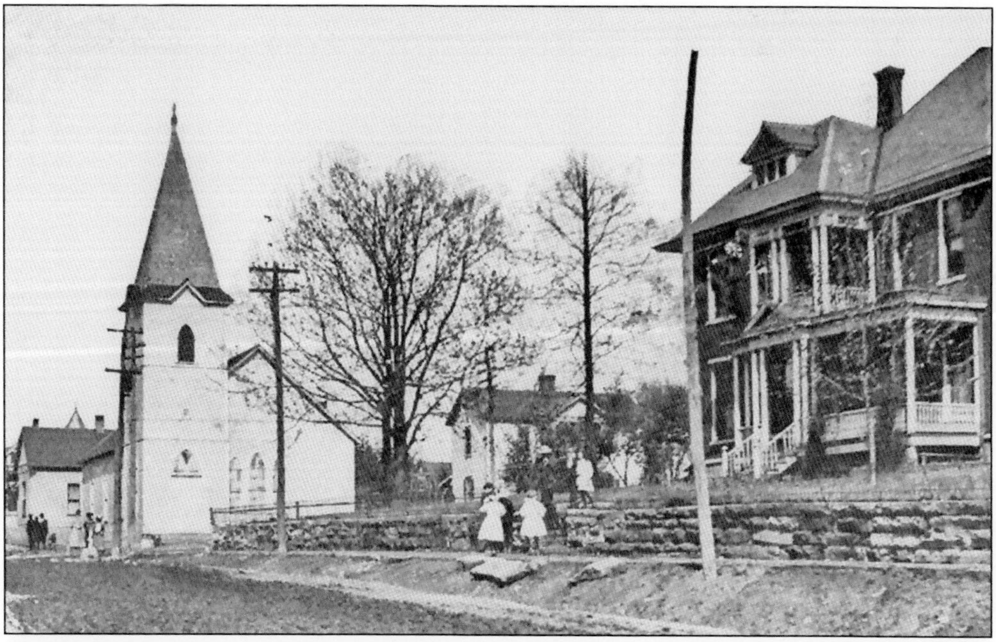

The Methodist Episcopal Church in Central City originated in 1883, and worship was held in a local schoolhouse. In 1889, the present lot was purchased, and the cornerstone was laid in 1890. In 1911, the brick church was built on the frame church's location, and in 1940, about the time of this picture, the church became the First United Methodist Church. (Christine Hinsey.)

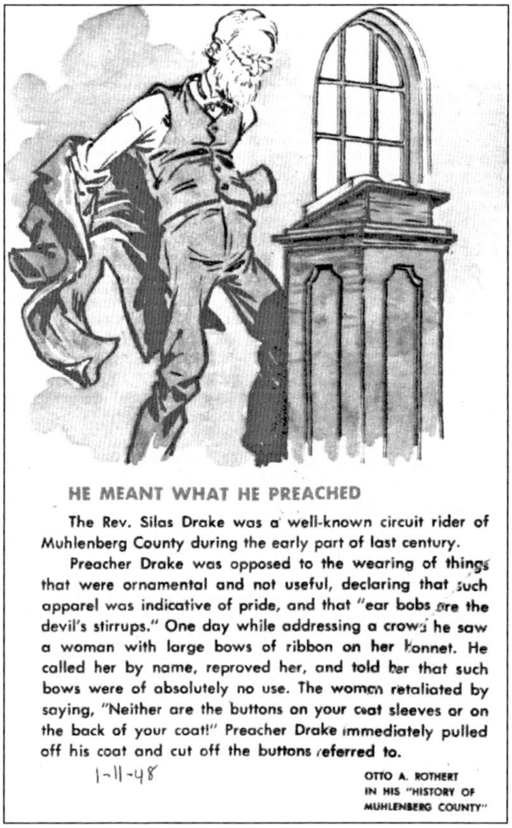

HE MEANT WHAT HE PREACHED

The Rev. Silas Drake was a well-known circuit rider of Muhlenberg County during the early part of last century.

Preacher Drake was opposed to the wearing of things that were ornamental and not useful, declaring that such apparel was indicative of pride, and that "ear bobs are the devil's stirrups." One day while addressing a crowd he saw a woman with large bows of ribbon on her bonnet. He called her by name, reproved her, and told her that such bows were of absolutely no use. The woman retaliated by saying, "Neither are the buttons on your coat sleeves or on the back of your coat!" Preacher Drake immediately pulled off his coat and cut off the buttons referred to.

1-11-48

OTTO A. ROTHERT
IN HIS "HISTORY OF
MUHLENBERG COUNTY"

Rev. Silas Drake, a 1900s circuit preacher, was opposed to the wearing of ornamental objects, declaring "ear bobs are the devil's stirrups." One Sunday, he chastised a woman for wearing large bows on her hat "for they were of no use." The woman retaliated, "Neither are the buttons on your coat sleeves or the back of your coat!" Reverend Drake immediately cut off his buttons. This image dates to around 1948. (Christine Hinsey.)

Members of the African Methodist Episcopal Zion convention gather in 1940. The numbers of members had greatly increased since the church's humble beginnings around 1868 with 15 members. Morris Rhodes Sr., his wife, Hannah, Charlotte Young, and Louis Smith Sr. gathered to form the foundation of the original church that moved to a permanent home in Drakesboro. (Christine Hinsey.)

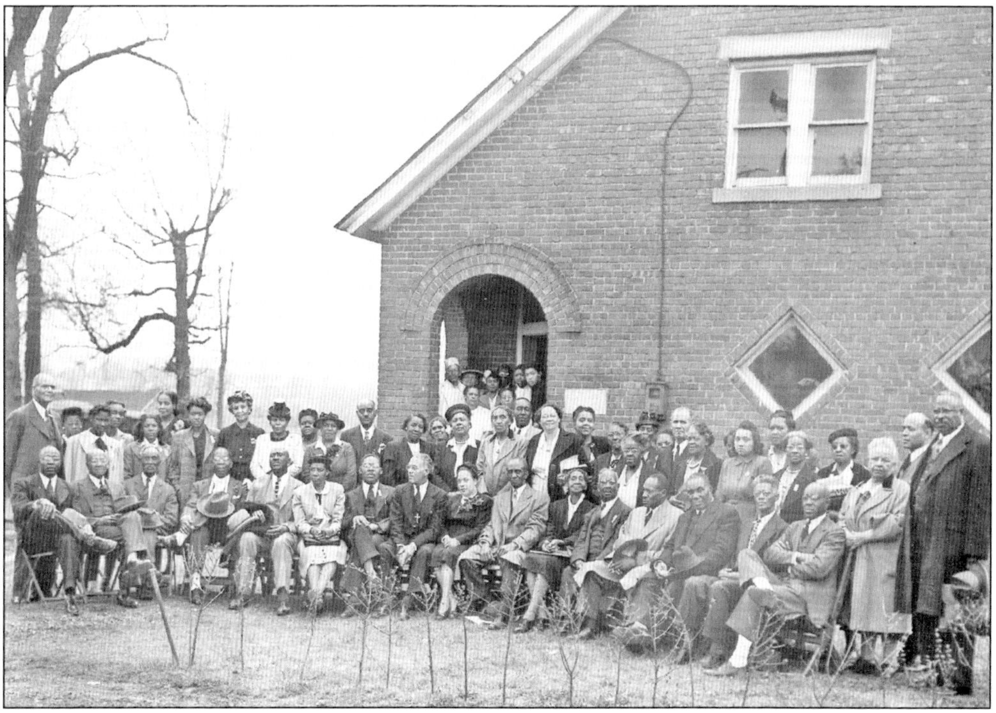

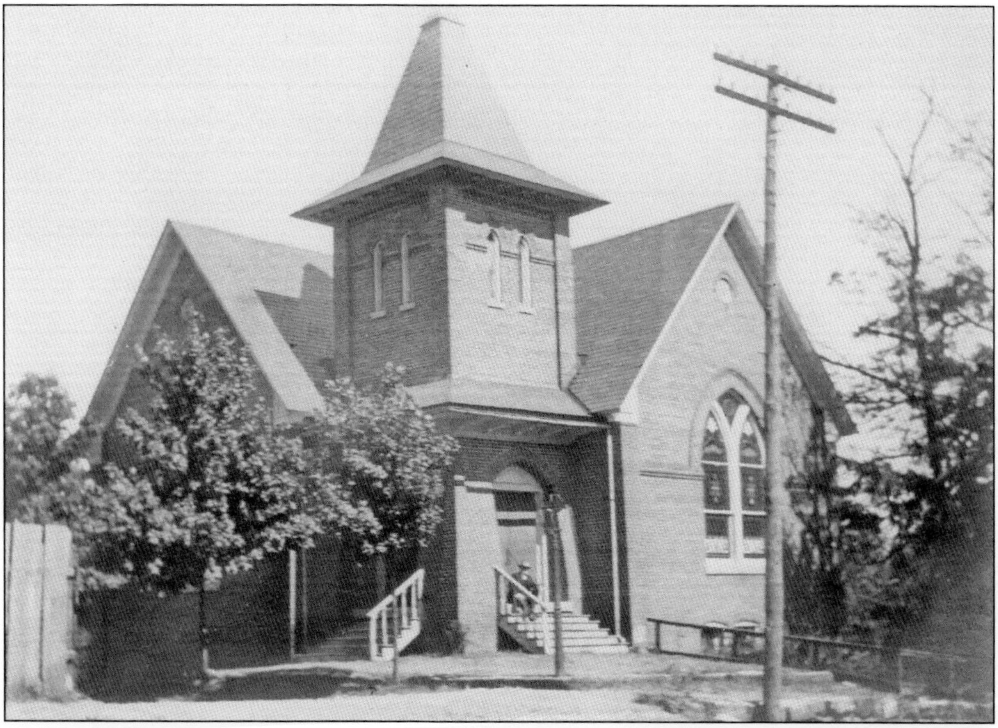

The Christian Church of Greenville, Kentucky, on the corner of Mill Street and East Main Cross, was built in 1855 and originally used by the Methodist Episcopal congregation. It became the First Christian Church in 1921. Many of the first churches in Muhlenberg County were known as union churches. These churches were built by two separate denominations that used the facility on alternate Sundays. (Christine Hinsey.)

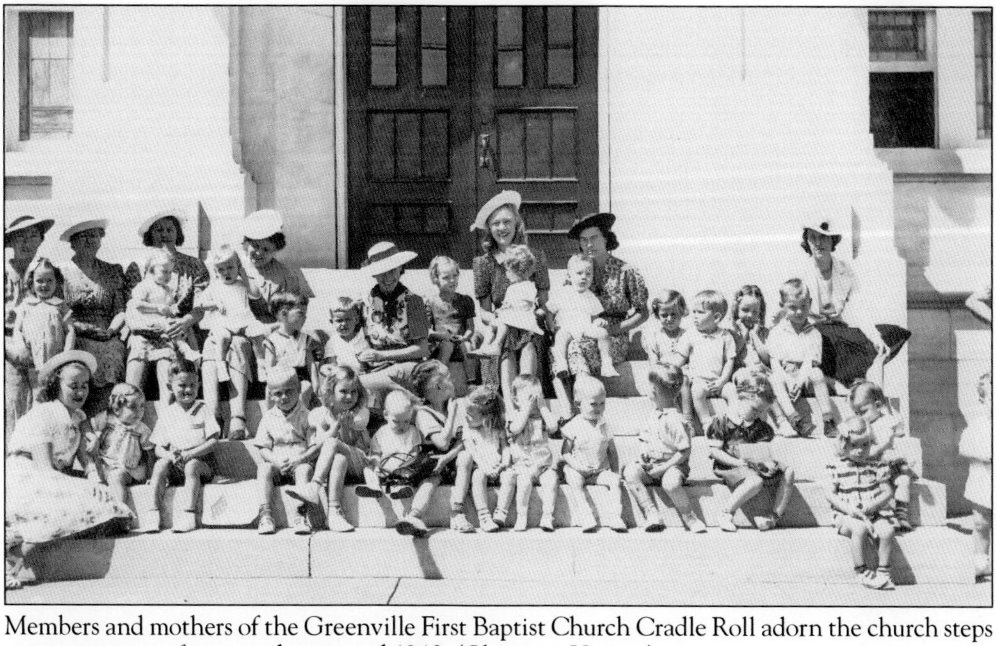

Members and mothers of the Greenville First Baptist Church Cradle Roll adorn the church steps in anticipation of picture day around 1940. (Christine Hinsey.)

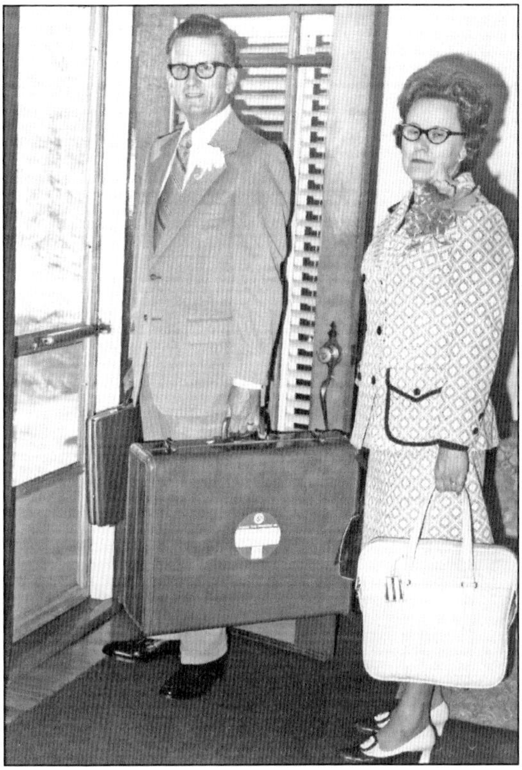

Rev. R. D. and Mary Ellen Mize prepare to leave for their 18-day trip to the Holy Land in 1972. The trip was a gift from the Cleaton Baptist Church, where Reverend and Mrs. Mize served since 1963. Church membership was recorded as 566 members in 1964. (*Times-Argus.*)

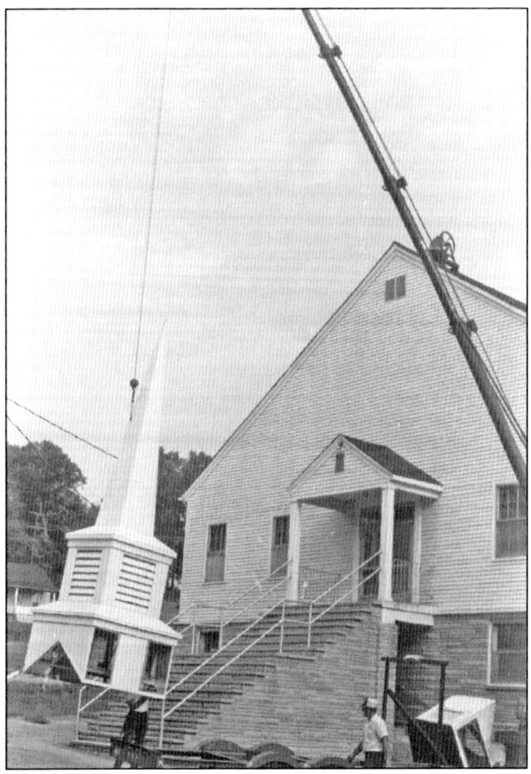

The Cleaton Baptist Church was established in 1844 and built in 1892. The church was originally called Belleview and was located on a hill overlooking Bevier. In 1924, the church body voted to move to the present site on Main Street in Cleaton. Here the church's new steeple is being attached to the roof. (*Leader-News.*)

Amy Longest, the first female superintendent of Muhlenberg County Schools, served in that capacity from 1914 until 1918. She obtained her formal education at Western Kentucky State Normal School, the University of California, the University of Chicago, and the University of Mexico. Longest was often seen driving her horse and buggy from school to school in the course of her duties. (Christine Hinsey.)

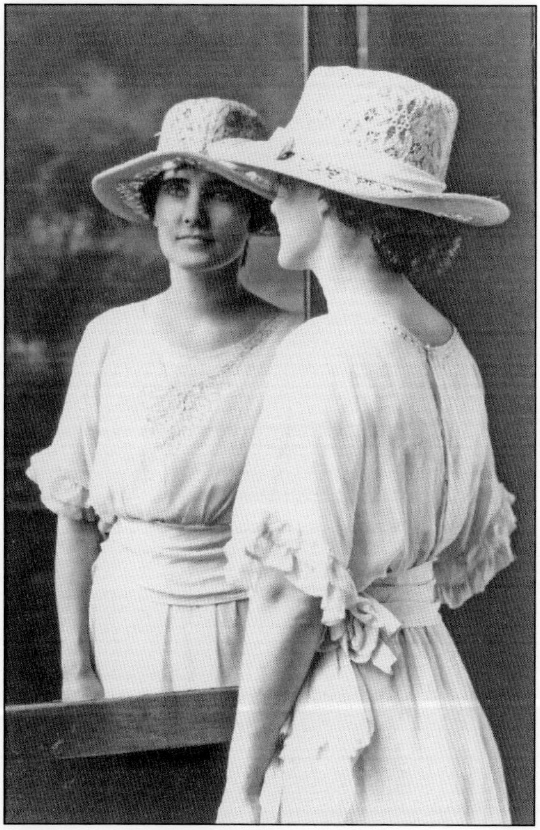

Amy Longest, superintendent of Muhlenberg County Schools, drives her buggy down Cherry Street around 1914 accompanied by Margaret Clovis, the county nurse. Longest's dedication and insight led her to express a need for a large, centrally located school 75 years before it ever happened. Longest Elementary School, named in her honor, sits on ground donated by her father. (Christine Hinsey.)

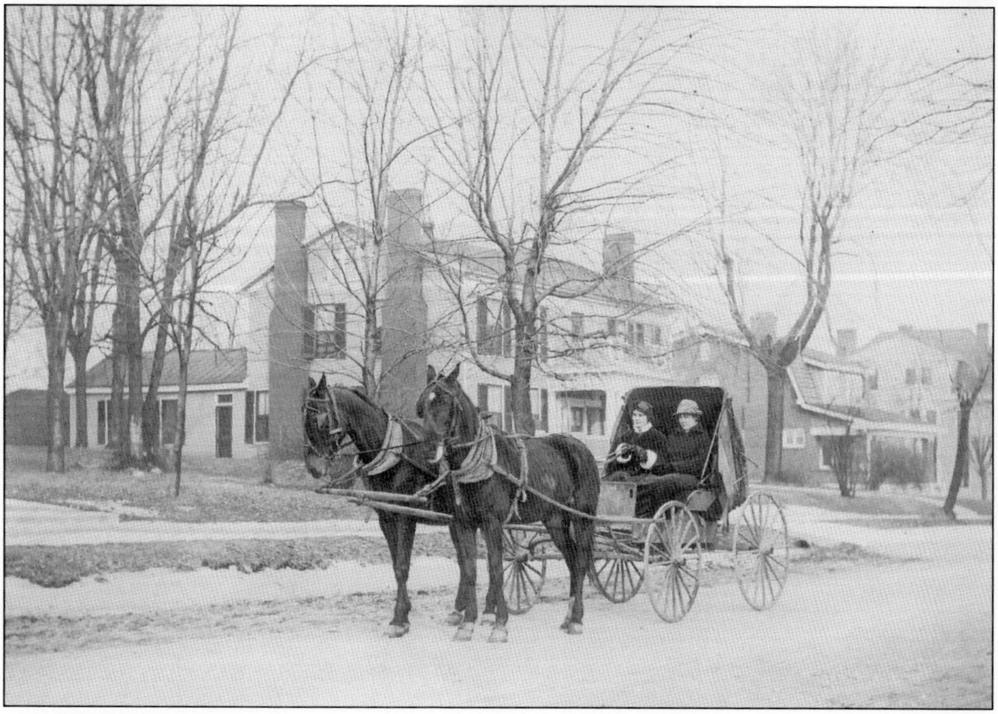

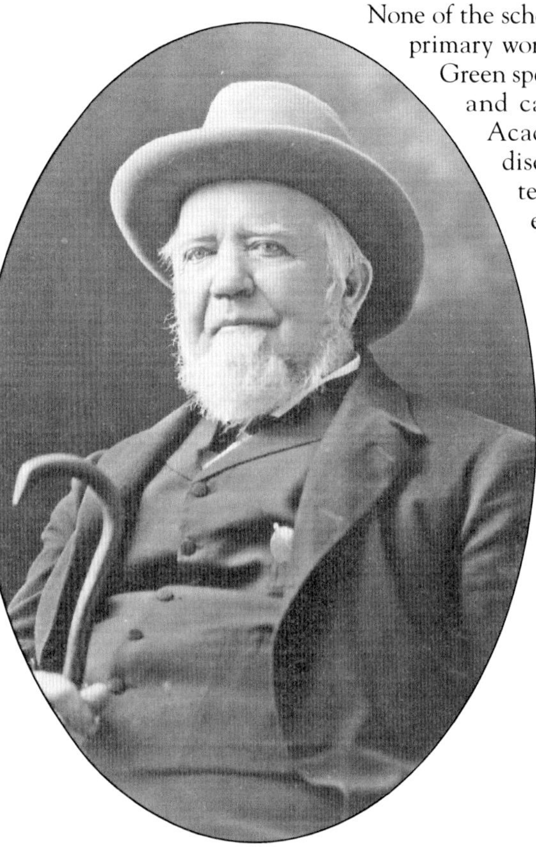

None of the schools in Muhlenberg County went beyond primary work until 1850, when Prof. William Lewis Green spent $50,000 to erect a beautiful dormitory and campus named the Greenville Female Academy. He organized it with the best discipline and supplied it with competent teachers toward the betterment of female education. He was considered the first teacher of higher education in the county. (Christine Hinsey.)

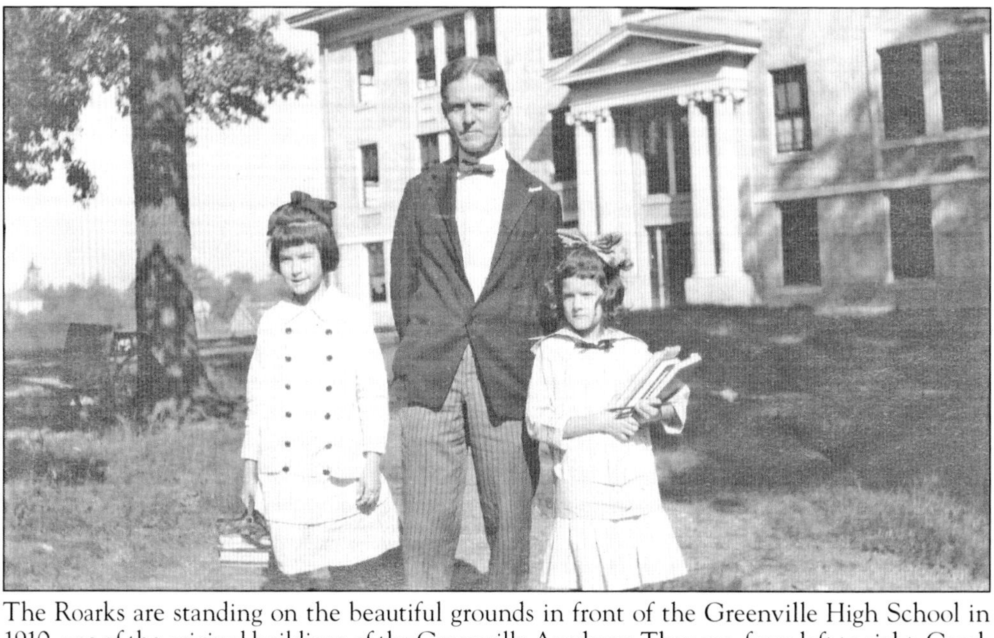

The Roarks are standing on the beautiful grounds in front of the Greenville High School in 1910, one of the original buildings of the Greenville Academy. They are, from left to right, Carol, Orien, and Mary F. (Carol McClure.)

The 1933 Hughes-Kirk School seniors pose on their trip to Diamond Springs. Harry Anderson holds a pipe in his mouth. The other members are not identified in order but are Howard Foster, Mary Ellen Porter, John A. Lile, A. H. Mohon Jr., Rodney Collier, Willie Hareld, Hines Cox, Grace Cisney Brown, Lillie Melton, Nell Conatser, Shelby Jones, Austin Pearson, and Lucillius Mohon, with Marcia Nell Grayson Wells absent. (H. L. Anderson Jr.)

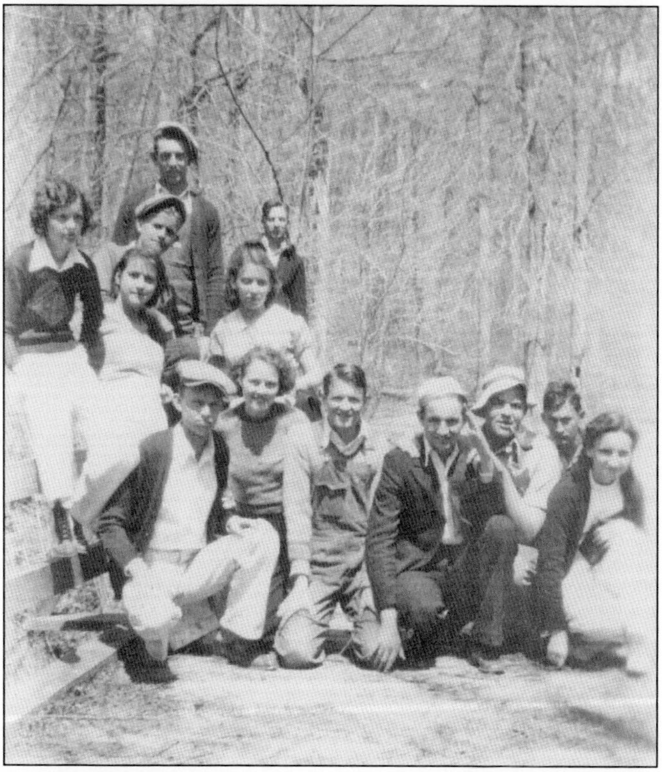

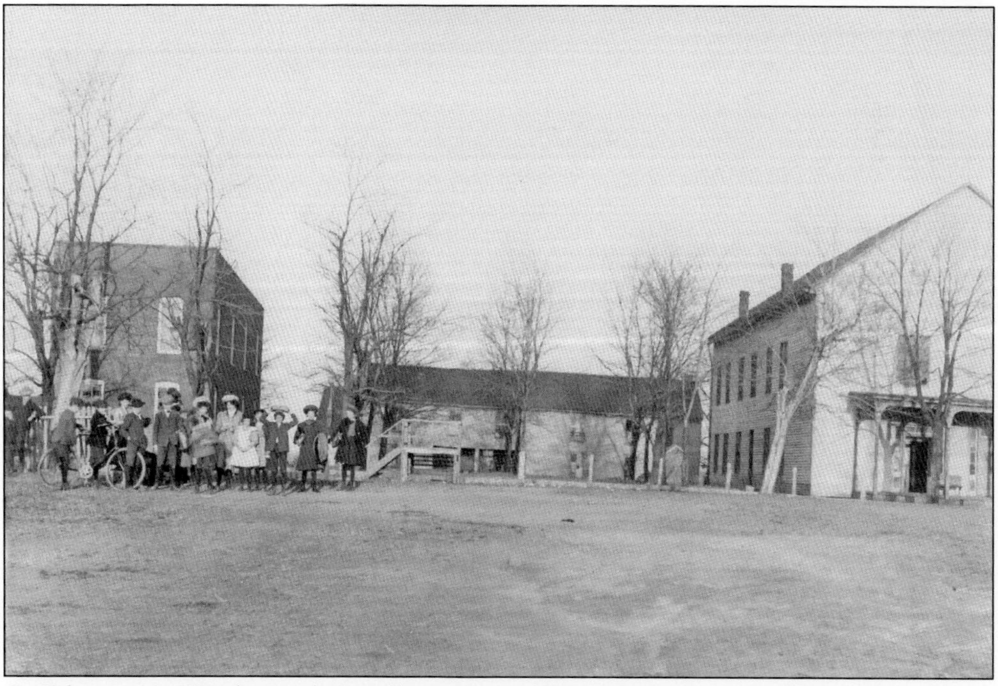

On February 23, 1874, the South Carrollton Male and Female Institute was established. It is pictured around 1880. In 1886, it became known as the West Kentucky Classical and Normal College. From 1850 to 1900, five colleges opened and closed in Muhlenberg County. (Christine Hinsey.)

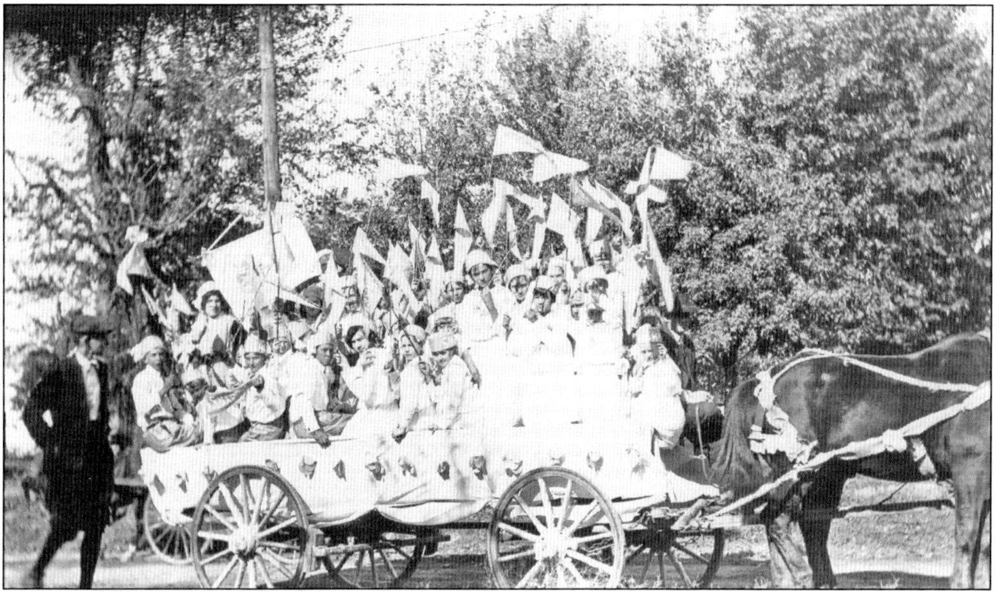

Amy Longest organized the first school parade in Greenville in 1912. Longest was innovative and insightful and knew how to instill a sense of excitement and adventure into her students. Her own spirit of adventure eventually took her to White Mountain, Alaska, to teach. In September 1930, she returned to attend the Kentucky Education Association and to visit her home state once again in the springtime. (Christine Hinsey.)

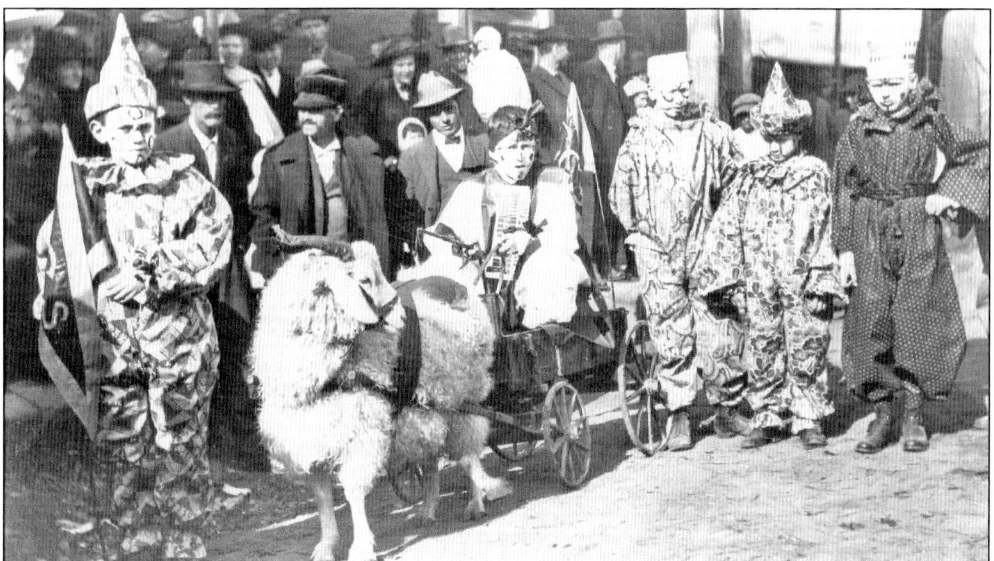

Students dressed as clowns await the signal to move their goat carts and join the parade down Main Street during the county's first school fair. People lined the streets for blocks in Greenville during the spring of 1912 to watch the excitement and enjoy the fun and refreshments. (Christine Hinsey.)

The 1921 Greenville High School seniors were members of Miss Featherstone's Cicero class. Enjoying their outing are, from left to right, Louise Williams, Raymond Vinson, Mary Marie Hayser, Roscoe Oglesby, and Carol Roark. (Carol McClure.)

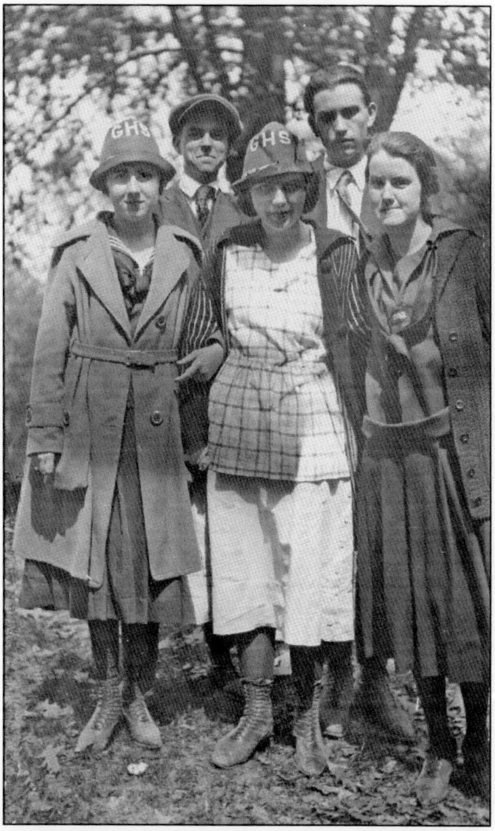

The Moonlight School was built by W. G. Duncan around 1895 to educate the illiterate adults in Graham. This system was the first access many had to an education. Moonlight schools were so named by adult education pioneer Cora Stewart because classes only met on the nights the moon was bright enough to light the students' paths. "Each one, teach one" was the program's motto. (Carol McClure.)

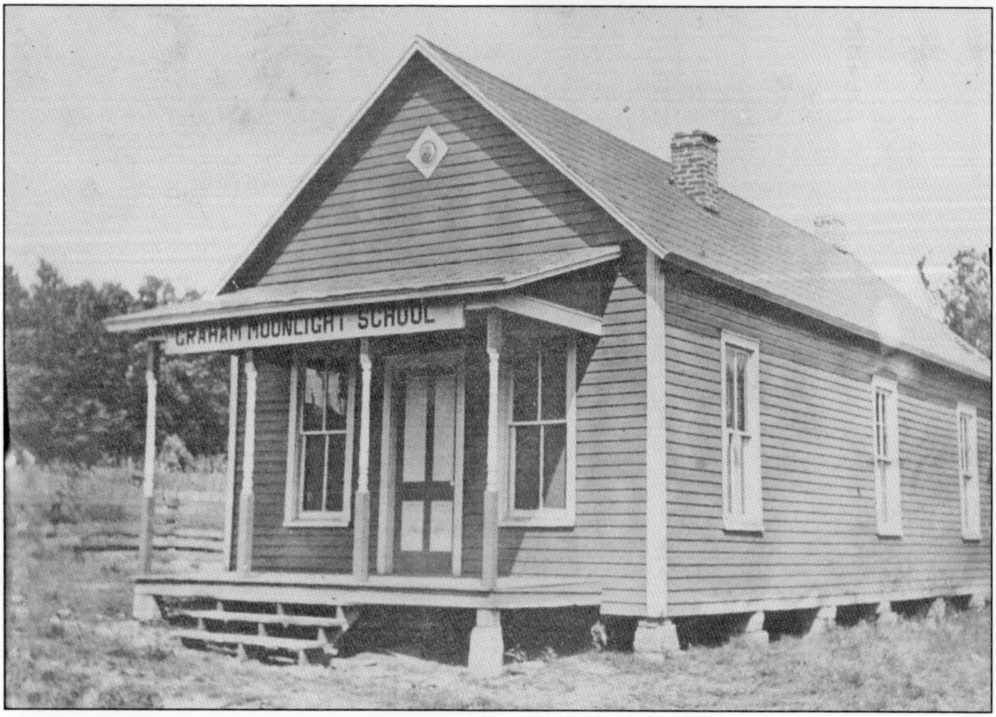

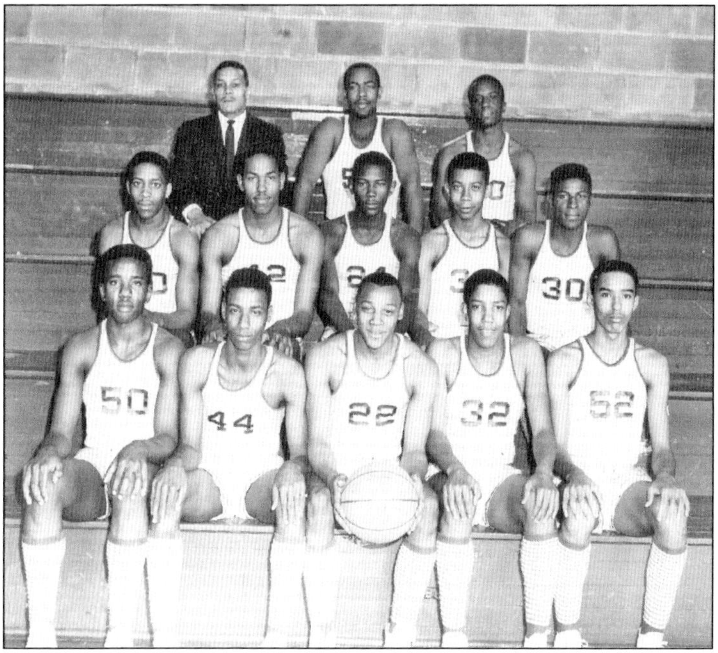

Prior to integration in Muhlenberg County, black students attended separate schools. The only identified basketball team members in this 1961 Drakesboro Community High School photograph are John Elliott (left front) and John Drake (far right front). In 1963, Elliott and Drake transferred to Greenville High School, where they played for the Greenville Black Hawks and graduated with the senior class of 1965. (*Times-Argus.*)

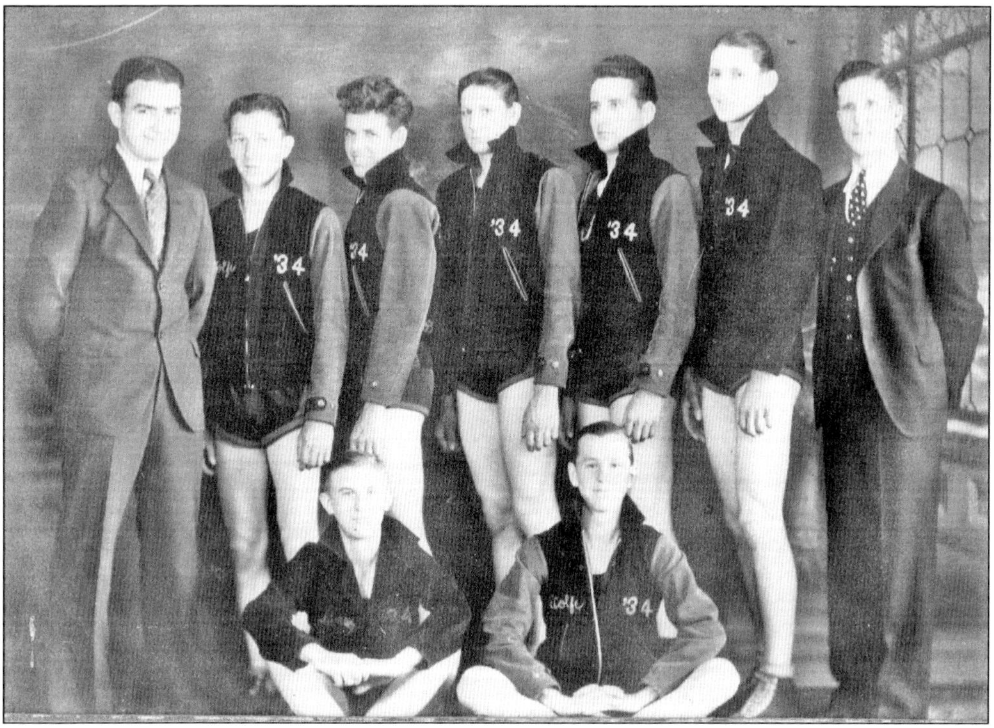

Members of the Drakesboro High School basketball team in 1934 are, from left to right, (first row) unidentified and ? Wolfe; (second row) unidentified, ? Wolfe, Elbert Revlett, unidentified, George Shinn, Oscar "Lefty" Roberson, and J. A. Wright. (Don Roberson.)

Leslie Shively Smith, a teacher and author, was born to a father who had been born into slavery. He stressed the value of education, pride, and humbleness. She followed his instructions and became a teacher so she could teach others. She taught for 40 years before retiring in 1972. In 1979, around the time of this image, her book *A Black History of Muhlenberg County* was published to rave reviews. (Christine Hinsey.)

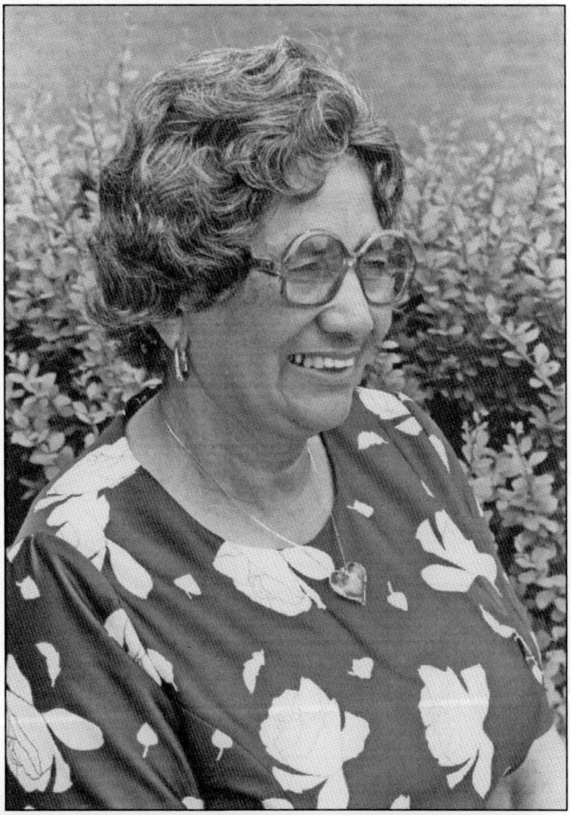

Admiring the historical marker denoting the location of the Old Greenville Cemetery around 1975 are, from left to right, William Donan, James Hahn, Lydia Geibel, and Helen Donan. In 1874, Ephraim M. Brank, M. C. Hay, and Alney Dennis, church trustees, donated the cemetery to the city. Pioneers are buried here along with Ephraim M. Brank, a hero of the War of 1812. (Christine Hinsey.)

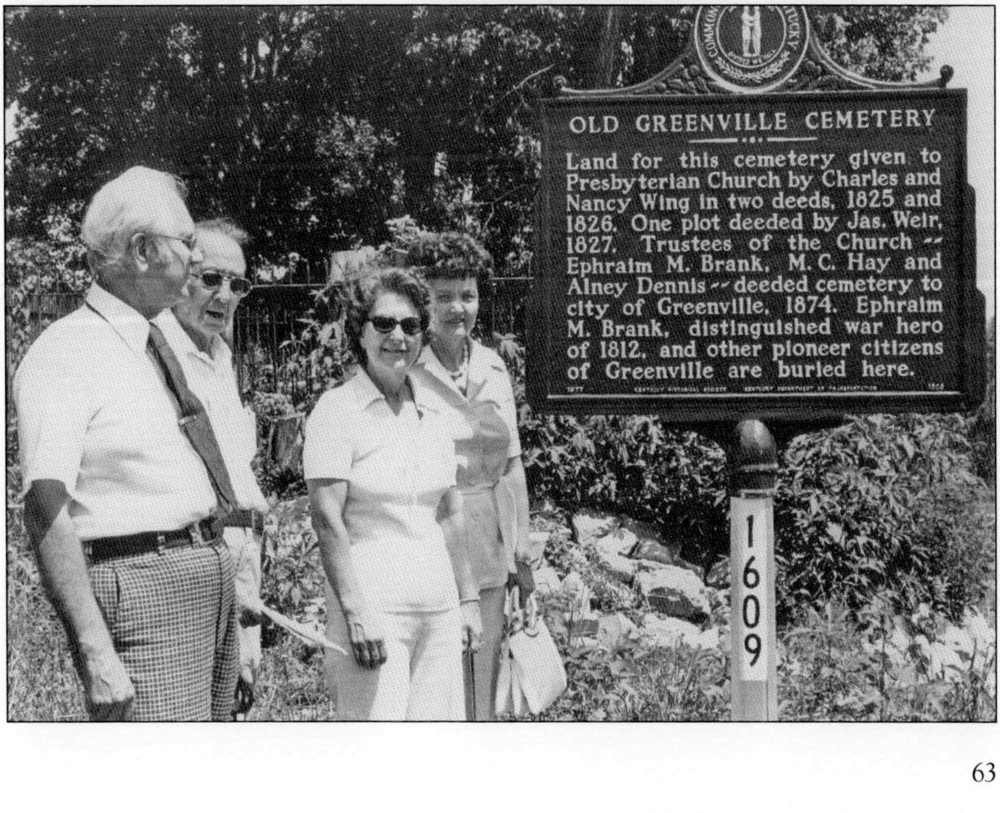

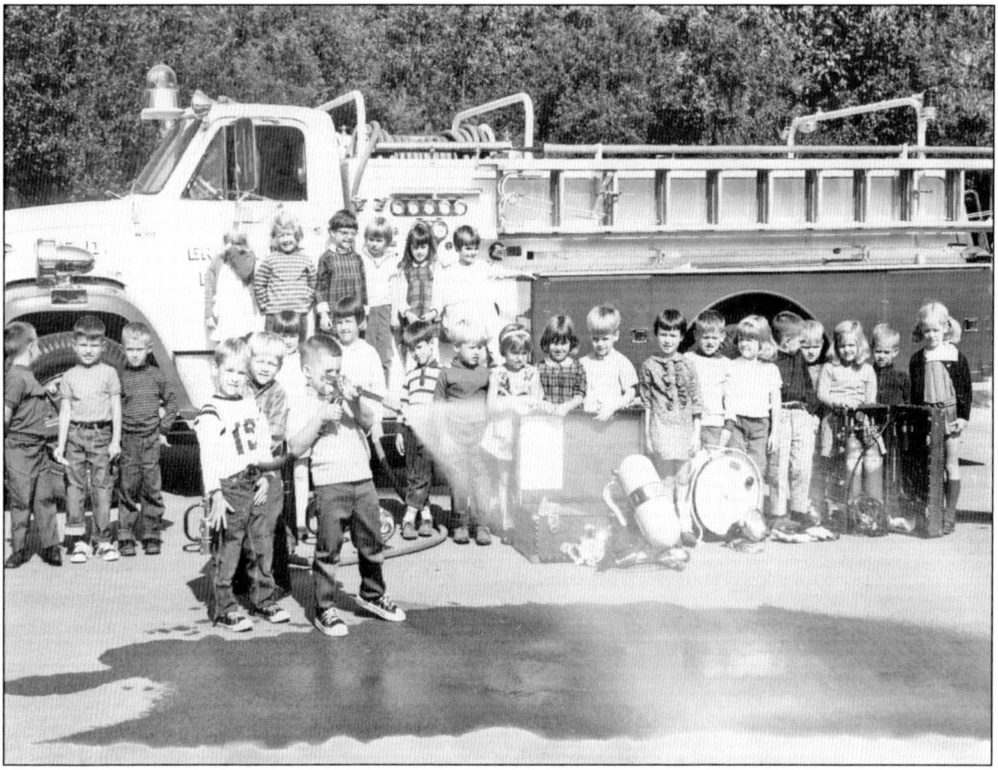

Methodist church kindergartners visit the Greenville Fire Department in 1968. In attendance were also fire chiefs J. W. McDonald and Bill McSpedden. (*Leader-News.*)

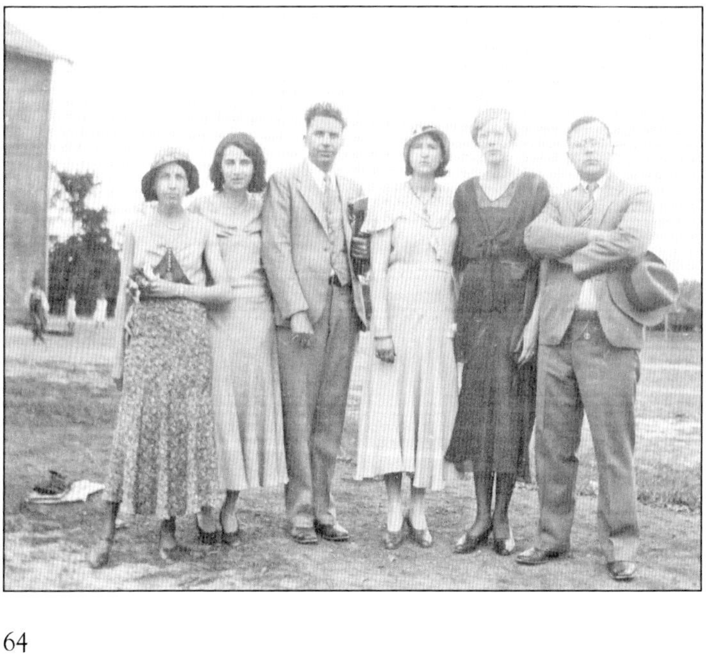

In 1931, Leonard Anderson and his wife, Demie, ran the teacherage for the Hughes-Kirk School. Teachers who had a long way to travel stayed at the teacherage during the week to work and traveled home on weekends. At the teacherage, conveniently located next to the school, they were furnished rooms and meals. Leonard Anderson, in the middle, is the only teacher identified. (Jan and H. L. Anderson Jr.)

Suvarah Anderson taught at the Hunt School in the Hunt Settlement in 1893 and made $30 per month. She was the great aunt of author Bobby Anderson, pictured with her in the 1930s. She taught him the survival skills of hunting, fishing, swimming, and writing. Suvarah was born in Gus in 1869 and married Frank Arnold in 1909. She had no children but loved everyone else's. (Jan Anderson.)

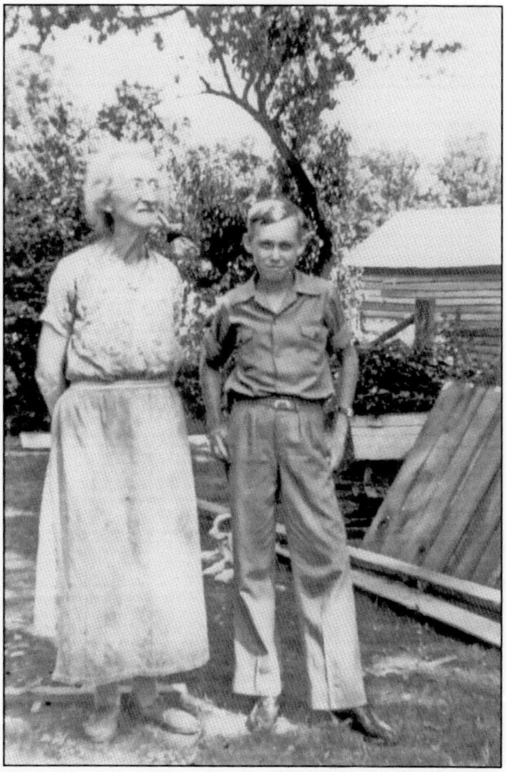

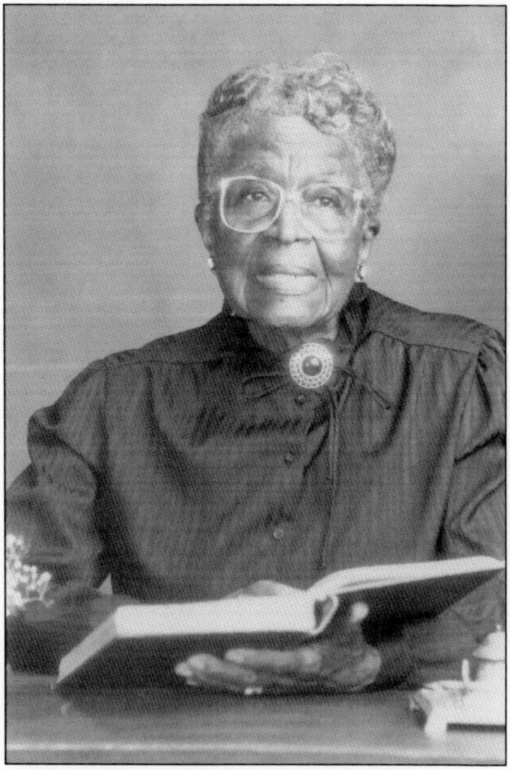

Mittie Render, pictured around 1980, was a serene lady who devoted her life to education. She taught at the first black school in Central City and was still employed as a teacher during the 1965–1966 school year. Mittie Render was also the first black woman to serve on the Muhlenberg Community Hospital board. In her honor, a street in Central City bears her name. (Muhlenberg Library Archives.)

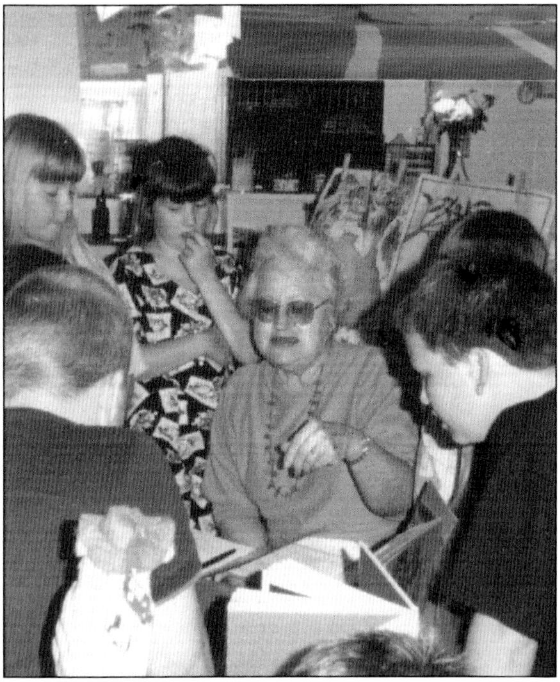

Roberta Chumley of Greenville (1920–2006) is shown in this 1960s photograph discussing a project with children visiting the Duncan Center, where she was a board member. Roberta taught school for many years and continued to contribute to her community through her rewards program and performing arts and concert series. Roberta Chumley also ran Chumley's Jewelry Store in Greenville with her husband, Cecil, until it closed in 1984. (Christine Hinsey.)

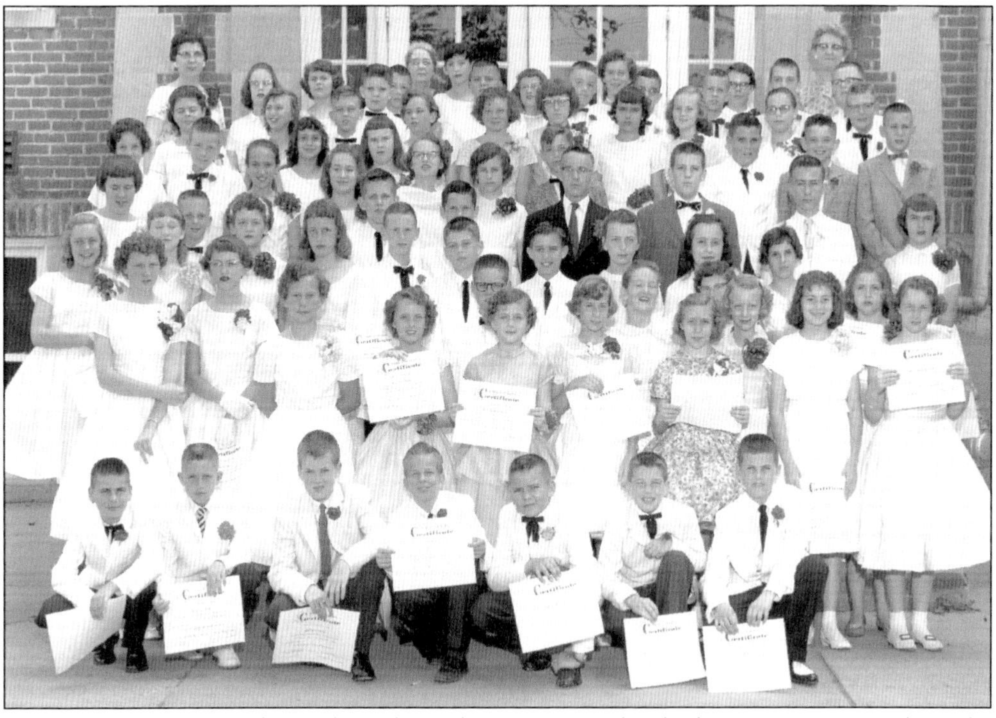

The 1958–1959 Greenville sixth-grade graduates prepare for the big step into seventh grade. These baby boomers broke all previous records for enrollment in all schools in the state and the country. The sheer numbers of their ranks necessitated the need for more teachers and larger classrooms, This sixth-grade class successfully graduated from high school as the class of 1965. (Don Roberson.)

Four

MEDICAL MOMENTS

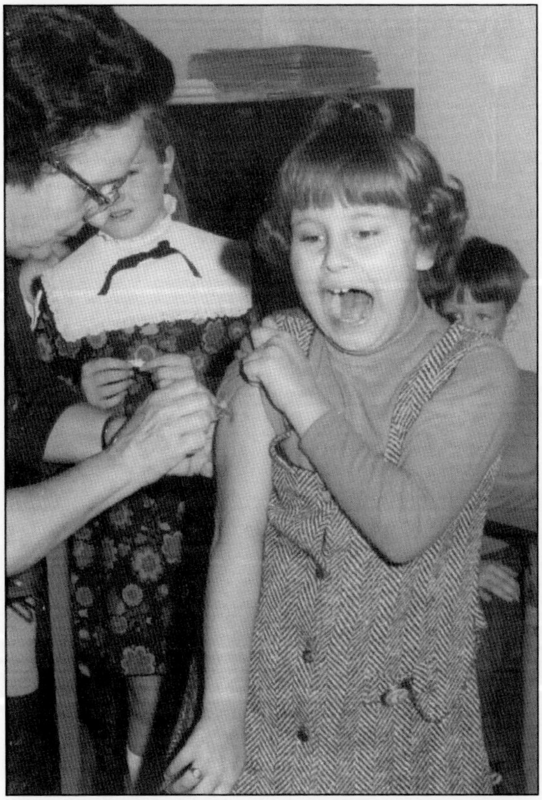

Greenville Elementary School student Wilda Willis shrieks as her classmate Pam McPherson looks on. In 1970, Sue Uzzle, County Health Department RN, had the challenge of inoculating the third graders against rubella, commonly known as the German or three-day measles. For hundreds of years, rubella was seen as a common disease that just about every child would get. Most children would develop a slight fever and rash, so the disease did not seem too serious. That changed in 1941, when an ophthalmologist notice that an alarming number of children developed cataracts following a rubella outbreak. Further investigation revealed rubella, contracted during pregnancy, could cause blindness, deafness, heart disease, or mental retardation to a fetus. Research led in 1969 to the development of the rubella vaccine, which was combined with the measles and mumps vaccine (MMR) in 1972. Mass school immunizations began to protect children from the devastating effects of the disease. (Harbin Memorial Archives.)

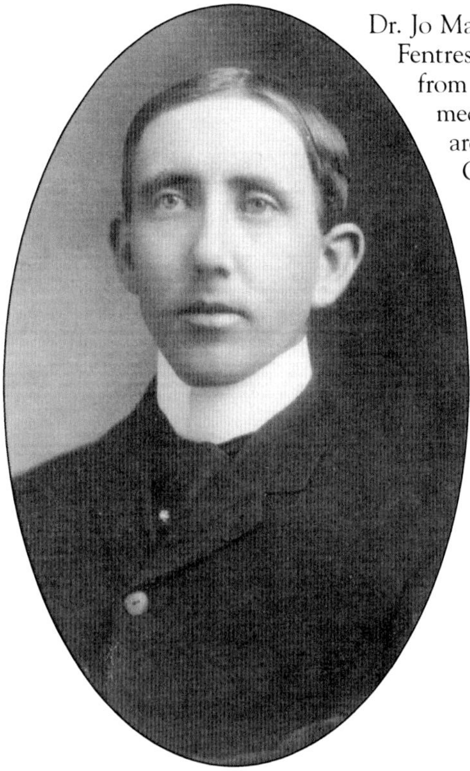

Dr. Jo Marvin Ferguson was the great-grandson of John Fentress, the founder of South Carrollton. He graduated from South Carrollton College in 1899 and attended medical school in Louisville, Kentucky. He returned around 1912 to open his medical practice in Central City, Kentucky. He is pictured around 1900. (Molly Alward.)

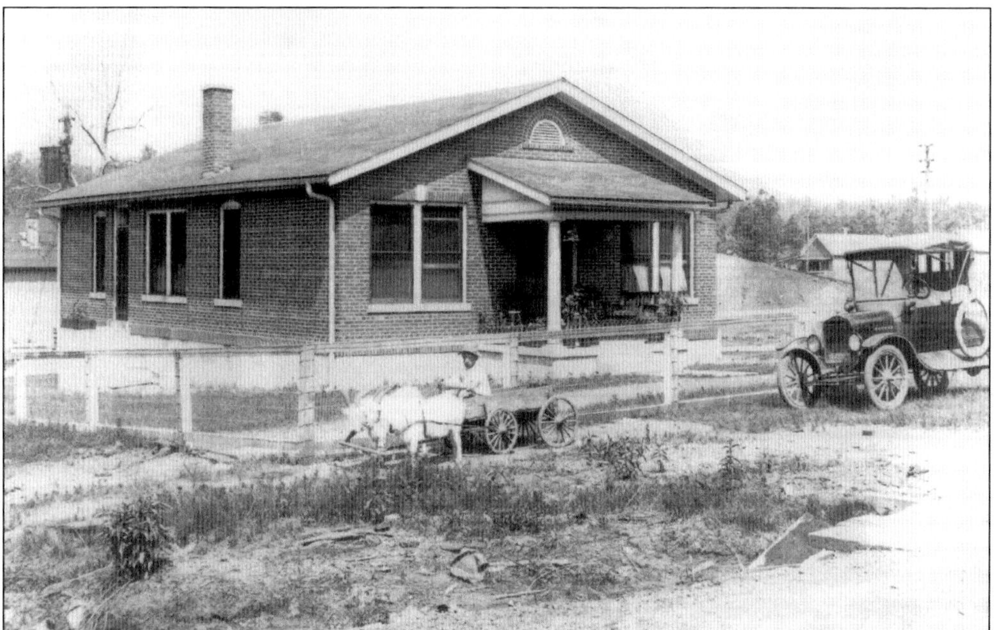

A hospital built in Graham by the W. G. Duncan Coal Company also served as a pharmacy and a post office. Duncan also built a poolroom, a theater, a skating rink, a trap-shooting range, a baseball field, a school, and several churches. Hob Steele is pictured in the goat wagon in front of the hospital around 1900. (William Raymer.)

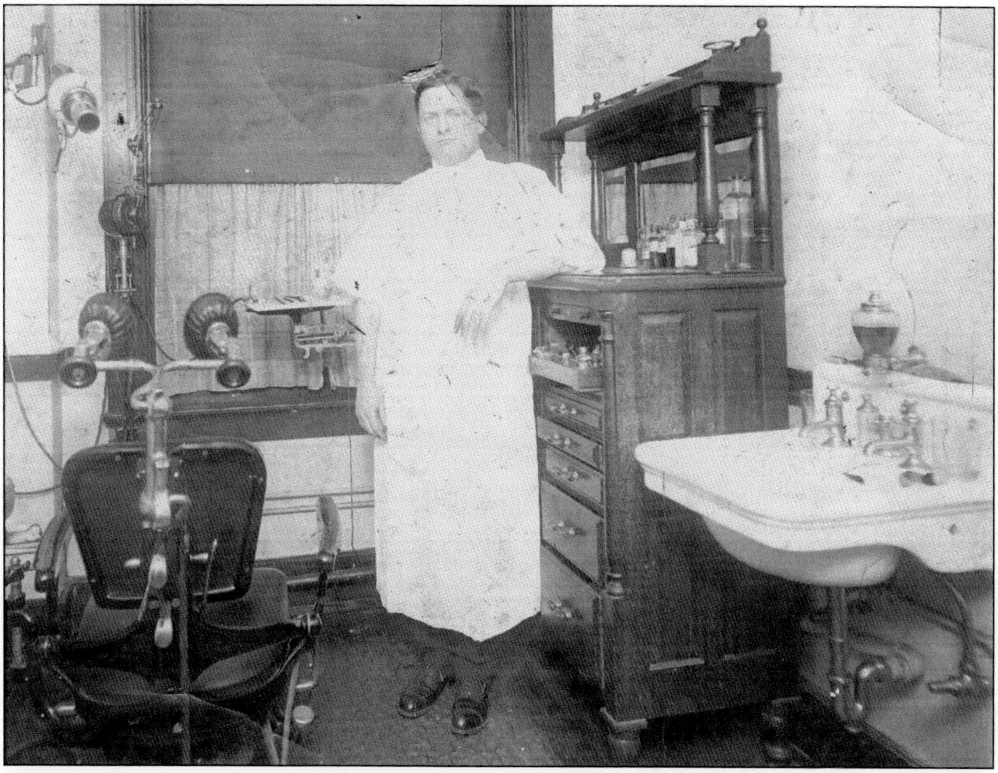

Prior to 1900, there were no licensing requirements for dentistry, but in 1911 Dr. J. L. Roark proudly offered professional dental services in his office. The office was equipped with the most modern of equipment from electricity and running water to a dental chair for comfortable positioning during procedures. Novocaine had been introduced as a dental anesthetic in 1905, and the era of painless dentistry had begun. (Carol McClure.)

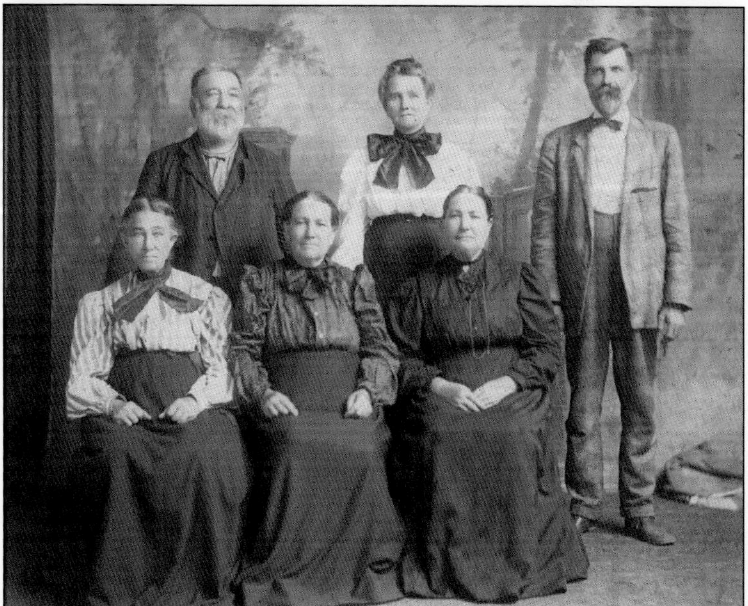

Pictured in this c. 1912 photograph are, from left to right, (first row) Angelina Thompson, Charity Chandler, and Belle Reed; (second row) John Thompson, America Durall, and Dr. J. T. Woodburn. Dr. Woodburn was a leading physician in the county and the mayor of Central City. He and Dr. W. R. McDowell formed the Woodburn and McDowell Drug Company together in Central City. (Molly Alward.)

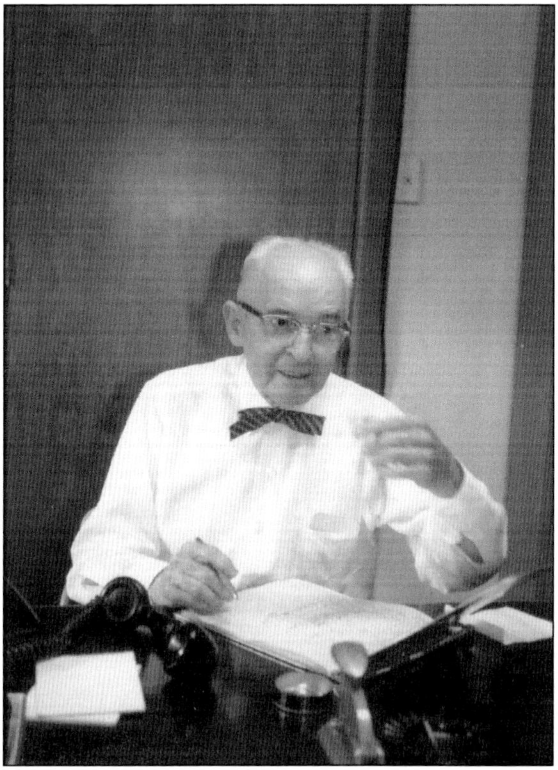

Central City doctor J. P. Walton (left) and general practitioner Dr. Hylan Woodson (below) of Greenville saw the world of medicine change on an almost daily basis from the time they began their individual practices in the 1930s and 1940s until their retirements. They saw antibiotics become numerous, tuberculosis sanitariums close, a polio vaccine developed, chemotherapies instituted, and small pox wiped out. Eventually office calls replaced house calls, and the familiar doctor's bag complete with bandages, syringes, pills, and bad-tasting medicines was replaced by prescriptions to be filled at the corner drugstores. But with all the new medicines, treatments, and equipment that would continue to arrive on the scene, the seasoned doctors knew some things they carried with them would remain irreplaceable—the knowledge, compassion, and skills of caring, competent physicians. Both images were taken c. 1955. (Muhlenberg Community Hospital.)

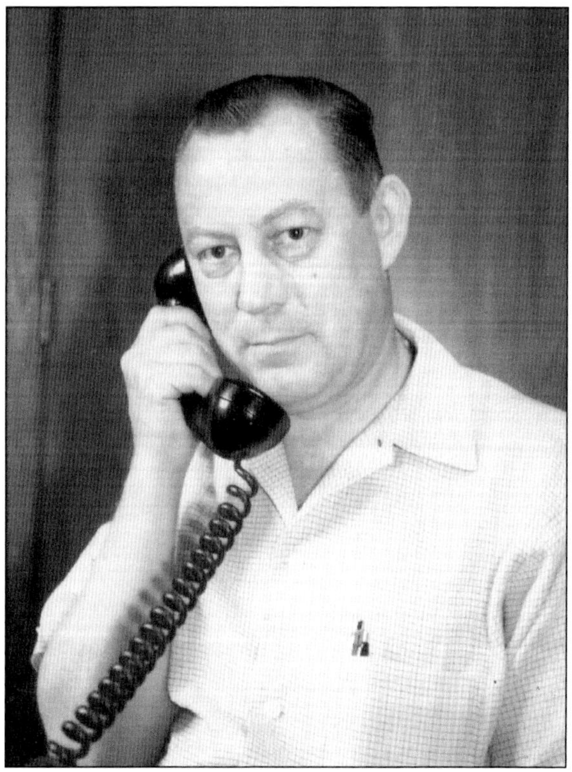

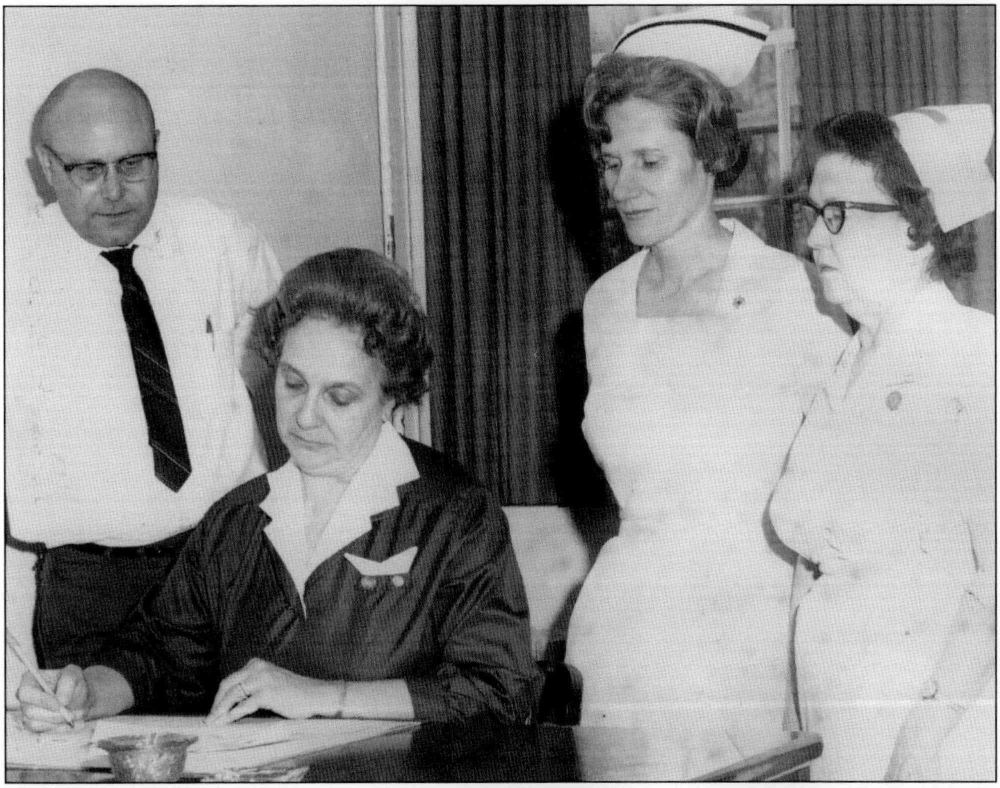

Muhlenberg County court clerk J. C. Nofsinger and two registered nurses look on as county health department nurse Sue Uzzle reads the proclamation honoring her birthday and her service to Muhlenberg County around 1972. Uzzle retired after 38 years of nursing in the community. (*Leader-News*.)

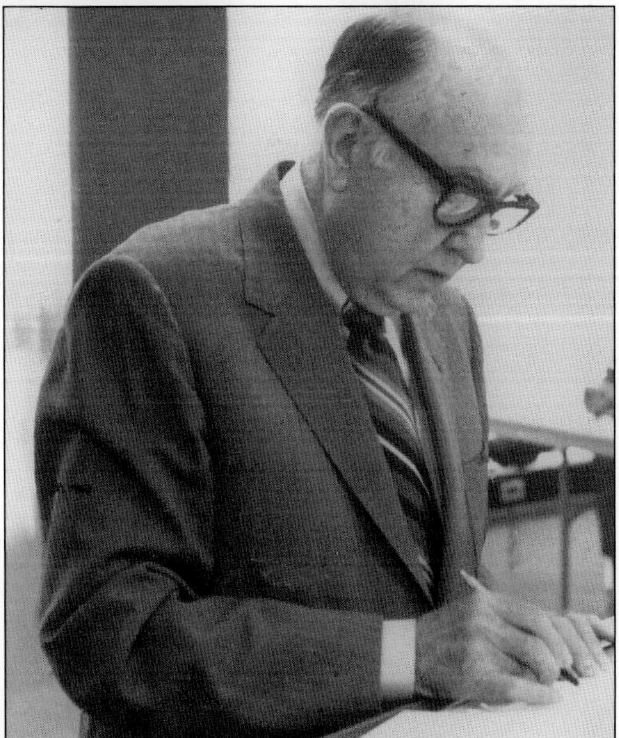

Surgeon G. L. Simpson of Greenville writes an order on a patient's chart at Muhlenberg Community Hospital. Dr. Simpson was present to cut the ribbon for the groundbreaking ceremonies for the hospital in 1938, and he was once again accorded that honor for the 60th anniversary celebration of the hospital in 1998. (Muhlenberg Community Hospital.)

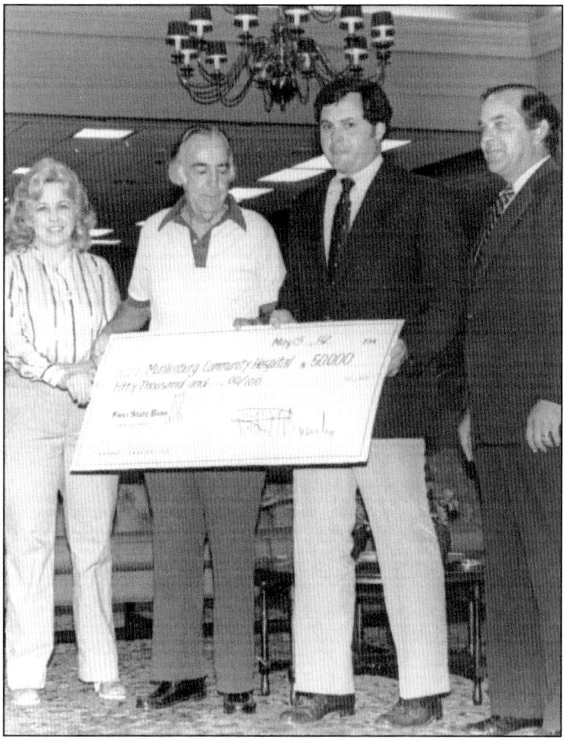

Challenge '82 was a hospital and community fund-raising effort to build a new addition to the hospital and expand its services. Through the generous contributions of interested individuals, businesses, hospital employees, and physicians, $1 million was raised. Pictured at left are, from left to right, Cleo Roberson, registered nurse and director of community relations, and Sam Jarvis, chairman of the board, receiving a $50,000 check from Lee Owen, president of First State Bank, and Tom Brumley, chairman of the bank board. Below, doctors, board members, and friends participate in a hospital fund-raiser. From left to right are (first row) John Howerton and doctors H. Woodson, W. Keith, J. Brashear, G. Simpson, and R. McGhee; (second row) Steve Dukes, doctors S. Jugo and Dr. G. Brockman, friend William Cisney, and doctors G. Givens, J. Boggess, and R. Diaz. (Muhlenberg Community Hospital.)

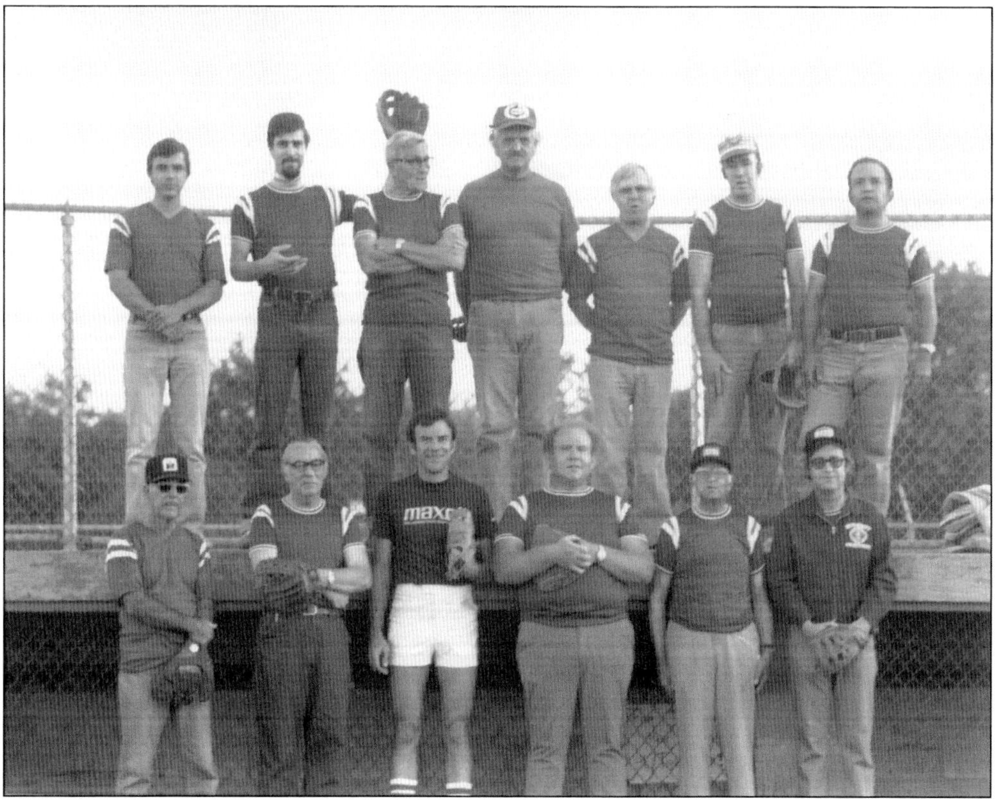

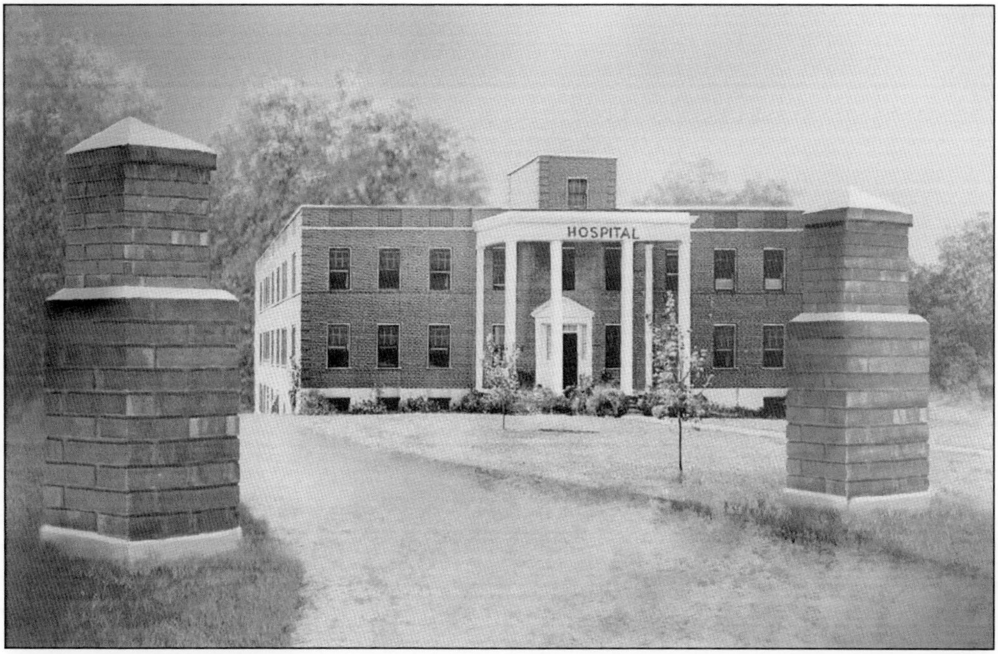

The first Muhlenberg Community Hospital was built on land donated by Orien Roark and was completed in 1938. Ten percent of the cost was paid with county donations, and 90 percent was paid for by the Works Progress Administration (WPA). The new hospital had 25 beds and cost $40,000 to complete. (Carol McClure.)

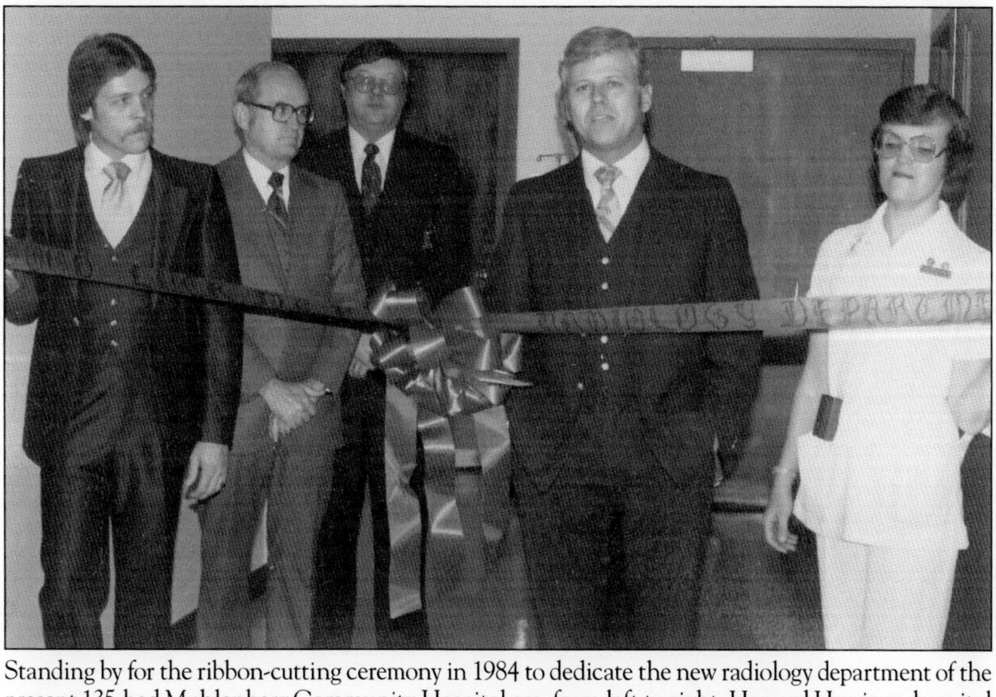

Standing by for the ribbon-cutting ceremony in 1984 to dedicate the new radiology department of the present 135-bed Muhlenberg Community Hospital are, from left to right, Howard Harrison, hospital engineer; Dr. Joseph Stokes, radiologist; Dr. Glen Hicks, radiologist; William Parrish, hospital administrator; and Sheila Johnson, radiology department head. (Muhlenberg Hospital.)

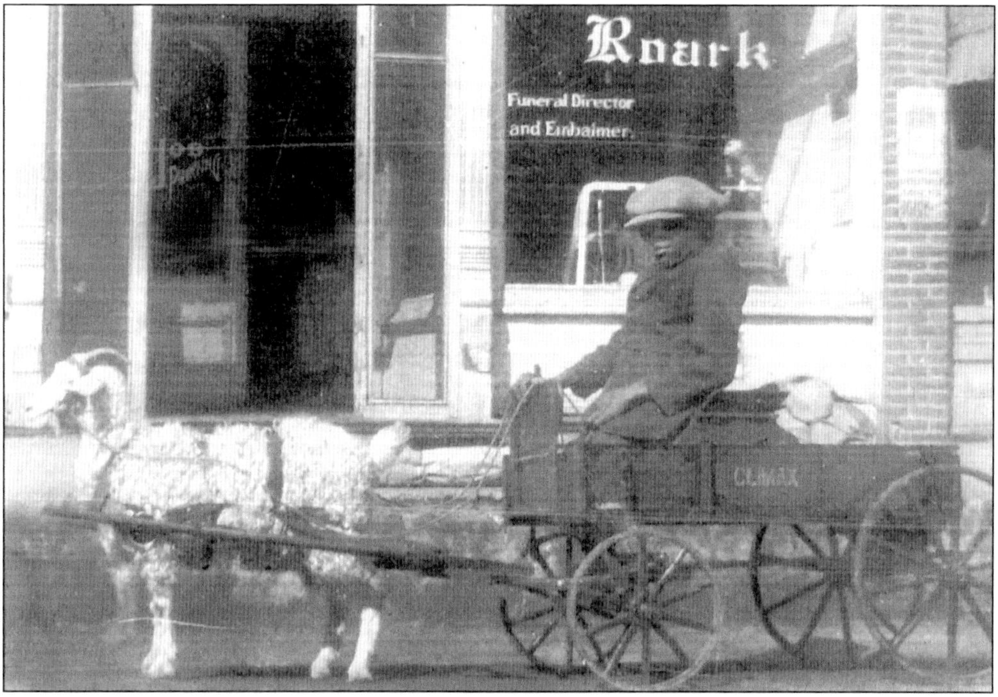

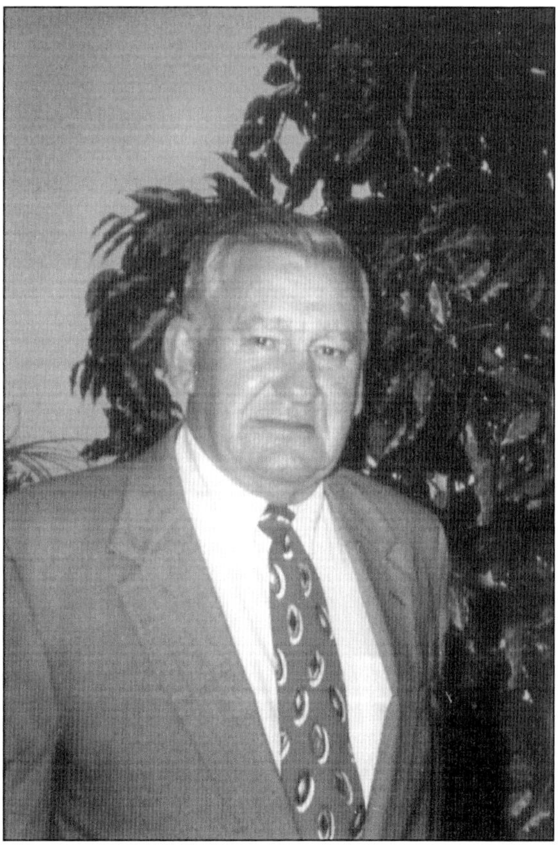

In 1888, Everett Doolin was injured in a childhood accident and left crippled. Without advanced technology, he was dependent on his family's own inventiveness for help. They replaced his useless legs with a goat cart, and Everett continued on. (Christine Hinsey.)

Tom Christerson of Central City, at 71 years old, made history when he became the second recipient in the world of an AbioCor implanted replacement heart. His will to live, his determination, and the skills of his surgeons bought him another 17 months. He and his wife celebrated their 55th wedding anniversary, and he held his first great-grandchild. "I'm no hero," explained Tom. "I just wanted to live." And live he did to the fullest and helped many others in the process. He, like notable others who began this county, became a pioneer and a hero. He is pictured around 2001. (Patti Pryor.)

Five

Public Service and Energy

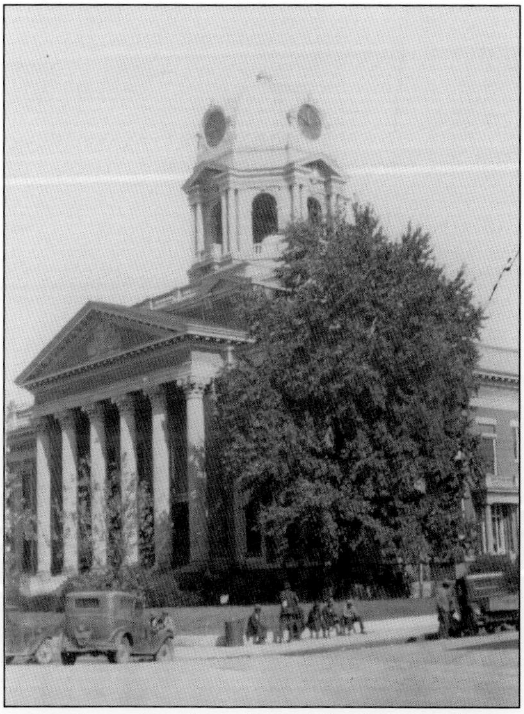

The Muhlenberg County Courthouse stands in the middle of Greenville as a symbol of craftsmanship and foresight that has served the county since 1907. The first courthouse was made of hewn logs in 1799 and was replaced by a second structure made of bricks around 1812. In 1836, another brick courthouse was constructed that was two stories high. The fourth and present courthouse, completed in 1907, stands on the site of the 1836 structure. The first of the court minutes of 1799 note that Muhlenberg County was formed from the counties of Logan and Christian. The minutes further detailed that John Bradley was appointed sheriff, Charles Fox Wing was appointed clerk, Alney McLean was recognized as county surveyor, John Anderson was appointed constable, and Richard Tyler was granted permission to keep a tavern. So began formal public services and accountability to the citizens of Muhlenberg County. (Christine Hinsey.)

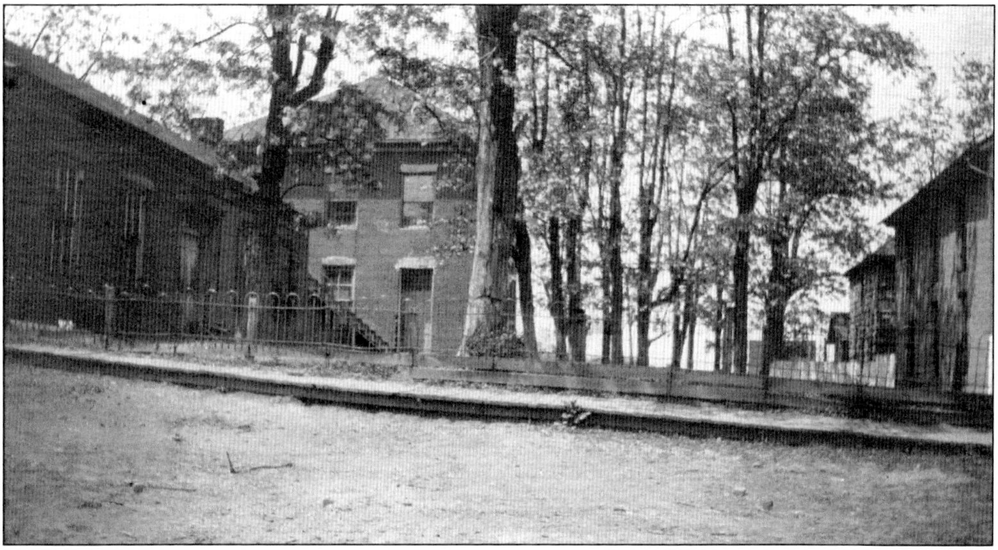

This is the two-story brick courthouse erected in 1834, prior to the present-day courthouse. When this courthouse was demolished to make way for the present structure, county surveyor Alney McClean divided Col. William Campbell's donation of 30 acres on the town square into 56 lots, which were sold off to raise money to pay for the construction. (Christine Hinsey.)

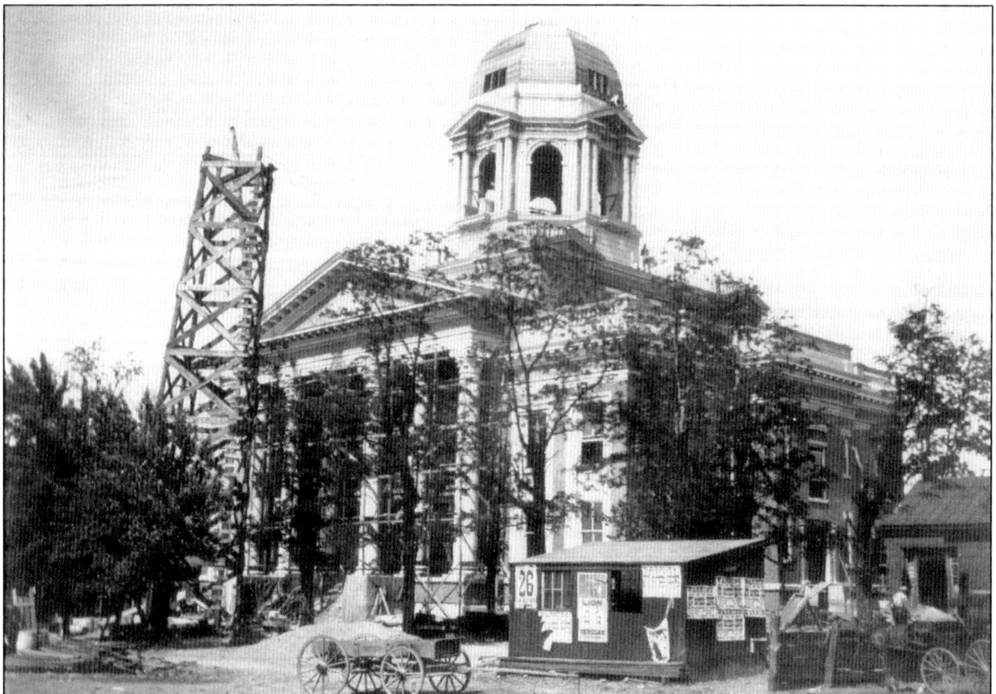

The background scaffolding shows construction in progress on the 1907 Muhlenberg County Courthouse. Presiding over court in 1907 were county judge R. O. Pace and county attorney W. O. Belcher. Magistrates were R. T. Johns, J. W. Stuart, C. W. Cisney, Bryant Williams, and O. T. Kittinger. The building committee members were chairman T. J. Sparks, T. B. Pannell, W. G. Duncan, J. W. Lam, and W. A. Wickliffe. The final cost of the structure was $74,340. (Christine Hinsey.)

A postcard sent to Sue Barkley on September 19, 1906, from her friend Roy Wells shows him standing outside the old Muhlenberg county jail. The inscription jokingly says, "I am still on the outside, but I don't know how long I will stay out." The jailer's residence is pictured on the right. (Christine Hinsey.)

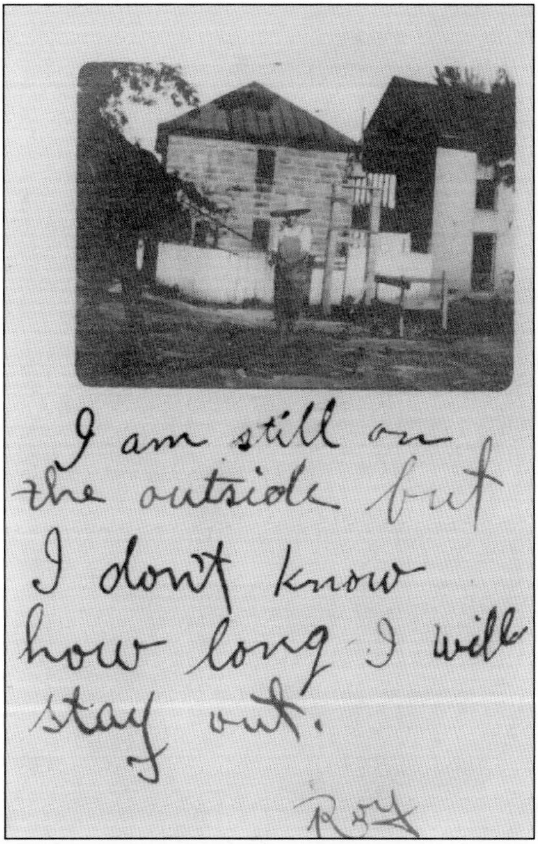

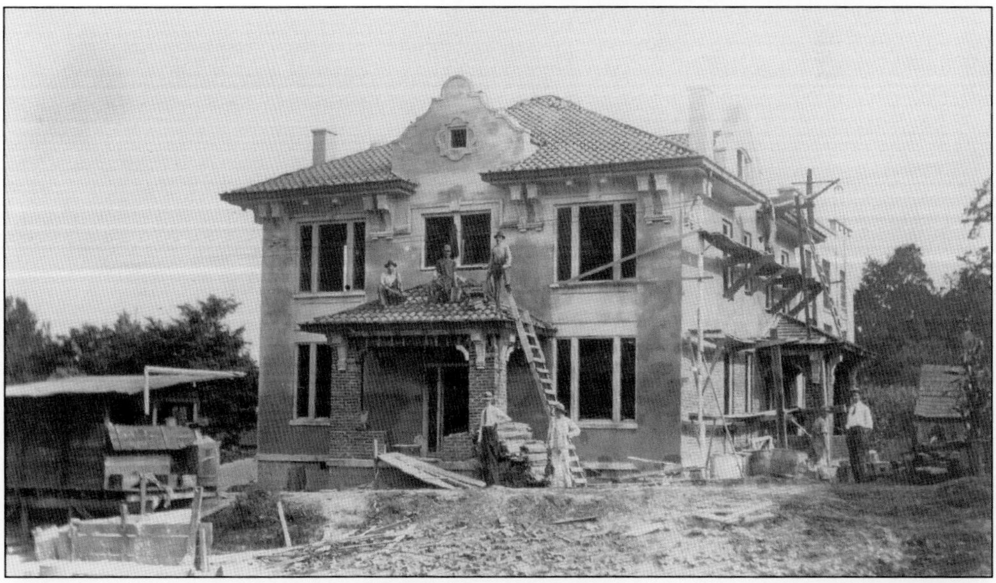

Muhlenberg County's first jail cost $200 and was approved and paid for on June 24, 1800. The second jail was a brick structure built in 1864 and demolished in 1912. It was replaced by the stucco-and-tile structure pictured above, which stood as the jail and the jailer's residence until 1987. (Christine Hinsey.)

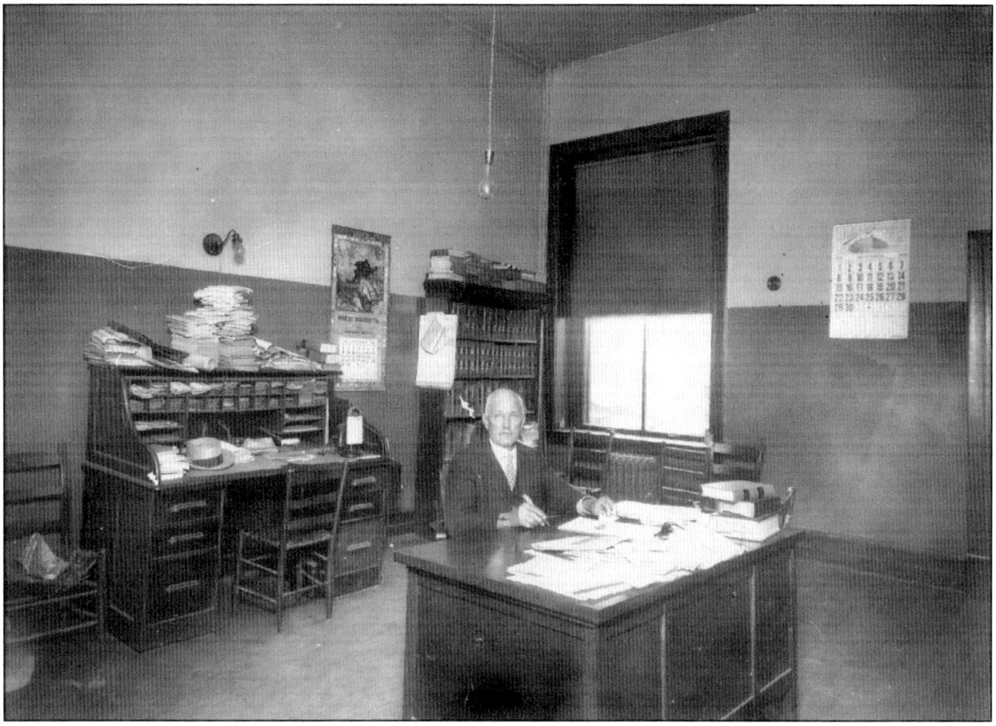

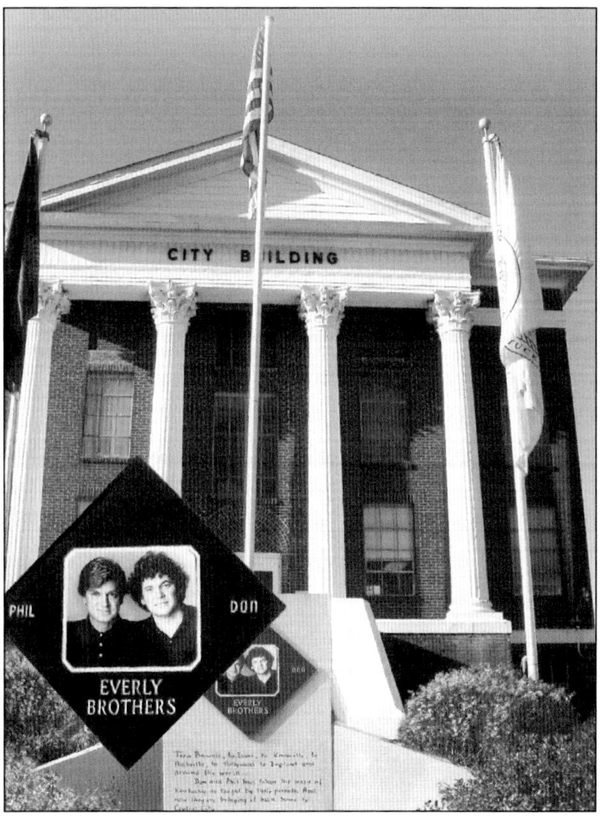

William Jackson Ross (1860–1934) served as principal of Sacramento Academy around 1890. After receiving his law degree, he practiced in Greenville and also served as county attorney. He was widowed twice; in 1908, he married his third wife, Pinkie Wells, and fathered his third set of children, including Alfred C., W. H., Ralph, and Gordon Ross, Joyce Rae Anderson, and Margaret Ann Wallace. Velma Oates was his child with first wife, Mary Ellen. (H. L. Anderson Jr.)

The City Building in Central City has served as a home to the city's business offices, the chamber of commerce, and the police department. In the 1950s and 1960s, the building also served as a meeting place for the county's preteens and teens, who gathered at the youth center upstairs every Saturday night for dancing and socializing. (Christine Hinsey.)

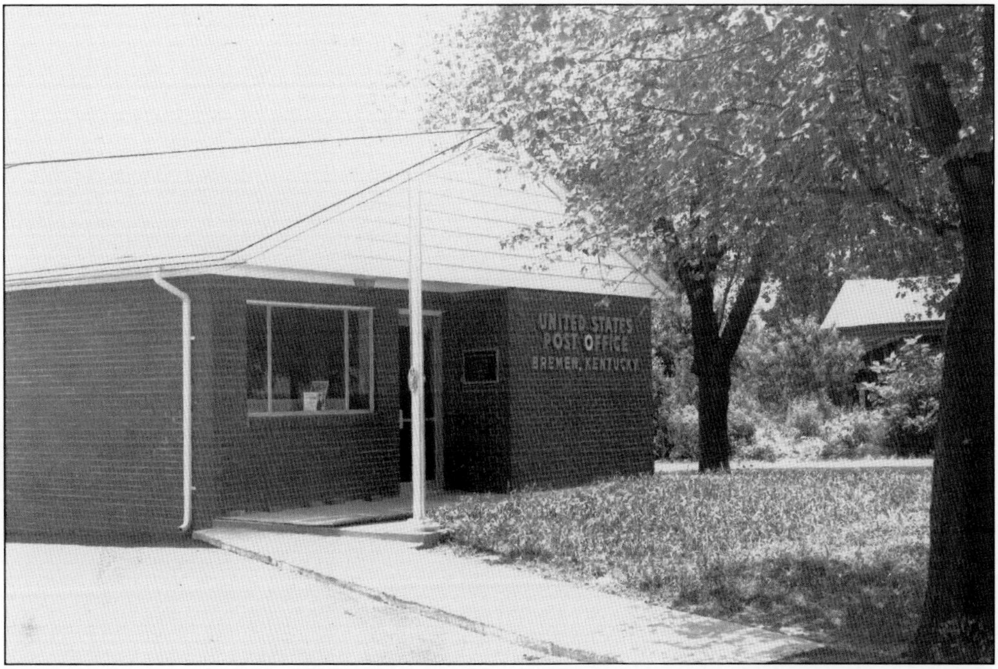

The Bremen post office has been in business since 1832. The name Bremen was given to the town and the post office in honor of Bremen, Germany, the hometown of Peter Shaver's father. Shaver was the first of many postmasters of the town, and in 1982, Hazel G. Tooley became Bremen's 29th postmaster. (Muhlenberg County Library Archives.)

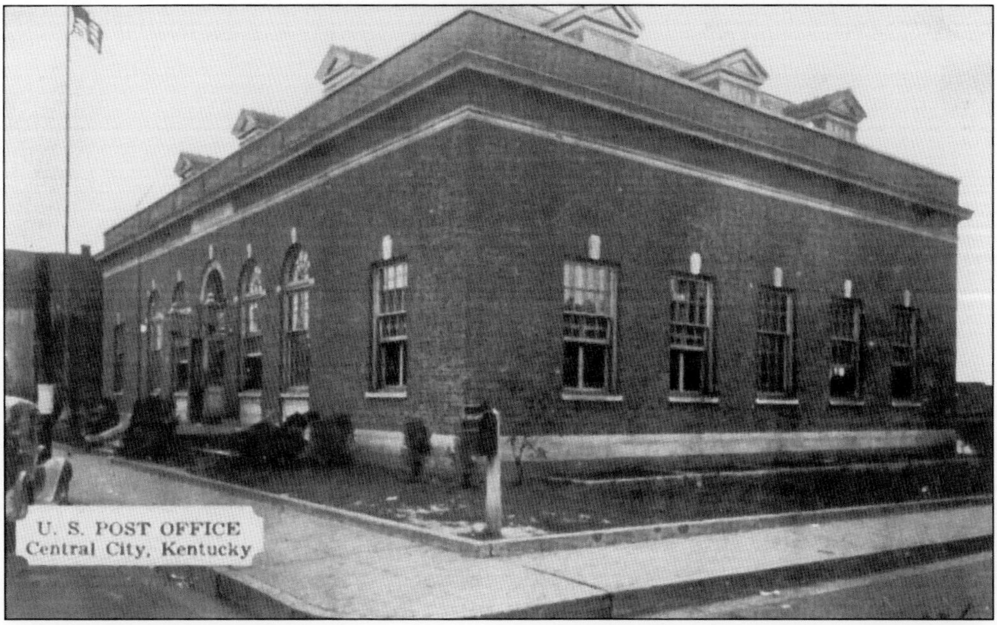

In 1913, Muhlenberg County had 34 post offices, 8 star mail routes, and 4 rural free delivery routes. Central City's first post office was built in 1871 and by 1884 already had rural route delivery from Central City to Gishton and Bethel Church, returning by way of Cherry Hill Church. The image is from around 1935. (Muhlenberg County Library Archives.)

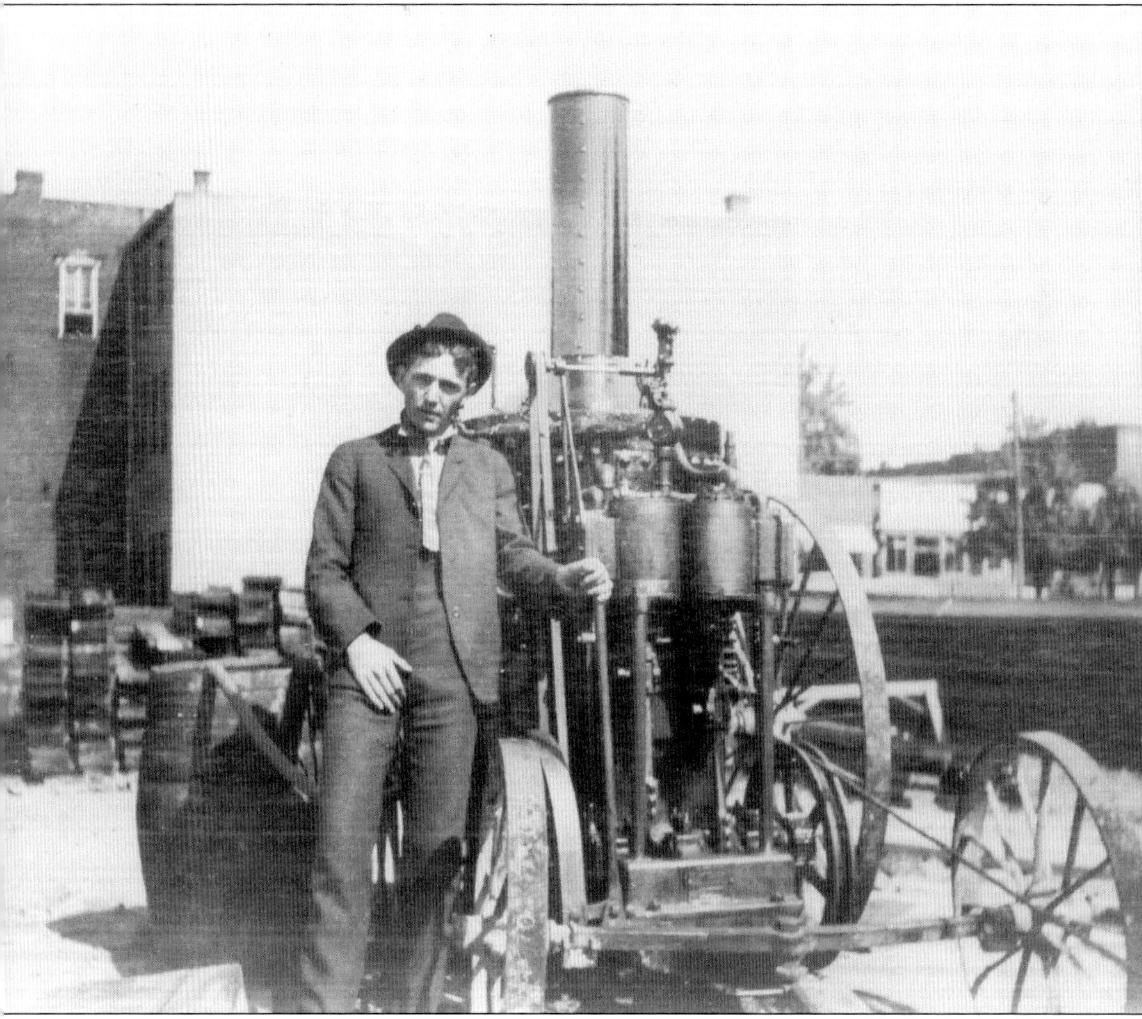

Prior to 1900, the internal combustion engine had not yet been invented, so there were no fire trucks. The only horsepower in the county was generated by real horses pulling the wagons that carried water barrels and the essential water pump. The fire hoses were on a separate cart pulled by strong men who ran with the horses to the scene of the fire. Once the men arrived on the scene, the hoses were attached to the water pump to shoot pressurized water into the flames. The only job of a fire department in the early days was to simply extinguish the fire and limit the damage to nearby structures. In 1930, Melbourne Jenkins was Greenville's only fireman and drove the town's only fire truck home to Cherry Street for lunch every day. (Muhlenberg County Library Archives.)

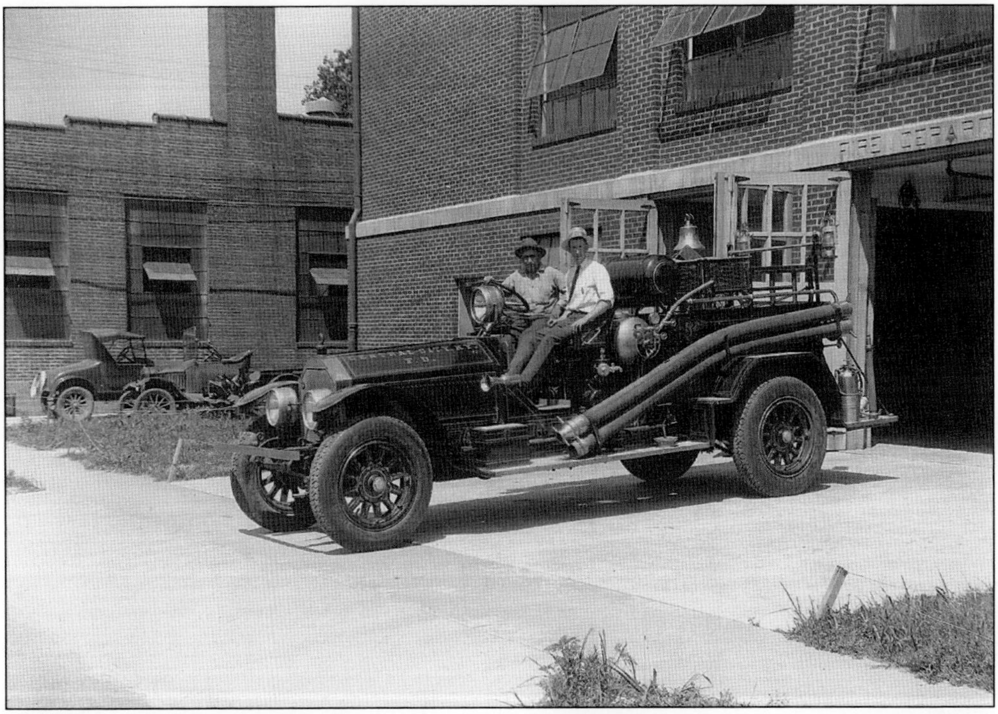

Bill Molloy and Alfred Mathis drive a fire truck out of the Central City Fire Department garage around 1925. (Christine Hinsey.)

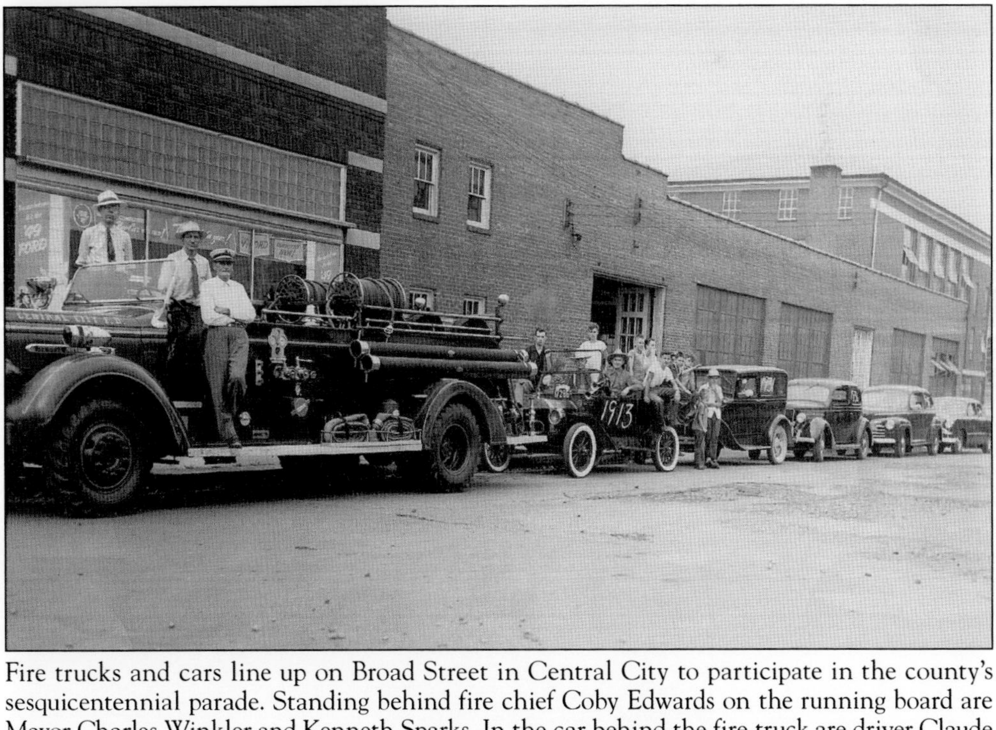

Fire trucks and cars line up on Broad Street in Central City to participate in the county's sesquicentennial parade. Standing behind fire chief Coby Edwards on the running board are Mayor Charles Winkler and Kenneth Sparks. In the car behind the fire truck are driver Claude Richey and passenger Vivian Lyle around 1948. (Muhlenberg County Library Archives.)

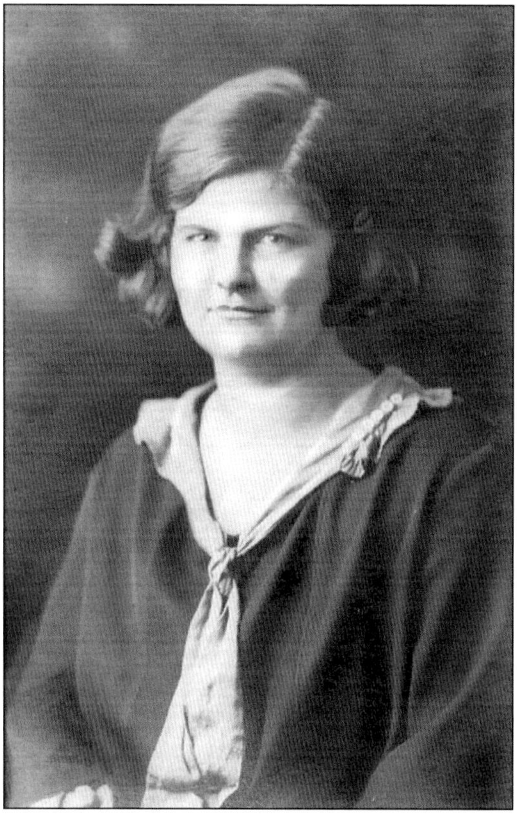

Mary Morgan, librarian and world traveler, poses for this picture around 1940. Morgan (1907–2001) was the daughter of Tallmadge and Hettie Morgan. After retiring as a Jefferson County school librarian, she returned to Muhlenberg County and served as librarian through the 1960s and 1970s. (Christine Hinsey.)

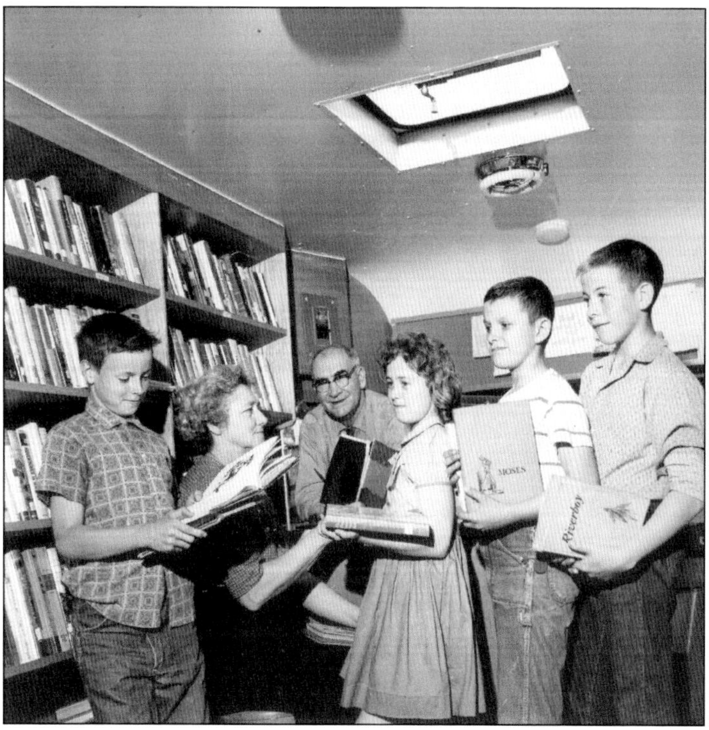

Children gather round Muhlenberg County bookmobile librarian James Pellow as they check out their selections. Excited customers at the Nebo School in 1963 are, from left to right, Stephen Mercer, teacher Mrs. L. B. Lynch, Katy Porter, Ronnie Jarvis, and Mike Stobaugh. Besides school stops, the bookmobile helps to make books accessible to shut-ins, the handicapped, and to those in nursing homes or correctional institutions. (Muhlenberg County Library Archives.)

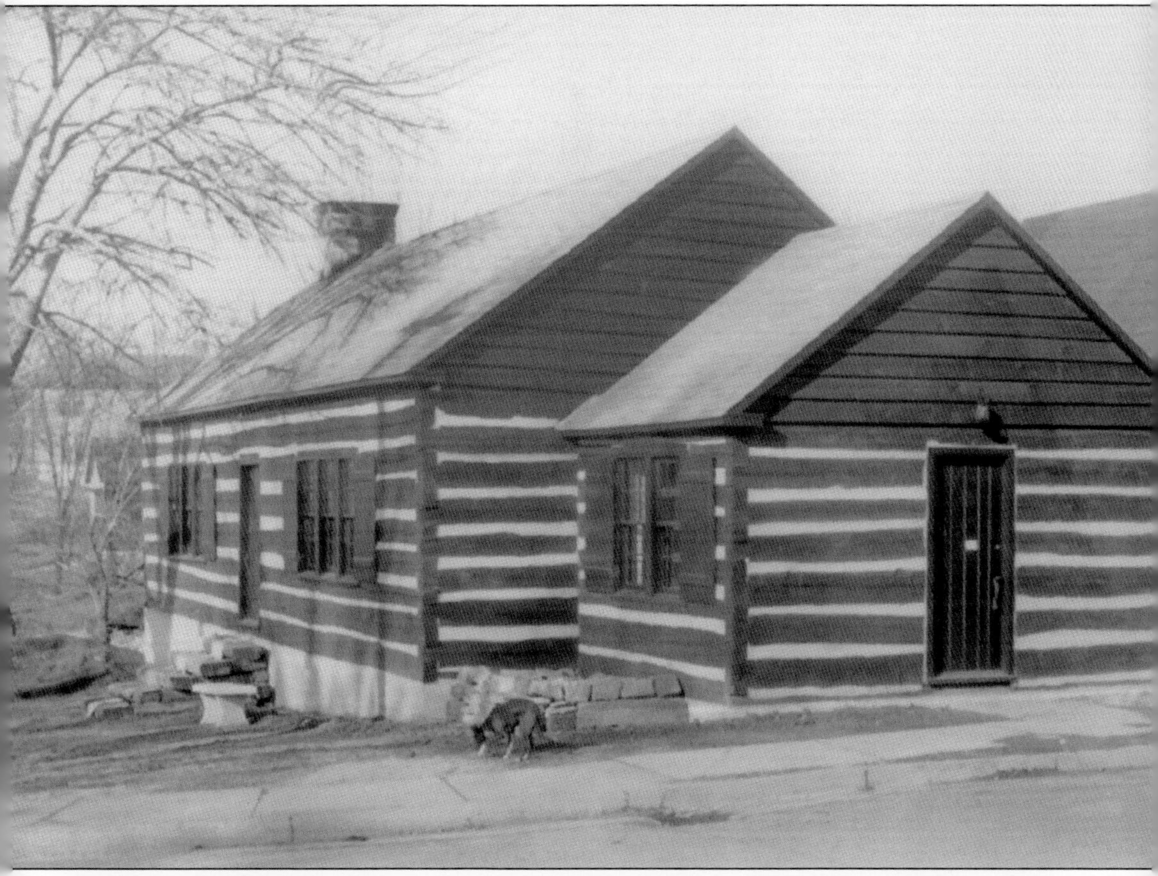

The Greenville Woman's Club began as the Ladies Book Club in 1908 with 12 charter members who met at various locations until their log clubhouse was finished in 1938. Their name was changed to the Woman's Book Club and in 1994 changed again to the Greenville Woman's Club. One of club's earliest projects was bringing the first health nurse to the county and paying her salary, which resulted in the establishment of the first county health program. Another project was the establishment of the public library in 1920. Club members Mrs. A. G. Duncan and Mrs. J. T. Reynolds were instrumental in the library's growth. Before moving to its present location on South Main Street, the library was housed in the courthouse and in the City Building. The club members also paid the librarian's salary. In 1936, the club raised $5,000 to help furnish the new hospital, and in 1943, members sponsored the sale of war bonds. Since 1962, the club's main focus has been on sponsoring scholarships for deserving county students. A 100-year legacy of giving proudly continues. (Christine Hinsey.)

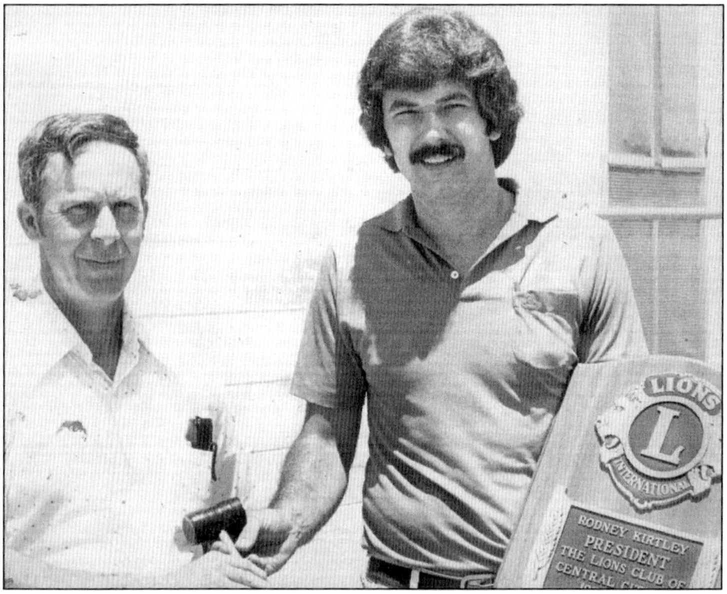

Jack Day (left), a Lions Club member and Central City teacher and coach, presents a plaque of appreciation to Rodney Kirtley for serving as Lions Club president around 1980. Always active on the county's behalf, Kirtley went on to become Muhlenberg County judge executive and instituted many far-reaching plans and programs that continue to benefit the citizens of the county. (*Times-Argus*.)

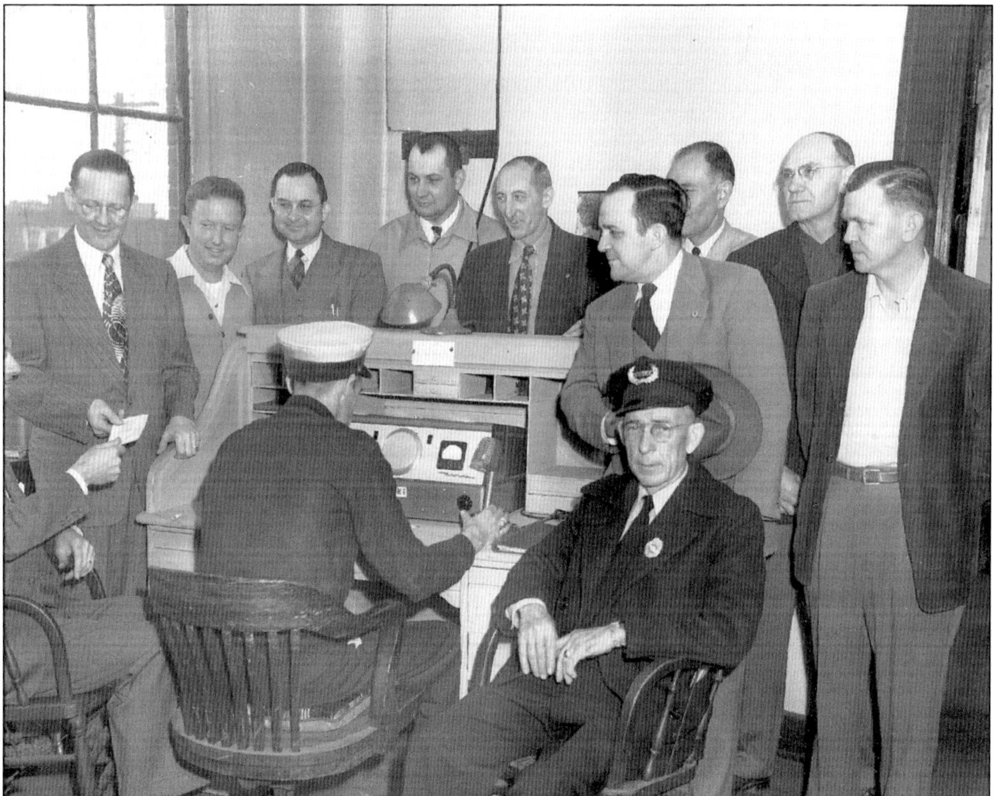

Central City Council members gather at the police department around 1950. Members are, from left to right, (sitting) Albert Harding, fire chief Bill Hardwick (back to camera), and police chief ? Gossett; (standing) L. M. Ross, Sherman Ferguson, Harold Capps, Kenneth Norris, Tony Wolfe, C. B. Greenwood, Jonas Rubenstein, Claude Richey, and Murel Gentry. (Christine Hinsey.)

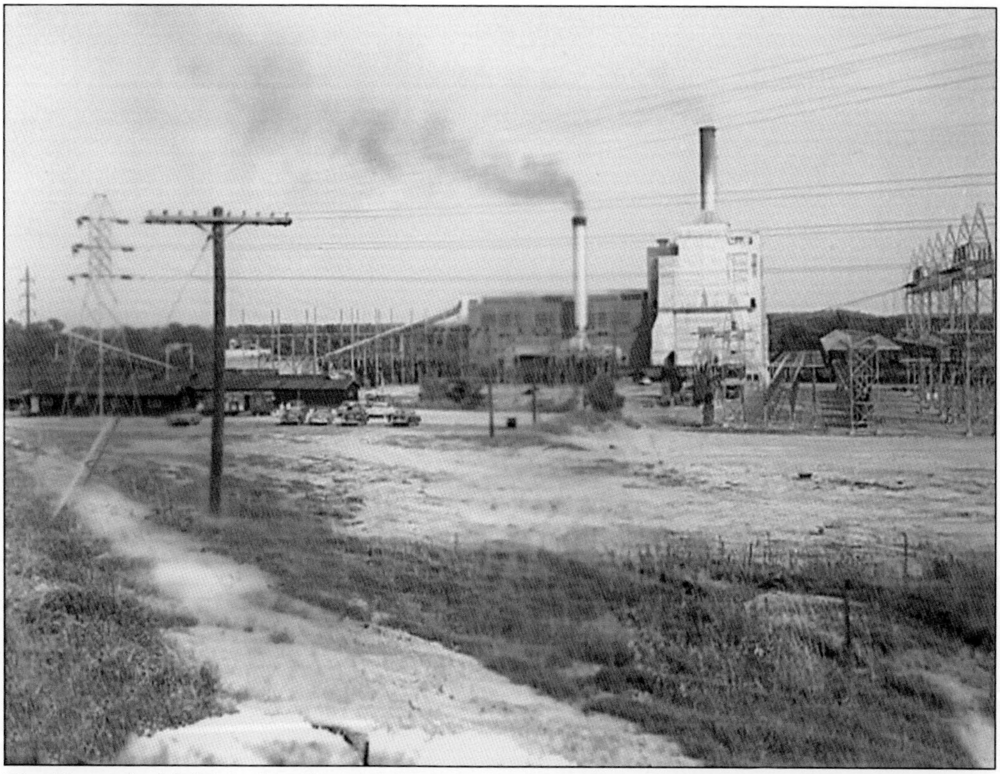

The Kentucky Utilities plant located at Moorman on the Green River is one of two power plants located in Muhlenberg County. The plant installed its first scrubber in 1975, which removes over 90 percent of the sulfur dioxide from the flue gas produced by burning coal. Approximately 1,600 tons of coal are transferred from truck to the plant daily, translating into 400,000 tons of coal burned per year. (Christine Hinsey.)

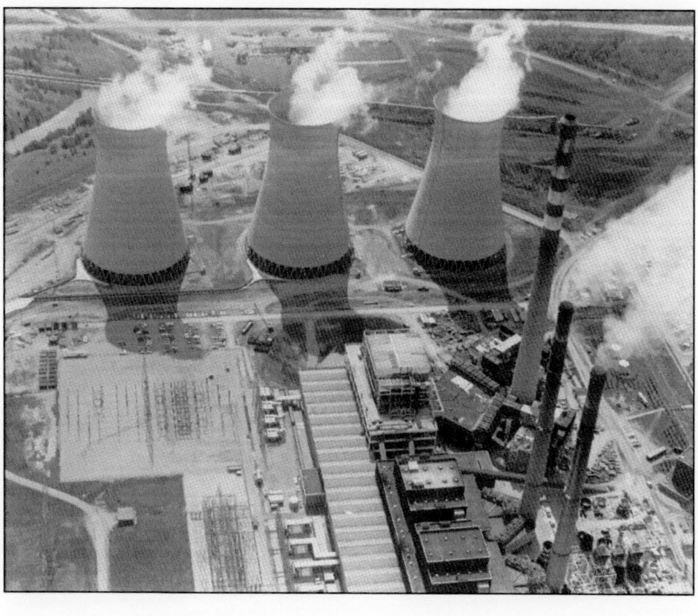

The Tennessee Valley Authority's Paradise Steam Plant was completed in 1970 and is still one of the world's largest fossil-fueled plants. The plant uses approximately 20,000 tons of coal a day, generates 15 million kilowatt hours per year, employees over 1,000 hourly employees, and pours $5 million into the local economy per year. Its payment to the state of Kentucky in lieu of taxes is approximately $37 million per year. (*Leader-News*.)

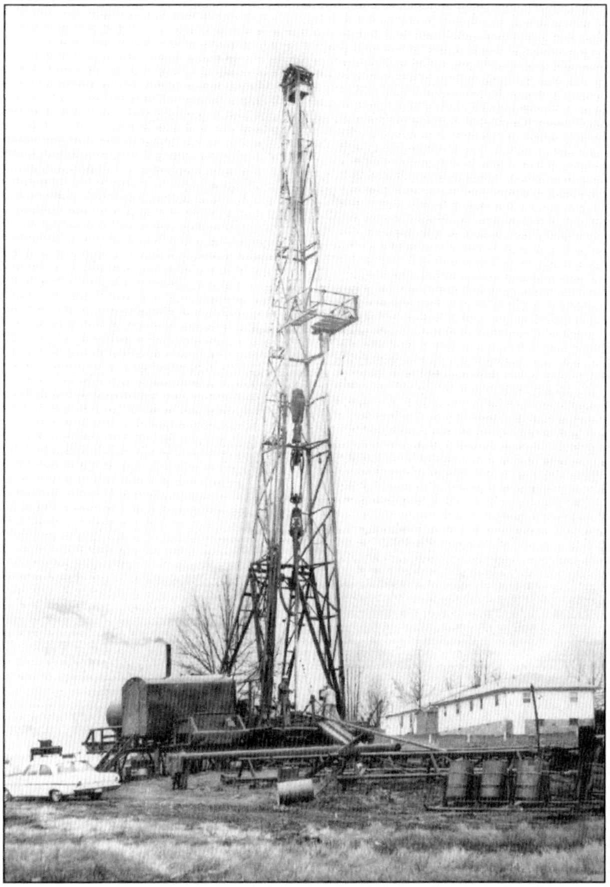

After the Civil War, Gen. Don Carlos Buell began his search for an oil field. He took a 40-year lease on Alexander's abandoned land, where he established the Airdrie Petroleum Company. Alexander's heirs sold the land to Buell, who discovered coal in such abundance that he ceased oil drilling and turned exclusively to mining. Many years later, Muhlenberg County would become the setting for lucrative oil exploration. (Christine Hinsey.)

The Rochester-Skilesville Lock and Dam No. 3 was opened in 1838. Skilesville, which was situated on the south bank of the Green River at the lock and dam 16 miles east of Greenville, was named after James R. Skiles, who introduced the first steamboat on Green River and spent a fortune promoting the navigation of the river. The lock and dam are pictured around 1950. (Christine Hinsey.)

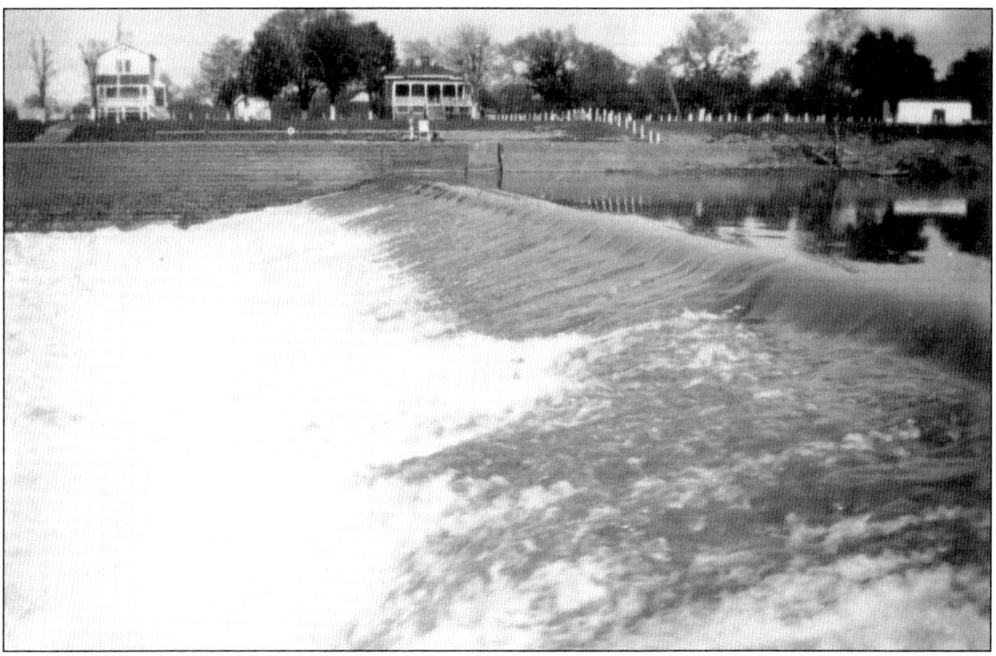

Six

Military Matters

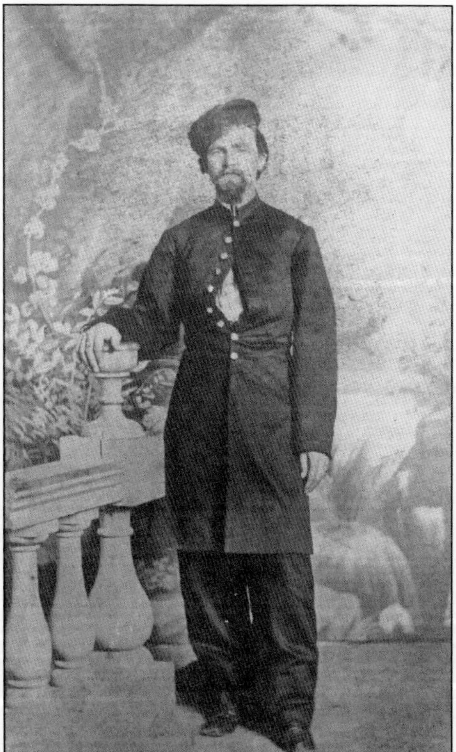

Lt. James L. Roark (1840–1893) enlisted in the Federal army in 1863. He, like the settlers before him, knew that freedom has never been free. The soldiers who came here with land grants for their service in the Revolutionary War knew the price of freedom. They knew the ability to stay free would demand sacrifice and courage. When the War of 1812 broke out, they enlisted again. When the Civil War reared its head, the men of the county split their loyalties but answered to the call just the same. In World Wars I and II, the Korean War, the Vietnam War, and every war since then, the men and the women of the county have offered up their lives to protect everything we hold dear. We could not stay free without the courage of their convictions. Winston S. Churchill said, "Courage is rightly esteemed the first of human qualities because it is the quality which guarantees all others." The courage of soldiers is the only guarantee we have that our freedoms will survive. (Carol McClure.)

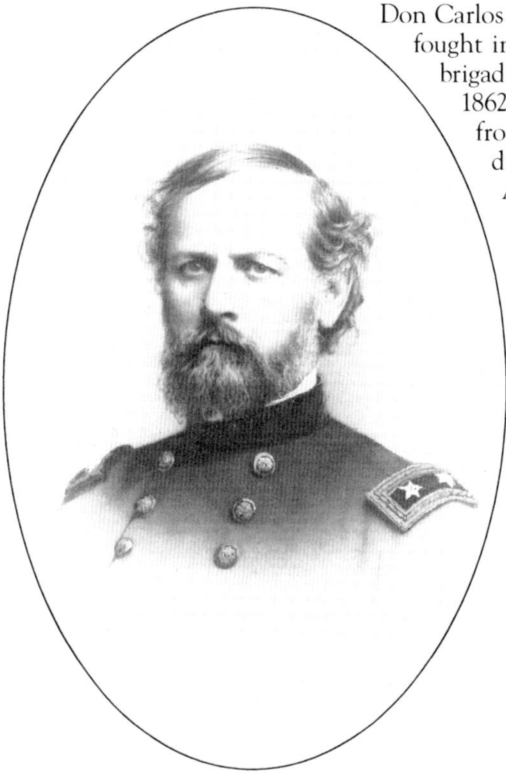

Don Carlos Buell graduated from West Point in 1841. He fought in the Mexican-American War and was made brigadier general of volunteers then major general in 1862. He and his troops saved Gen. Ulysses S. Grant from defeat at Shiloh, and he was credited with driving the Confederate army out of Kentucky. After the war, he retired to Airdrie to write his memoirs. (Christine Hinsey.)

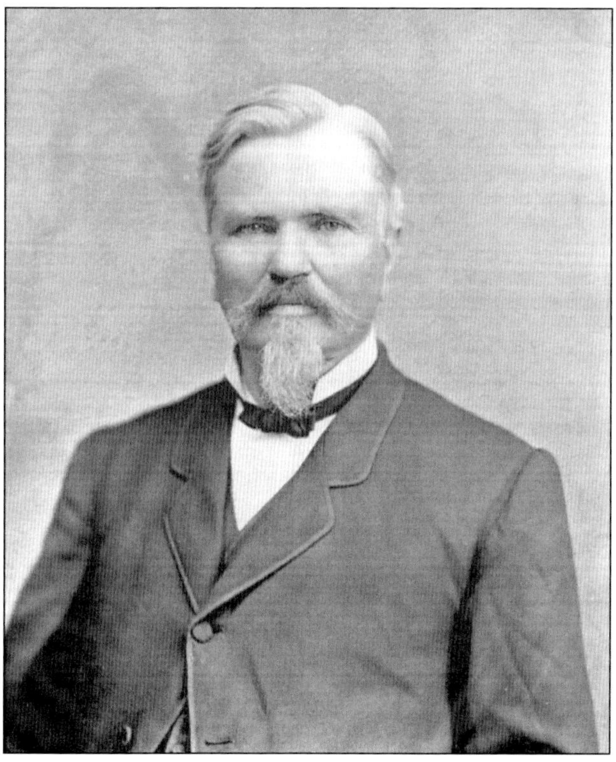

Gen. Simon Bolivar Buckner served in the Civil War as a lieutenant general of the Confederacy. After his capture and subsequent pardon, he returned to Kentucky to become editor of the Louisville *Courier*. In 1887, he was elected governor and later ran for vice president on the gold standard. He died in 1914. He was the only lieutenant general that Kentucky had on either side. (Christine Hinsey.)

On October 7, 1911, Civil War veterans gathered with their wives for a reunion. Probably less than 150 Muhlenberg citizens served in the Confederate army. Edward R. Weir Sr. was looked on as the leader of the Union men in the county. Attending are, from left to right, (first row) three unidentified, America Jane (Woodburn) Duvall, and unidentified; (second row) four unidentified, J. N. Duvall, and unidentified. (Molly Alward.)

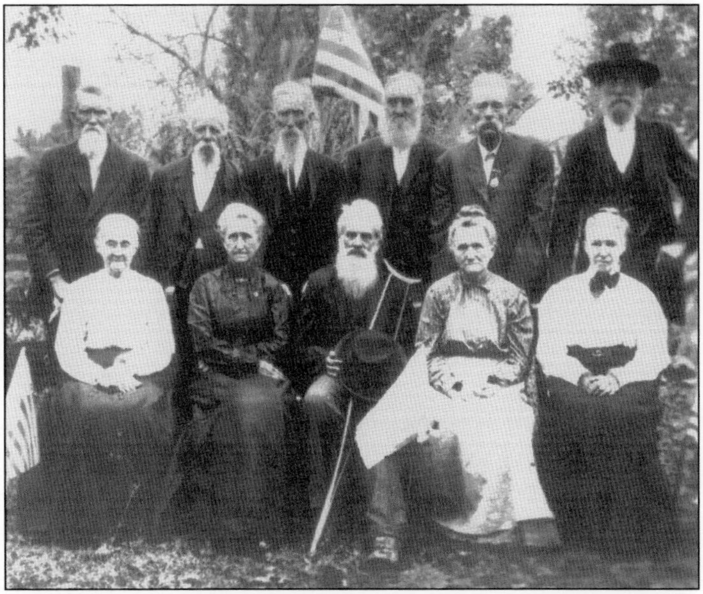

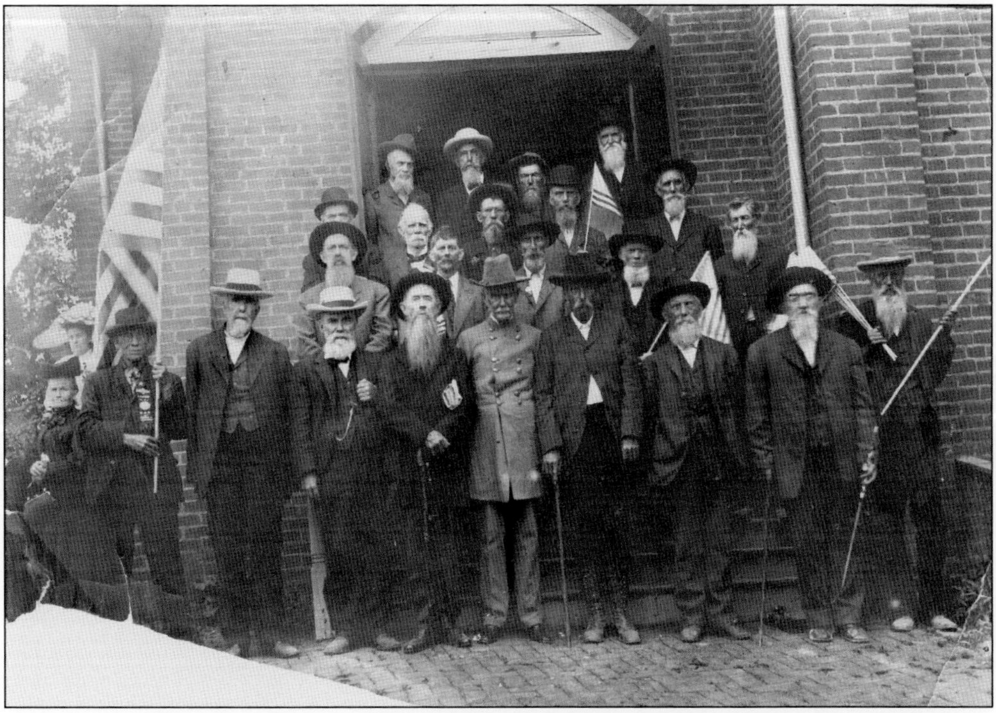

James Leonard Anderson Jr., a veteran of the Civil War, stands on the back row third from the left during the veterans' reunion in 1900. No other veterans are identified. James carried a festering musket ball in his thigh from a wound received in the war and lived with constant, unrelieved pain. He was unable to receive adequate veteran's benefits due to lack of sufficient army documentation. He died in 1911. (H. L. Anderson Jr.)

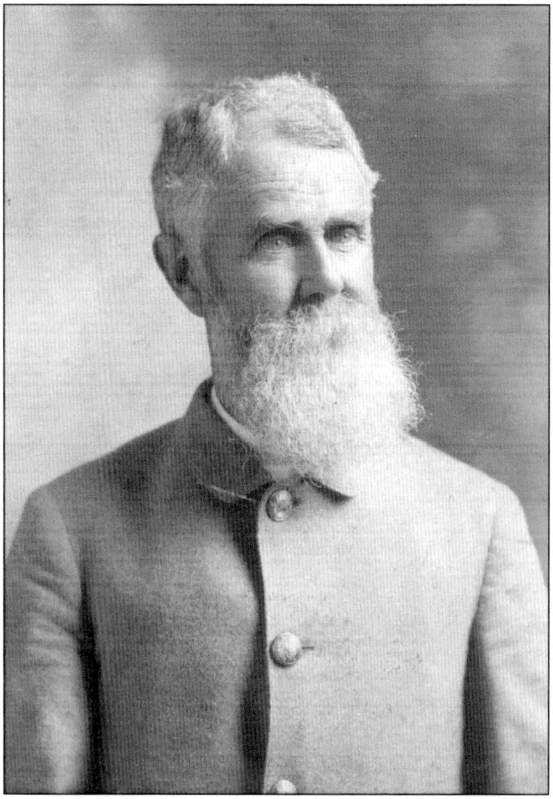

Lt. Col. Jeptha C. Johnson, age 29, enlisted in the Confederate army on March 28, 1862, at Searcy, Arkansas. He was severely wounded at Prairie Grove, Arkansas, on December 7, 1862. At the military hospital where he was treated, he met and married the young nurse who had cared for him. After rejoining the troops, Lt. Col. Jeptha Johnson was captured on July 4, 1863, at Helena, Arkansas. He was eventually pardoned and transferred to New Orleans, Louisiana, on January 9, 1865. (Carol McClure.)

Unidentified Muhlenberg County soldiers of the Spanish-American War pose together in 1898 as they prepare to leave for war. The Spanish-American War lasted from April 25, 1898, to August 12, 1898, for a total of 109 days. With the signing of the Treaty of Paris, Spain relinquished all claims to Cuba, Guam, and Puerto Rico and ceded the Philippines for a payment of $20 million. (Christine Hinsey.)

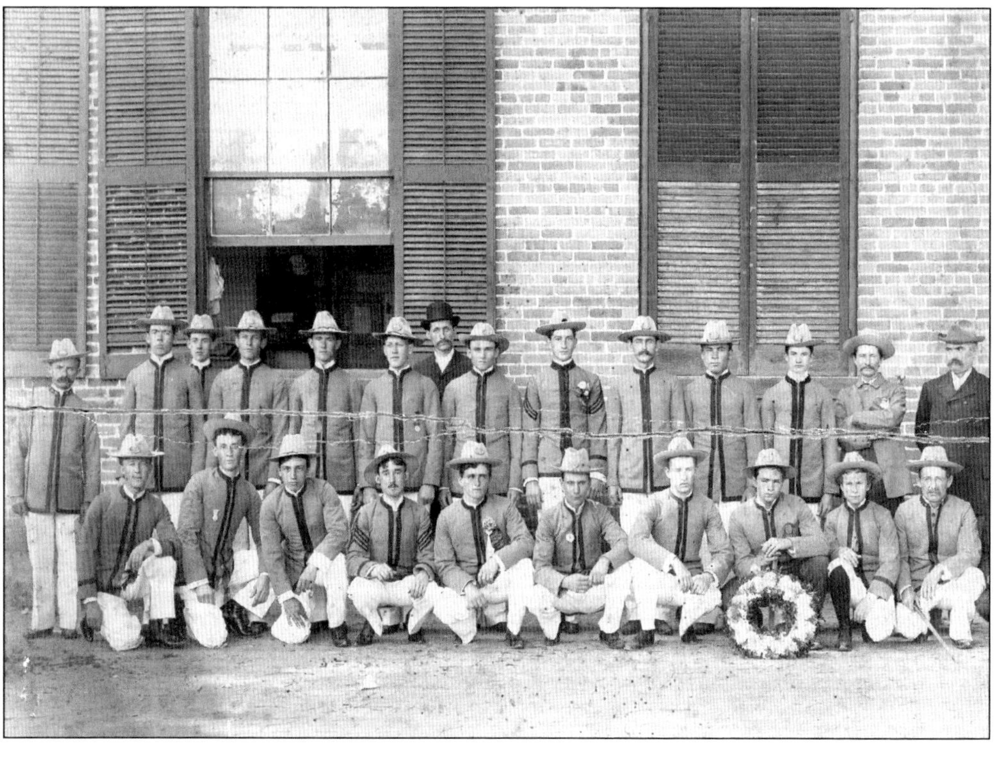

The Purple Heart, originally called the Badge of Merit, was established by Gen. George Washington in 1782 during the Revolutionary War. Only three men in Washington's time received it. On the 200th anniversary of Washington's birthday, the Badge of Merit became the Purple Heart, and in 1941, the Purple Heart became reserved for wounds received in action. Harland Anderson received his Purple Heart for the loss of his leg during World War II. (Jan Anderson.)

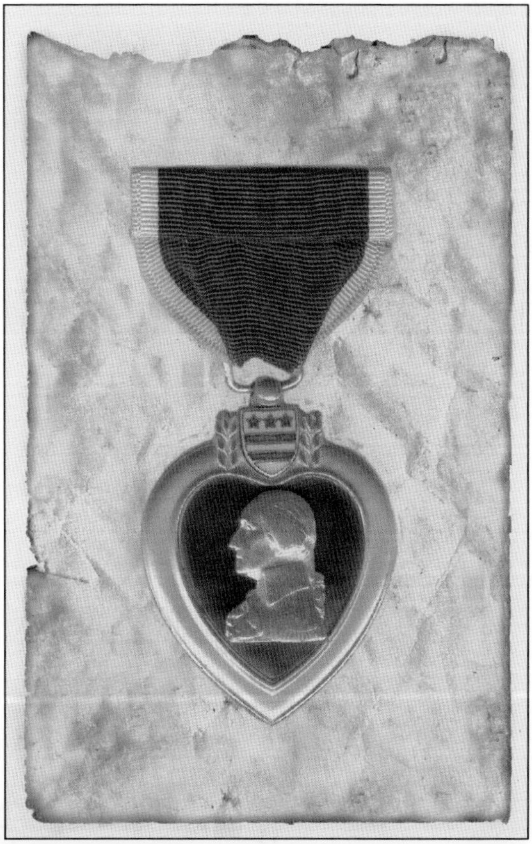

World War I draftees stand on the courthouse steps on Main Street in Greenville, Kentucky. With the American flag as their backdrop, they stand proudly with their hats in their hands, their ties straight, and their suitcases at their feet. (Christine Hinsey.)

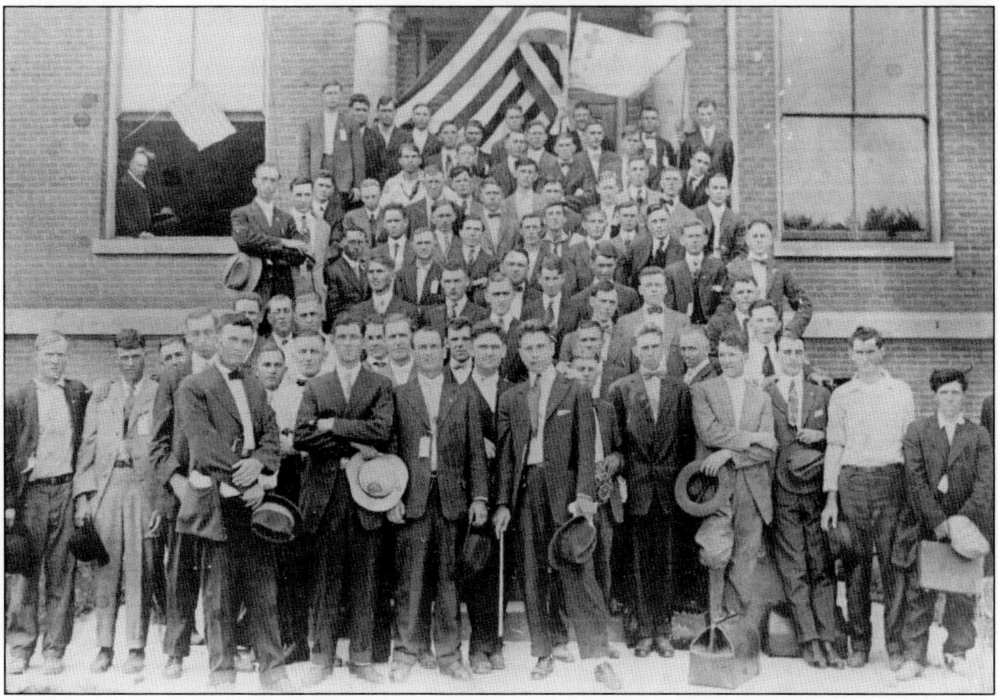

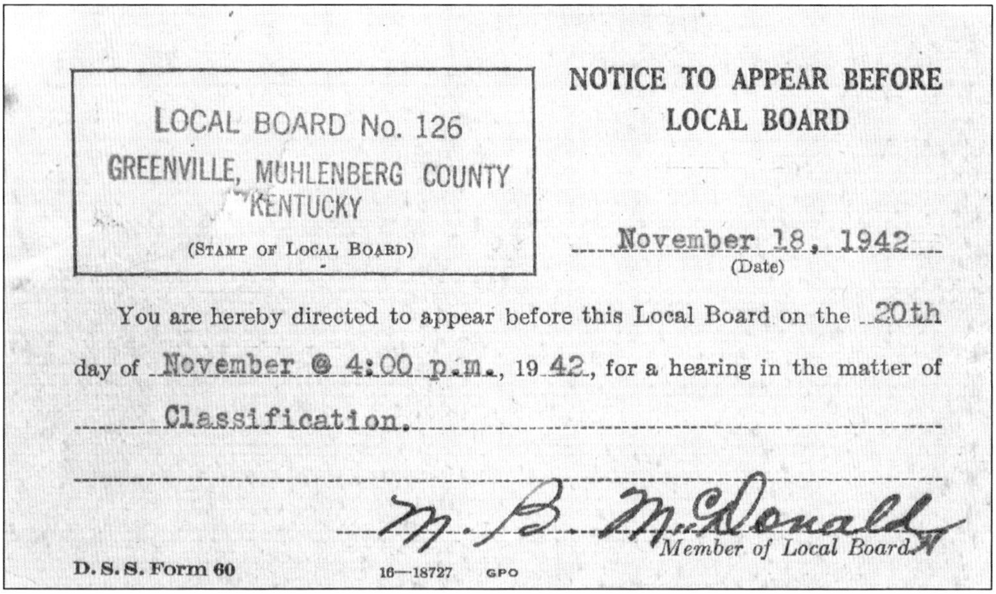
LOCAL BOARD No. 126
GREENVILLE, MUHLENBERG COUNTY
KENTUCKY
(Stamp of Local Board)

NOTICE TO APPEAR BEFORE
LOCAL BOARD

November 18, 1942
(Date)

You are hereby directed to appear before this Local Board on the 20th day of November @ 4:00 p.m., 19 42, for a hearing in the matter of Classification.

M. B. McDonald
Member of Local Board

D. S. S. Form 60 16—18727 GPO

This "notice to appear before the Muhlenberg County draft board for matters of classification" is dated November 18, 1942. The young men in the county 18 or older received this notice. Pres. Franklin Roosevelt signed the Selective Service Act of 1940, which created the country's first peacetime draft. The draft filled vacancies in the armed forces that could not voluntarily be filled. (Jan Anderson.)

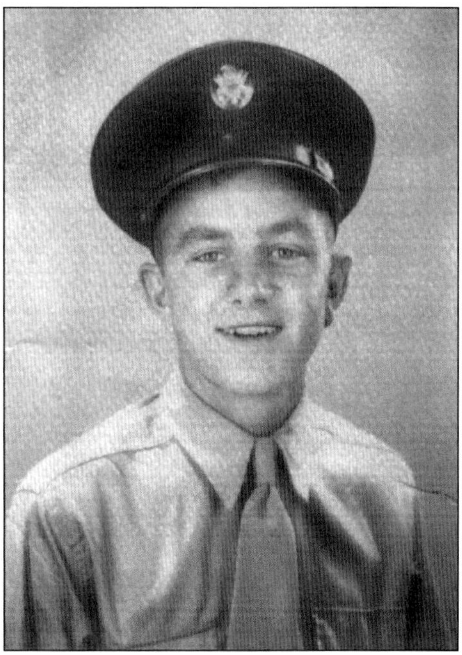

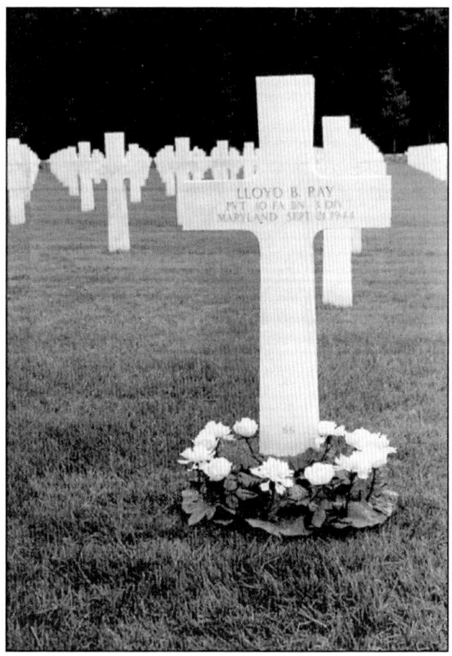

Pvt. Lloyd B. Ray, a Muhlenberg County native, was killed in action during World War II in a battle near Epinal (Vosges), France. He was buried, like so many other American men and women far from home, on the foreign soil they fought to protect. His plot is located at row 23, grave 66, at the Epinal American Cemetery in France. The cross lists his name, rank, serial number, and unit. (Larry and Venita Ray.)

In 1944, at age 19, Henry Dukes found himself on the front lines as a medical technician battling his way through Germany. Henry and 19 of his comrades were captured and shipped to Munich. Their food consisted of sawdust bread and grass soup. Red Cross rations traded for bread sustained them until their liberation. "That was the most remarkable day of my life," Henry said. He is pictured around 1943. (Loretta Grace.)

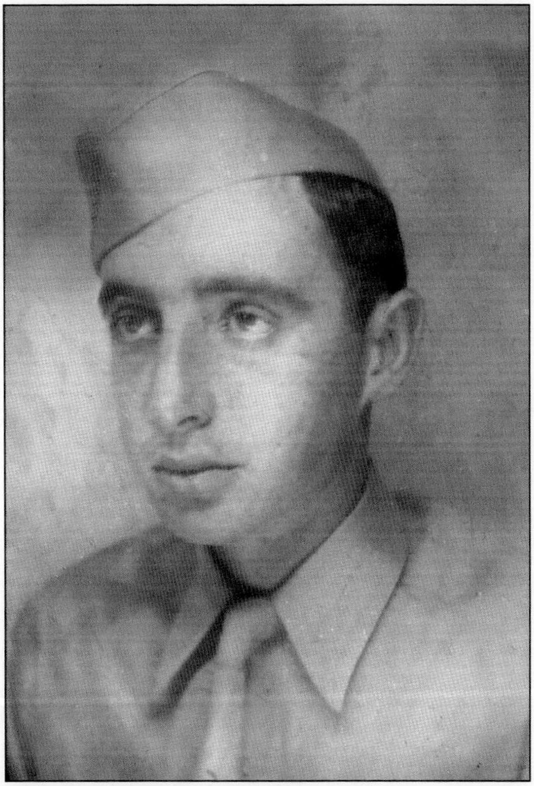

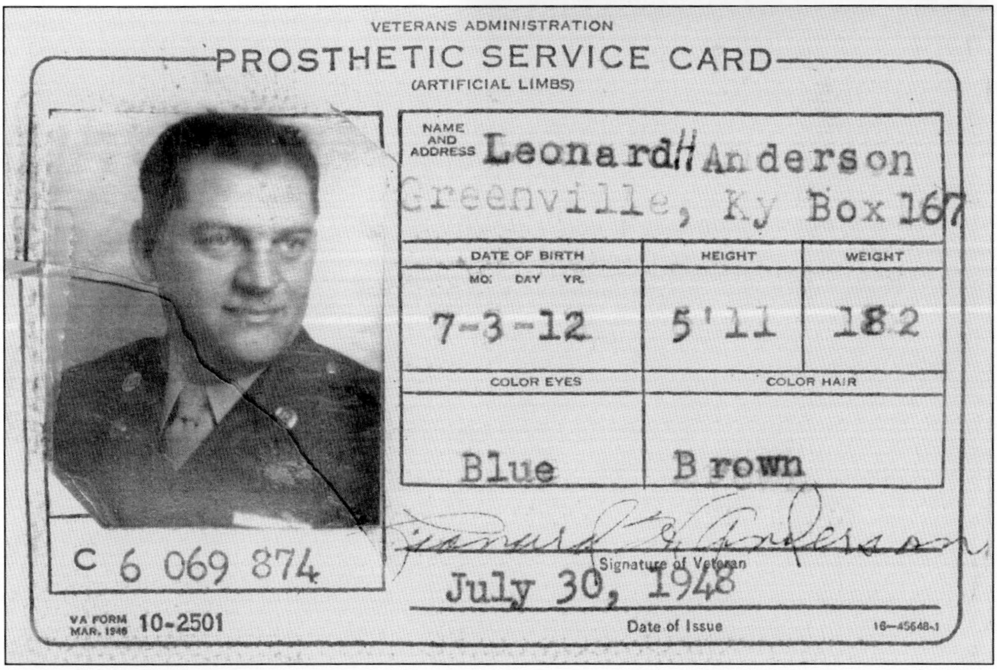

Leonard Harland Anderson received a prosthetic service card on July 30, 1948, from the U.S. government. The card was formal approval for a prosthetic device to replace the leg he lost in a battle on Okinawa in World War II. (H. L. Anderson Jr.)

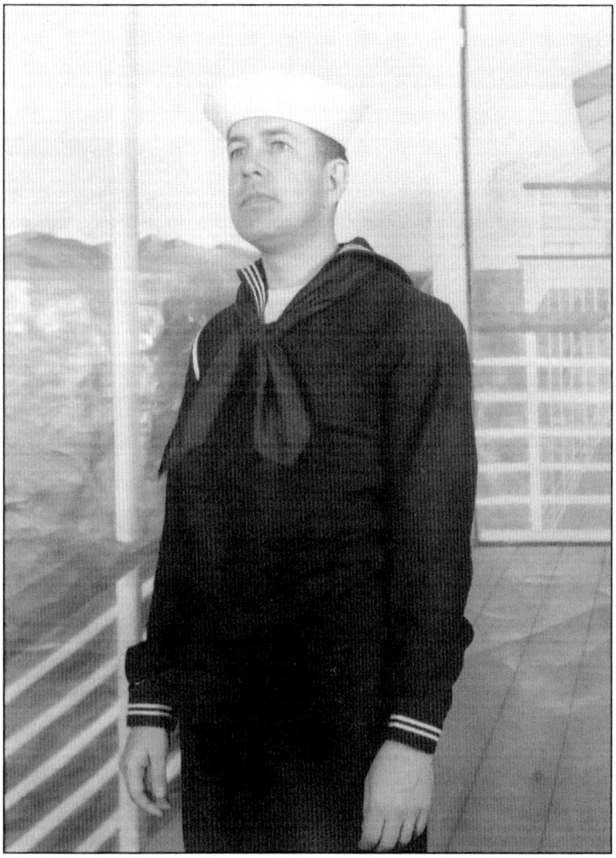

Hamilton R. Duncan stands on board in his navy uniform during World War II. Hamilton, the son of Andrew and Cynthia Robertson Duncan, was a benefactor to the city of Greenville. He was also treasurer of the W. G. Duncan Coal Company and oversaw its sale to the Peabody Coal Company in 1958. (Duncan Center.)

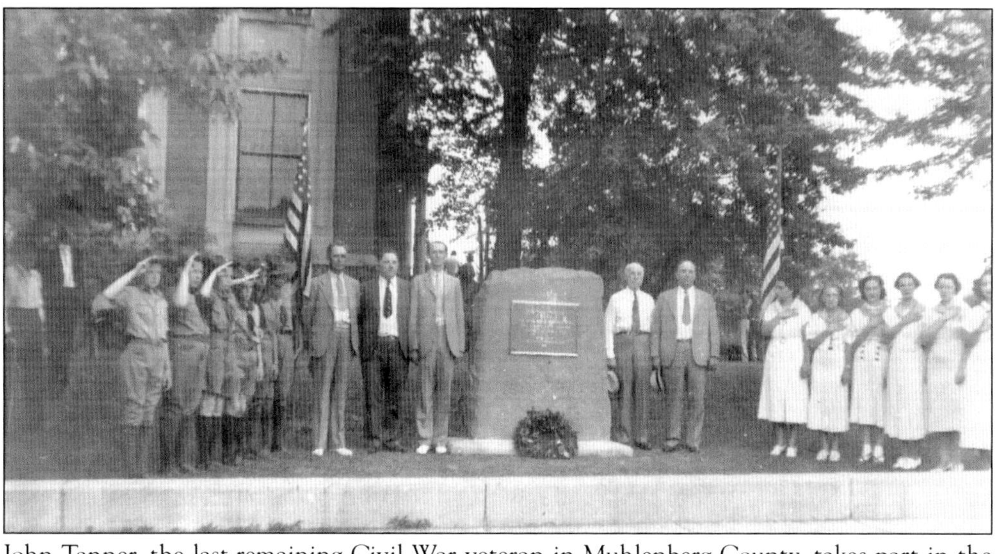

John Tanner, the last remaining Civil War veteran in Muhlenberg County, takes part in the unveiling of the World War I memorial marker on the courthouse lawn on May 30, 1937. John is standing beneath the shade tree to the left holding his cane. The memorial marker was furnished by the Greenville Kiwanis Club. Also in attendance are the Boy Scouts and the Girl Reserves. (Duncan Center.)

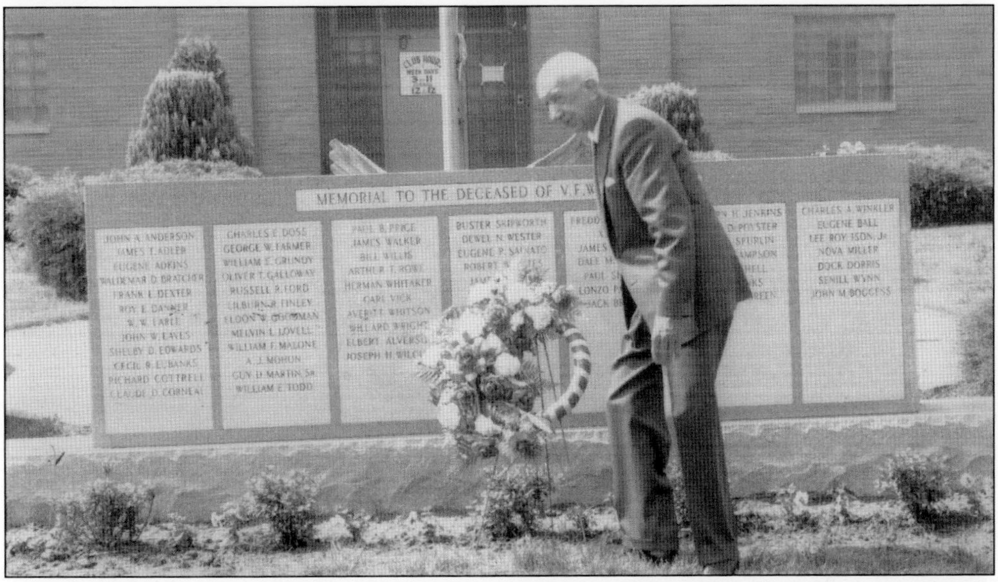

On a Veteran's Day around 1950, Rev. Arthur Gross, minister of the Greenville Presbyterian Church, places a wreath on the memorial to the deceased veterans of foreign wars at the Muhlenberg County VFW Post. (Muhlenberg County Library Archives.)

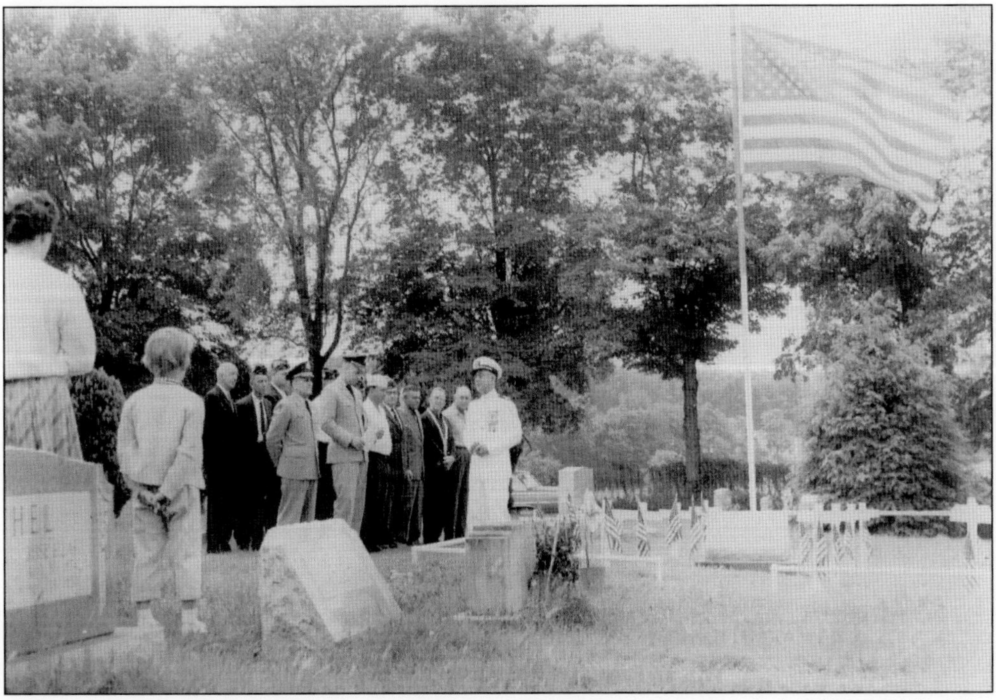

A Veteran's Day Memorial service in 1965 at the Evergreen cemetery is held by Muhlenberg Memorial Post 5478 of the VFW. Members taking part in the service are, from left to right, Bob Ed Vick, W. D. Bratcher, and U.S. Naval Reserve lieutenant J. E. Wood. The service was held adjacent to the VFW memorial lot to pay tribute to the county's war dead. (Christine Hinsey.)

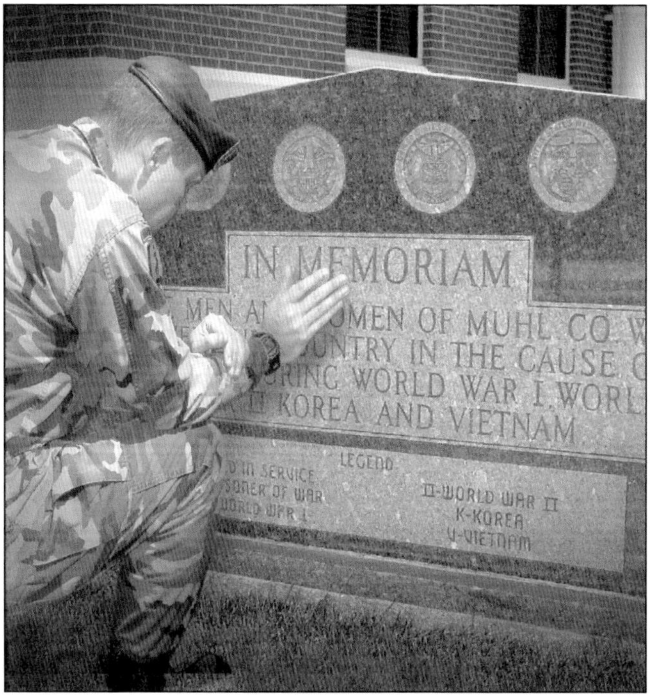

Past, present, and future, the war memorials stand as silent reminders beckoning one to remember those who have served the country selflessly in the cause of freedom. On the courthouse lawn in Muhlenberg County, soldier John Thompson kneels to pay his respect to fallen comrades. (Jan Anderson.)

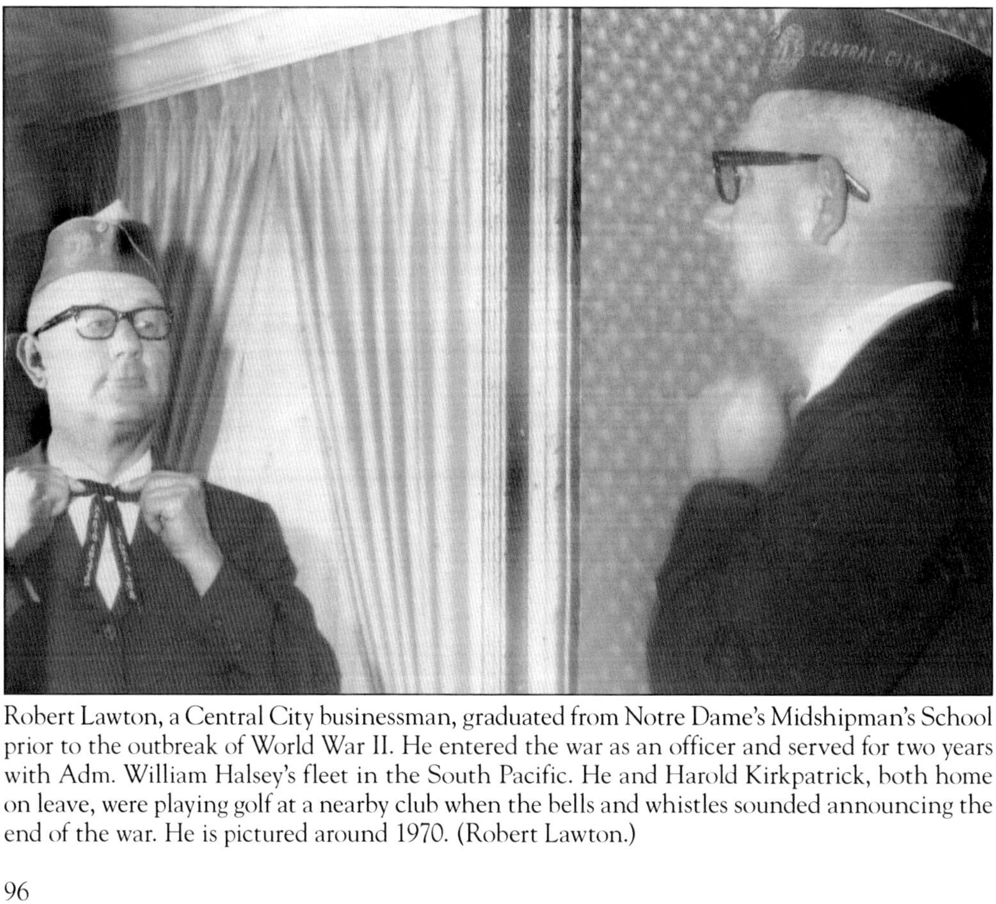

Robert Lawton, a Central City businessman, graduated from Notre Dame's Midshipman's School prior to the outbreak of World War II. He entered the war as an officer and served for two years with Adm. William Halsey's fleet in the South Pacific. He and Harold Kirkpatrick, both home on leave, were playing golf at a nearby club when the bells and whistles sounded announcing the end of the war. He is pictured around 1970. (Robert Lawton.)

Seven

SORROW AND HARDSHIPS

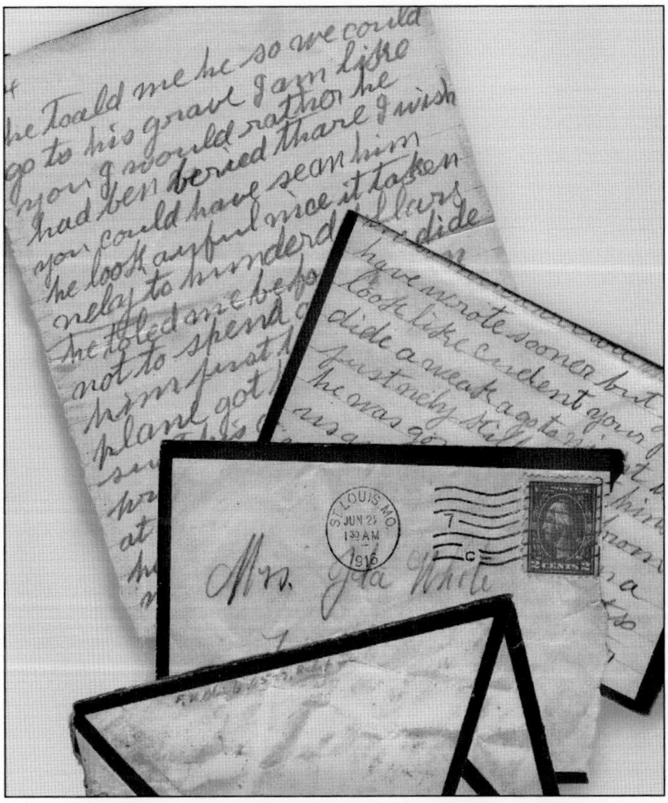

Mourning covers—black-edged, posted letters used during the 19th and early 20th centuries, were harbingers of death and messengers of grief. Mourning covers were used to mail death or funeral notices or as black-edged cards or letters to extend sympathy or to express appreciation for condolences received. These were similar to the cards provided by the funeral homes today, though they are no longer black-edged. These black-marked letters were accepted as one of the proper and important rites of mourning and grieving and often used for a full year by surviving family members. This mourning cover and its enclosed grief-stricken contents were correspondence in a series of letters addressed to Ida White in Rosewood, Kentucky. On June 23, 1916, this one from her mother in Missouri concerning the recent death of her father reads, "Ida, the semetary ant far from us. I bout to graves. They caust $25 dollers. I will haft to close and go to bed. I cant think of nothing but truble. Take care of yourself. From your mother." (Loretta Grace.)

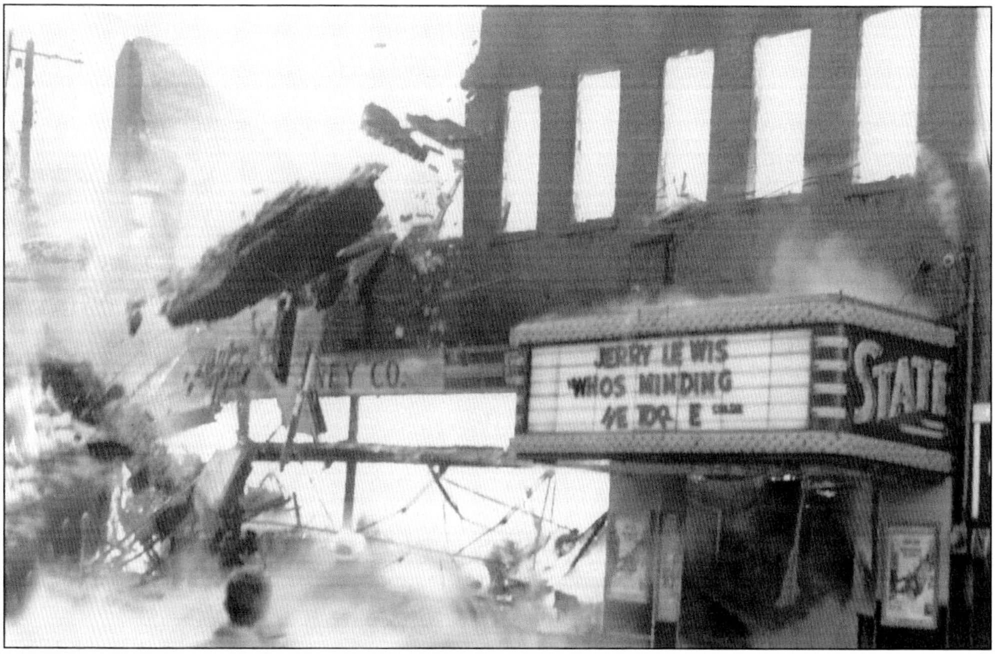

The second story of the structure collapses as fire devastates the State Theater and the J. C. Penney's building on Broad Street in Central City. Ironically, the 1962 theater marquee lists Jerry Lewis as starring in *Who's Minding the Store?* (Christine Hinsey.)

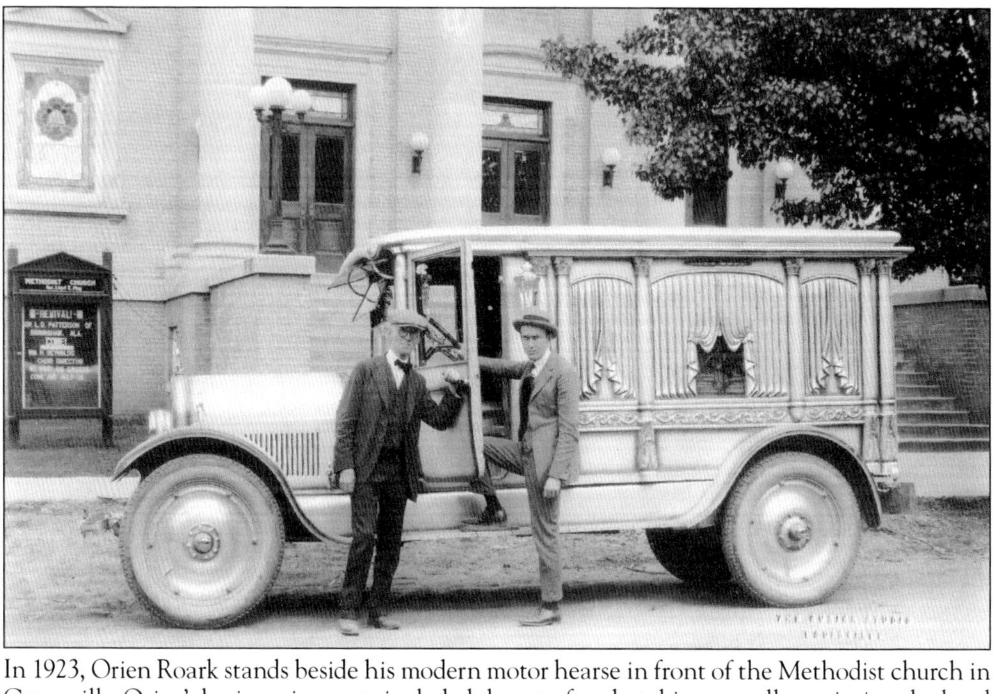

In 1923, Orien Roark stands beside his modern motor hearse in front of the Methodist church in Greenville. Orien's business interests included the art of undertaking as well as printing the local paper and running a retail store that carried everything a modern consumer of the 1920s could need, including coffins. Roark was proud of embalming Gen. Don Carlos Buell, who arrived in St. Louis perfectly preserved. (Carol McClure.)

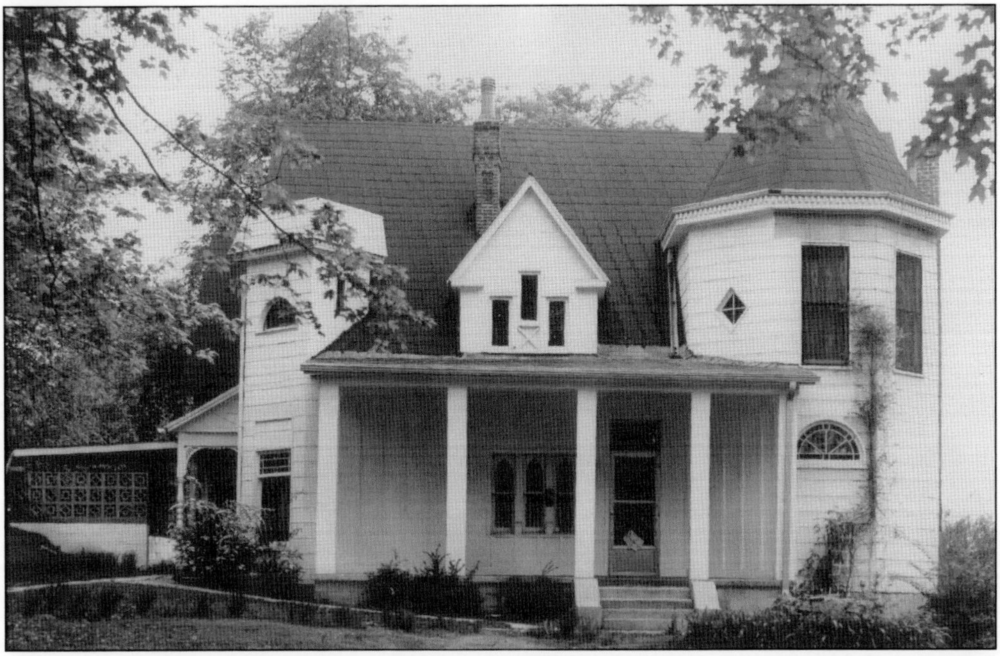

Once upon a time in Greenville, a man built a castle for his queen on town hill. She declined his offer of marriage, and brokenheartedly he sold the castle. So goes the story of William H. Reynolds, who never married and built other houses that he occupied alone for the rest of his life. The house, pictured above, was sold to St. Clair Eaves and eventually became the Washburn-Pannell Funeral Home around 1962. The Washburn-Pannell funeral business also had a chapel in Drakesboro and, shown below, in Beech Creek. (Christine Hinsey.)

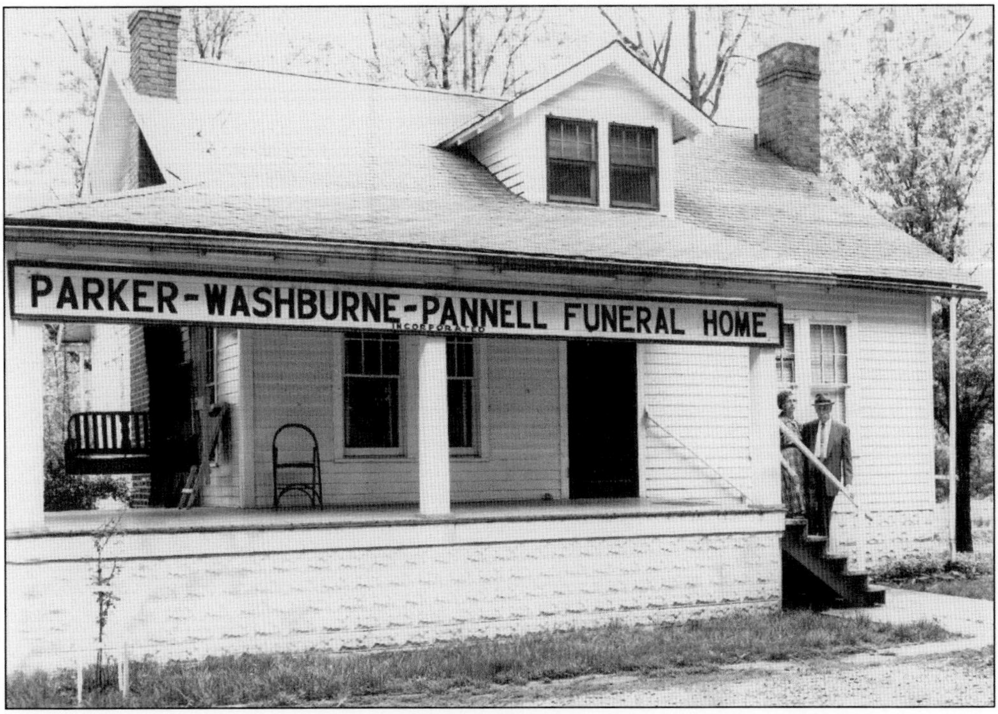

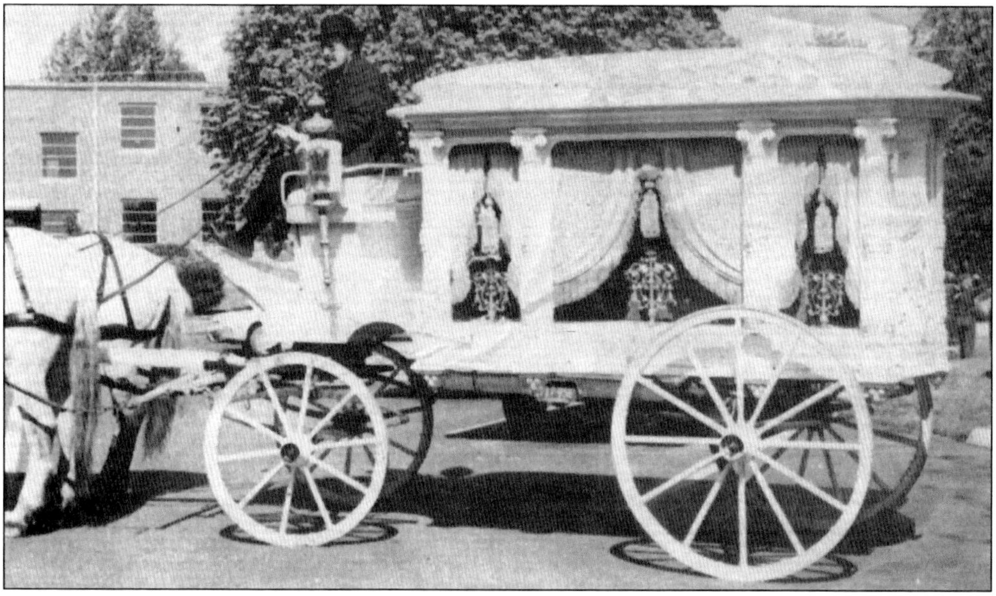

The horse-drawn carriage has been the symbol of the Tucker Funeral Home and services since 1909. The business was founded by Jesse B. Tucker in Bremen, Kentucky. His sons Norman and George expanded the business by adding the current Central City location and in 1959 opened a chapel in Sacramento, followed by another chapel in Beechmont, Kentucky, in 1969. Four generations of Tuckers have continued to serve the county and surrounding areas for over 90 years. Below is the Tucker's Funeral Home in Central City around 1970. (Both, Joe Ben Tucker.)

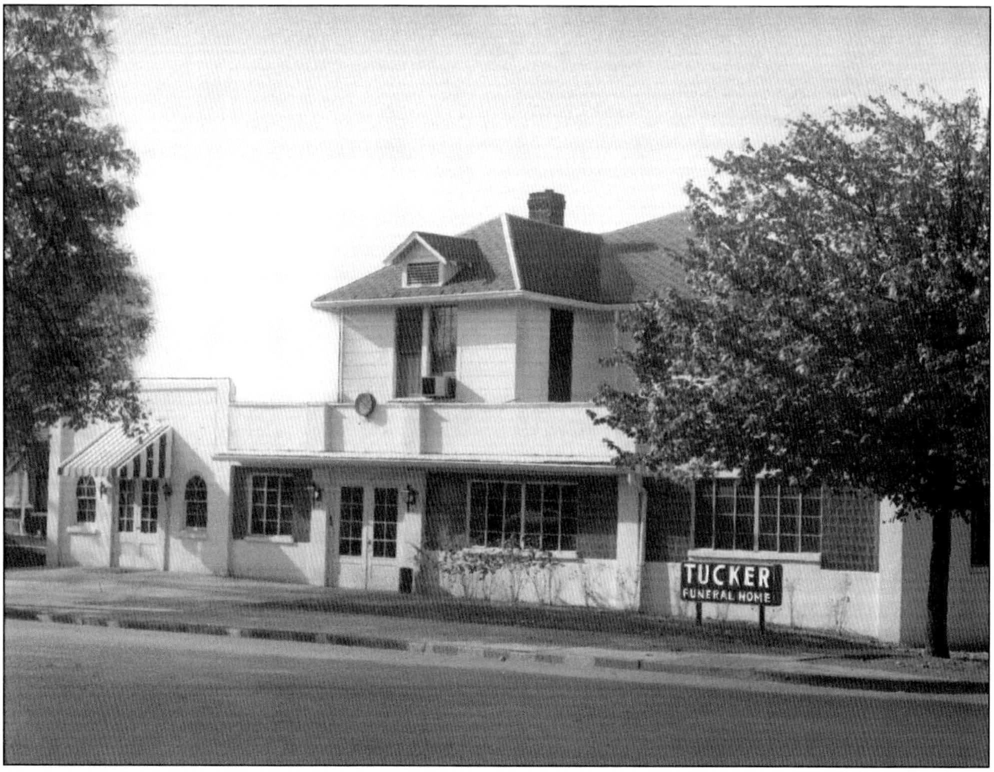

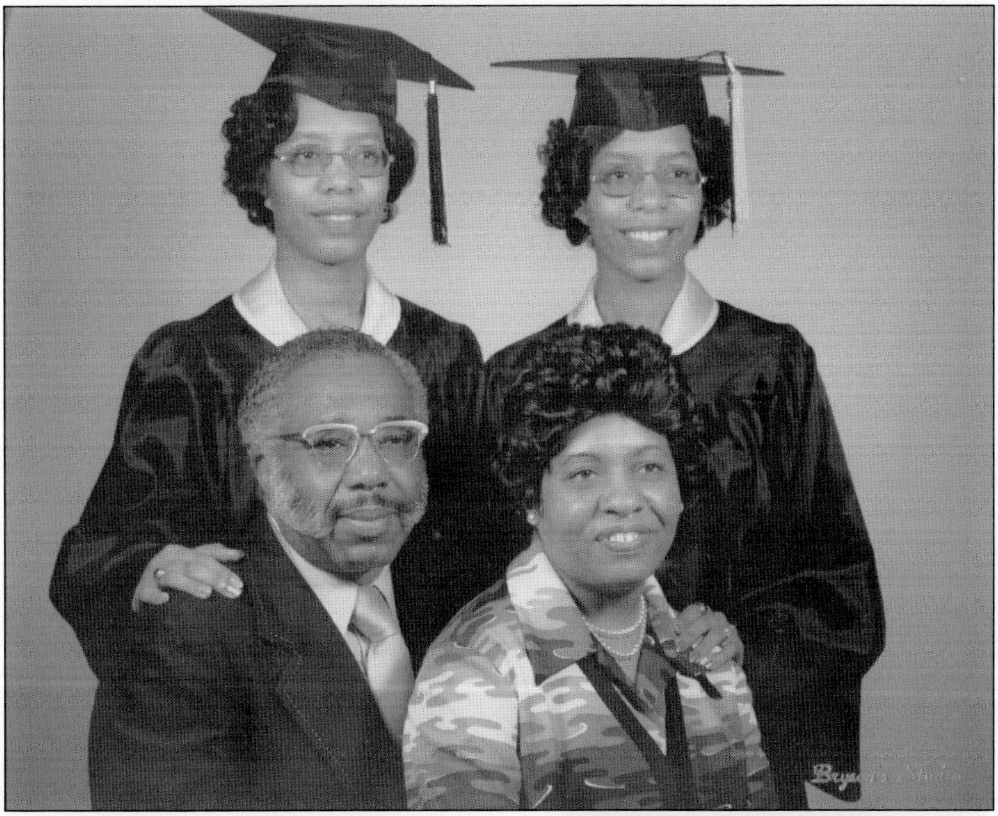

In the early 1960s, licensed funeral director and embalmer Bernes L. Bibbs founded the Bibbs Funeral Home along with his wife, Dorothy (Hightower) Bibbs, a local educator. The couple's Greenville business continues to be run by their twin daughters, Berna Dean Bibbs-Snipes and Dorothy Jean Bibbs-Kendrick, who are co-owners and licensed funeral directors as well as educators. They remain dedicated to continuing their parents' legacy of professionalism. (Bibbs family.)

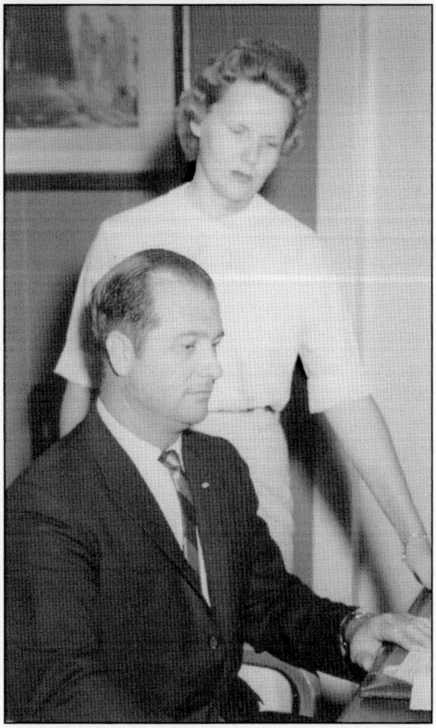

In 1954, J. Irvin Gary bought the Ernest Parker Funeral Home in Greenville and moved it as Gary's Funeral Home to its present location on Hopkinsville Street. Irvin Wright began helping his father J. Irvin when he was 12 years old by making trips in the night to assist with transporting bodies to the funeral home. Irvin Wright graduated from embalming school in 1952, and his wife, Ima Nell, is also a licensed funeral director. (Christine Hinsey.)

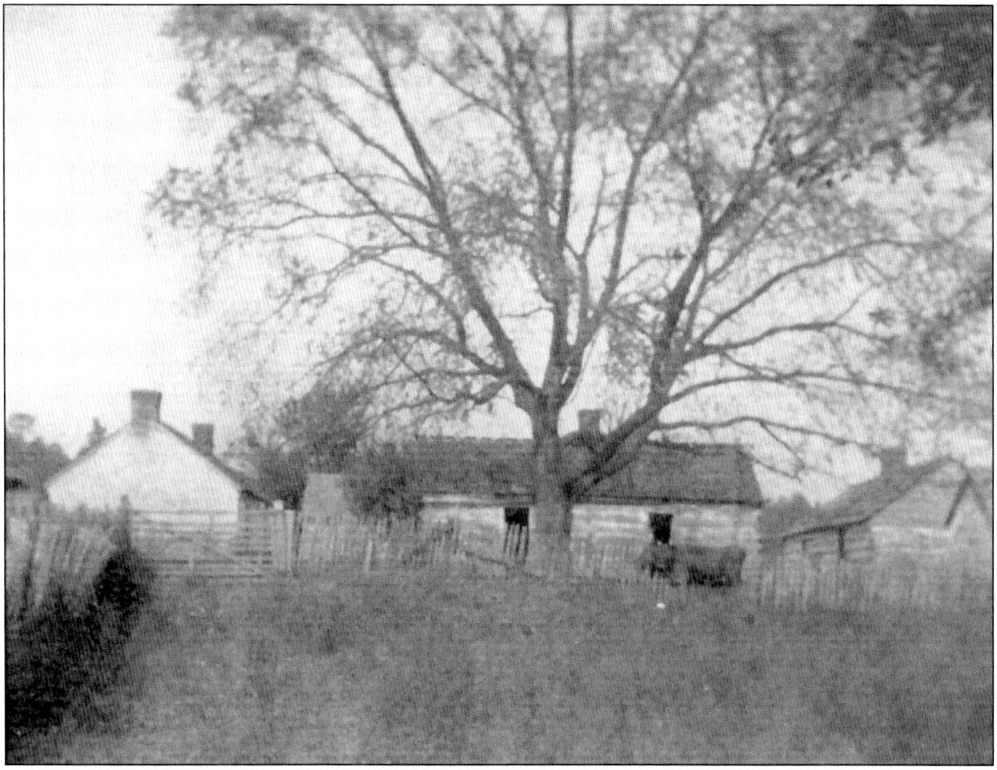

The poor asylum, pictured around 1865, was one of the richest farms in the county before becoming a refuge for the needy. Robert M. Martin was born there January 10, 1840, and became the epitome of the dashing figure of a Confederate cavalry leader. He was known for his humor and courage and remained the idolized leader of his soldiers and their desperate cause until the surrender at Appomattox. (Christine Hinsey.)

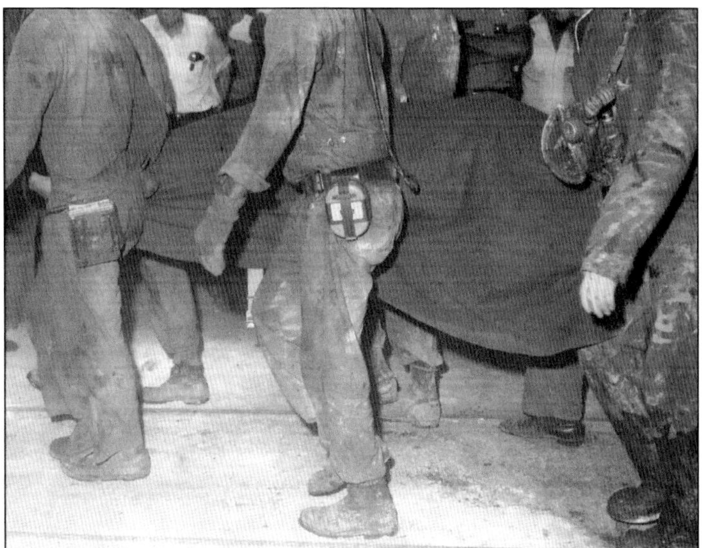

Unidentified rescue workers carry a fallen comrade from the scene of a mine tragedy in Muhlenberg County in 1968. These brave men exemplify the commitment that miners have to one another in times of danger. The worst mine disaster in the county occurred on February 1, 1910, claiming the lives of 35 miners. Rescue workers stayed on the scene day and night until the last miner was recovered. (Christine Hinsey.)

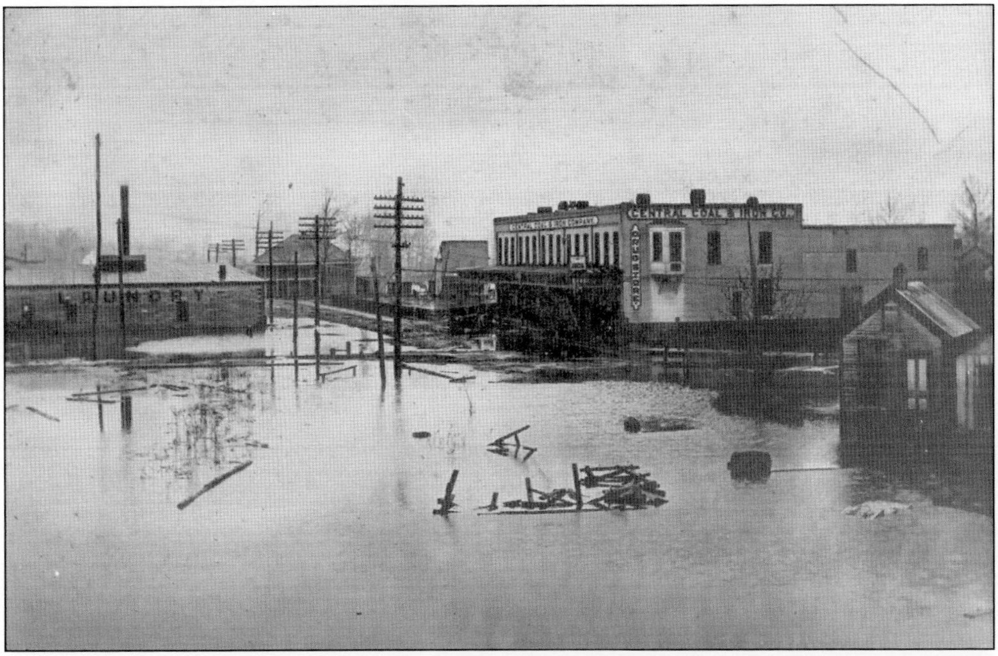

Above, debris is seen floating down the streets of Central City, Kentucky, after Cypress Creek overflowed its banks for the last time in 1935. Below, two unidentified young men take a break sitting in chairs swamped by the waist-deep Patton Town floodwaters while others contemplate their dire situation. Unrelenting rains caused severe flooding in the Central City and Patton Town areas in 1962. Families in the low-lying areas had to remove possessions from their homes to keep them from being damaged or destroyed by the rising water. (*Times-Argus.*)

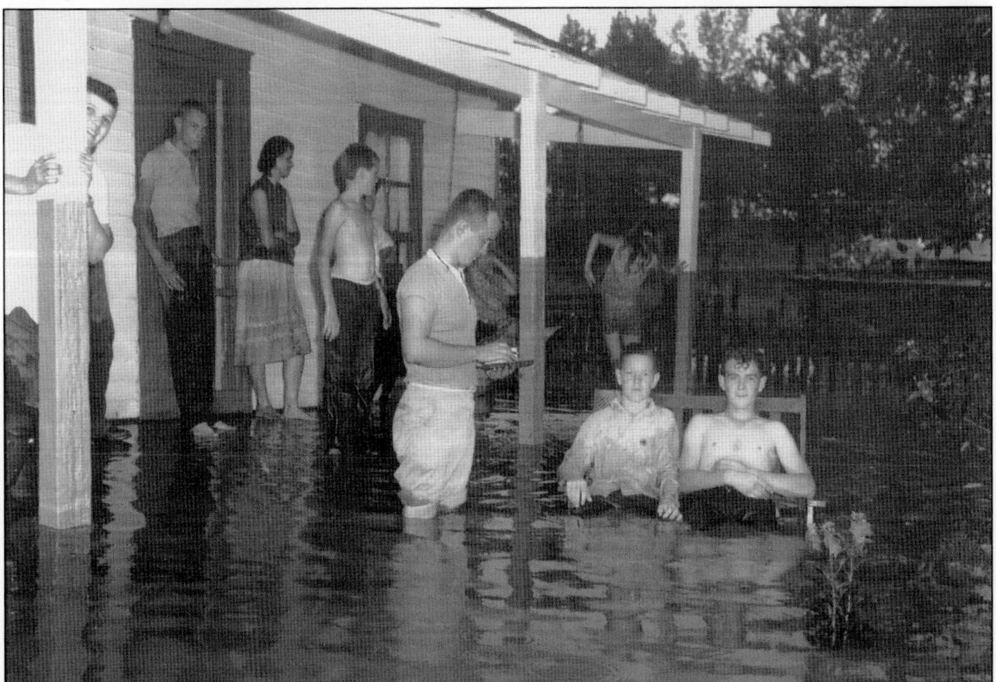

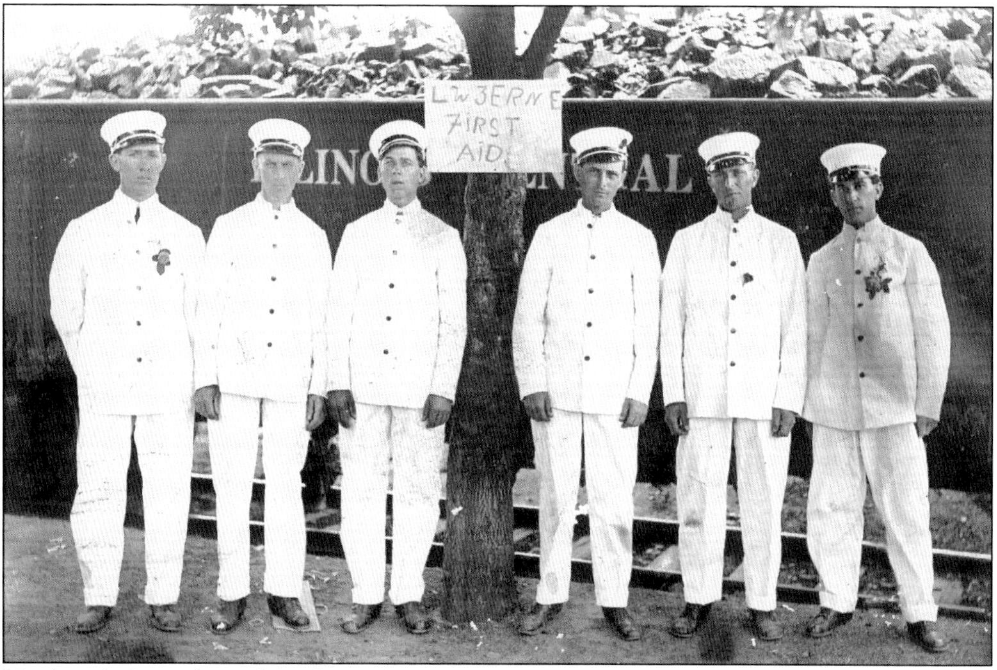

Unidentified members of the first aid team at Luzerne around 1910 wear professional uniforms that denote their function. Formal mine disaster training began in the United States in 1910 in an effort by the Bureau of Mines to prepare miners to assist each other in rescue measures during emergencies. By current guidelines, all rescue members must stay together at all times. Each member's training is considered vital to the unit. The squad must also stay hooked together by a lightweight chain in areas of smoke or low visibility. Below, Peabody Star Mine Rescue and Safety team members are, from left to right, Tom Littlepage, Delbert Richey, John Crockett, Jack Littlepage, Randy Duncan, Charles Willis, Kevin Miller, and Jerry Durall. (William Raymer.)

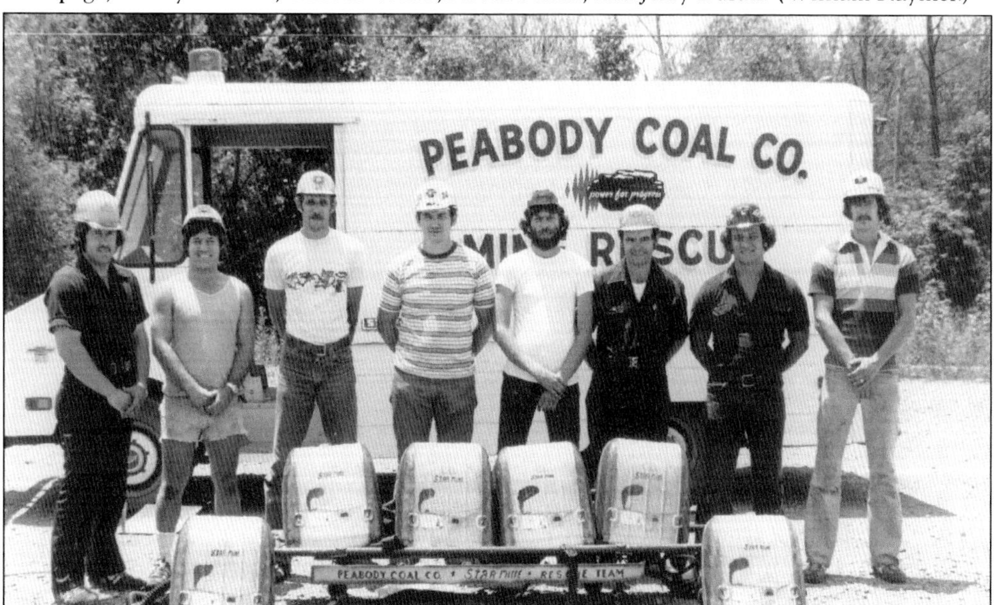

Eight

Coal Mines and Miners

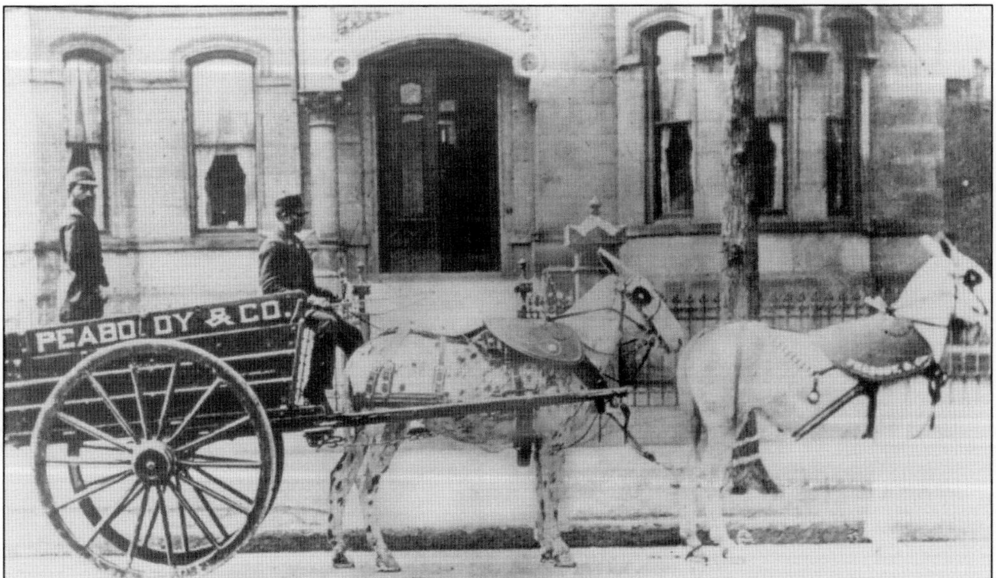

In 1883, Francis S. Peabody began his coal mining career selling coal door to door in Chicago using a horse and wagon. The demand for his quality coal increased rapidly, as did Peabody's ability to supply it. His initial business grew from the horse-and-buggy outlet to a contract with Commonwealth Edison to supply their coal needs. Unfortunately, securing that energy has always been a dangerous occupation. Accidents occur from roof falls, cave-ins, and explosions. Initially living conditions were deplorable, as miners and their families were obliged to live in company-owned homes, issued company money, and forced to buy necessities from company stores. Many miners grew old quickly and died years before their time with lungs diseased by coal dust breathed in day after day in unventilated shafts. But in 1920, the union became a reality and the name John L. Lewis became a chant of hope for the miners and a mantra of dread for some mine owners. Finally life began to improve for the miners. (Christine Hinsey.)

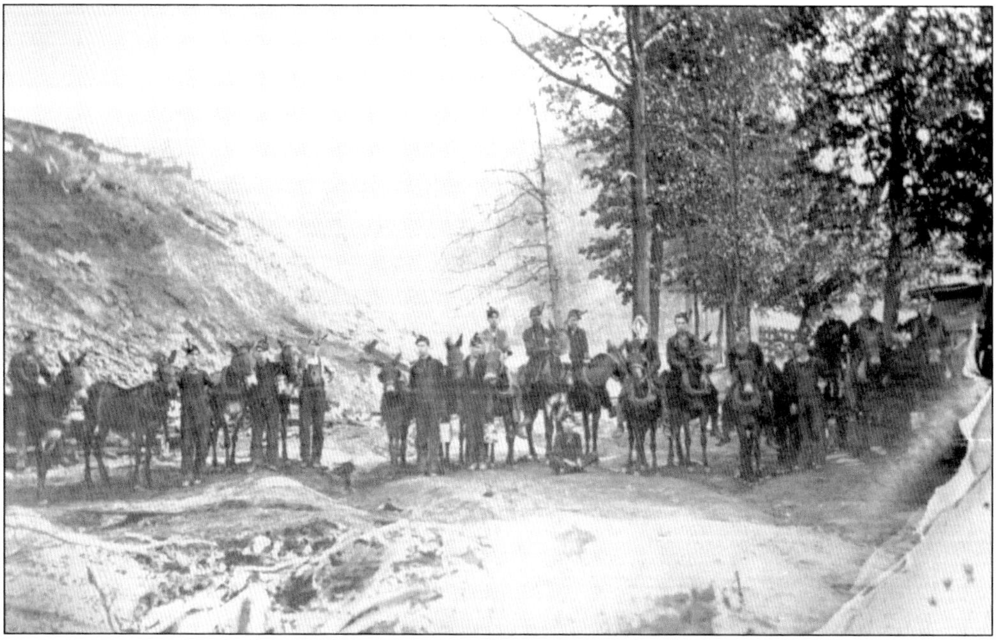

Mule drivers stand with their mules at the Luzerne Mine around 1915. Before the days of electricity, mules were used to haul coal from the mines in carts. Each miner had his own mule, and they worked as a team. Many of the mules were bred to be short and stocky to better fit under the low mine roofs and to haul heavier loads of coal. (William Raymer.)

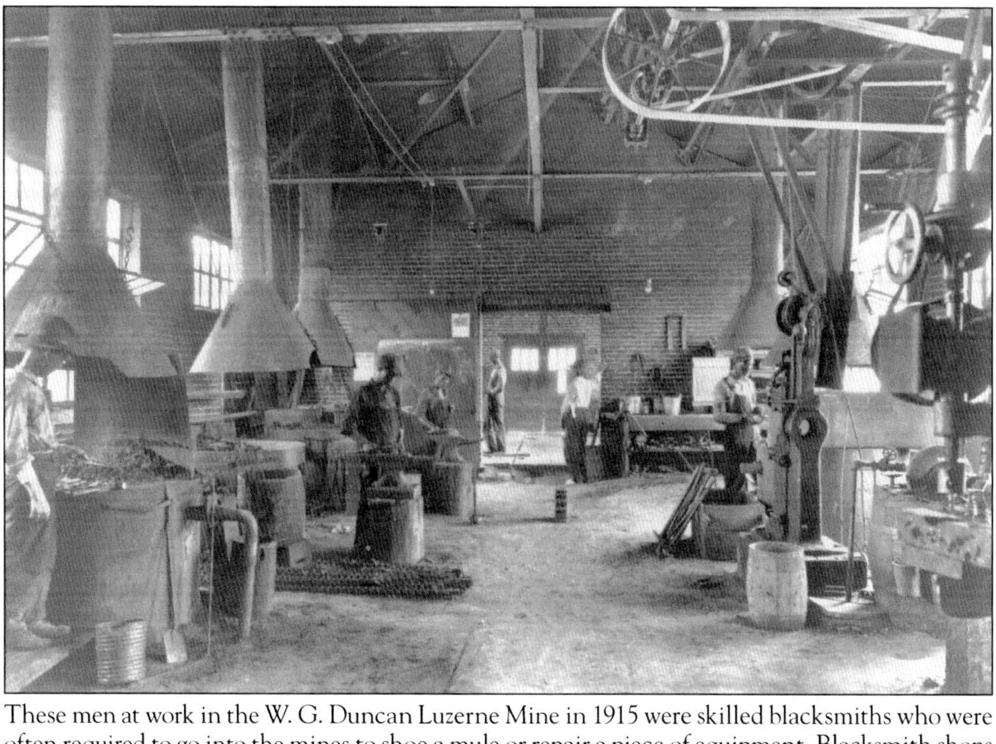

These men at work in the W. G. Duncan Luzerne Mine in 1915 were skilled blacksmiths who were often required to go into the mines to shoe a mule or repair a piece of equipment. Blacksmith shops and repair shops on site were a necessity for keeping the mines running. (William Raymer.)

Miners with their lunch pails under their arms prepare to leave for work around 1939. Early miners with their carbide lamps in place often walked 5 to 10 miles to work and back daily. Young men began working in the mines at age 16 making 44¢ a ton. In 1949, miners averaged $14 a day. In 1980, the miners averaged approximately $100 a day. (William Raymer.)

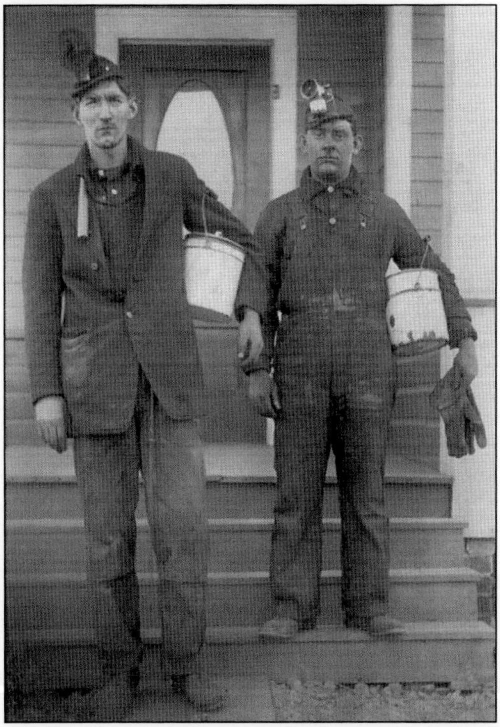

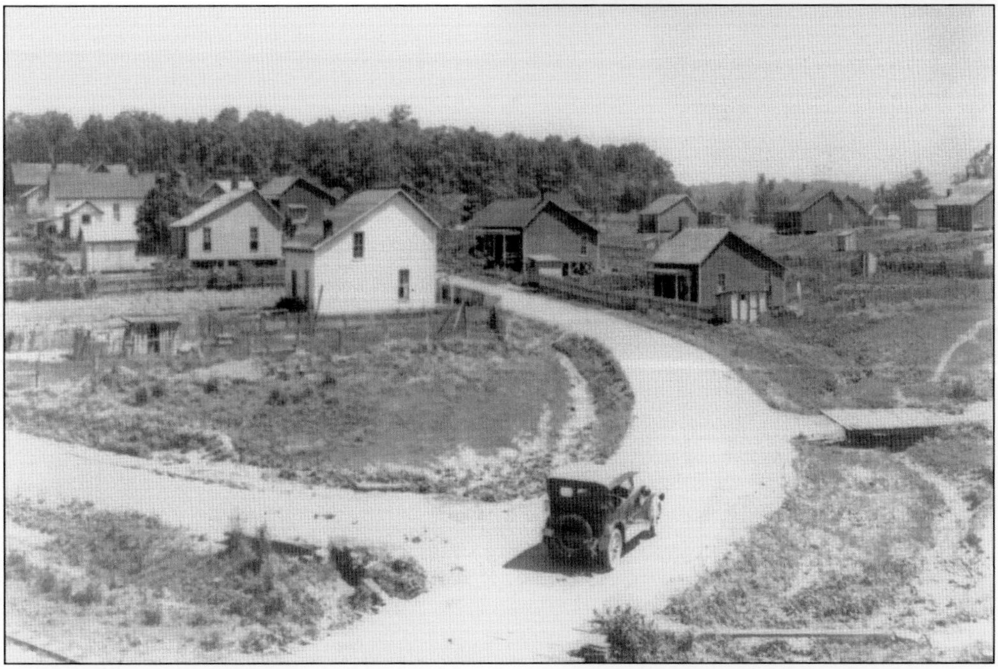

A car makes its way through the mining town of Luzerne in 1930. Many of the mining towns were terrible places to live, but W. G. Duncan built a pleasant community for his workers complete with nice houses, a hospital, schools, churches, ball fields, poolrooms, and a skating rink. He provided a teacher for the community and encouraged his workers and their families to continue their education. (William Raymer.)

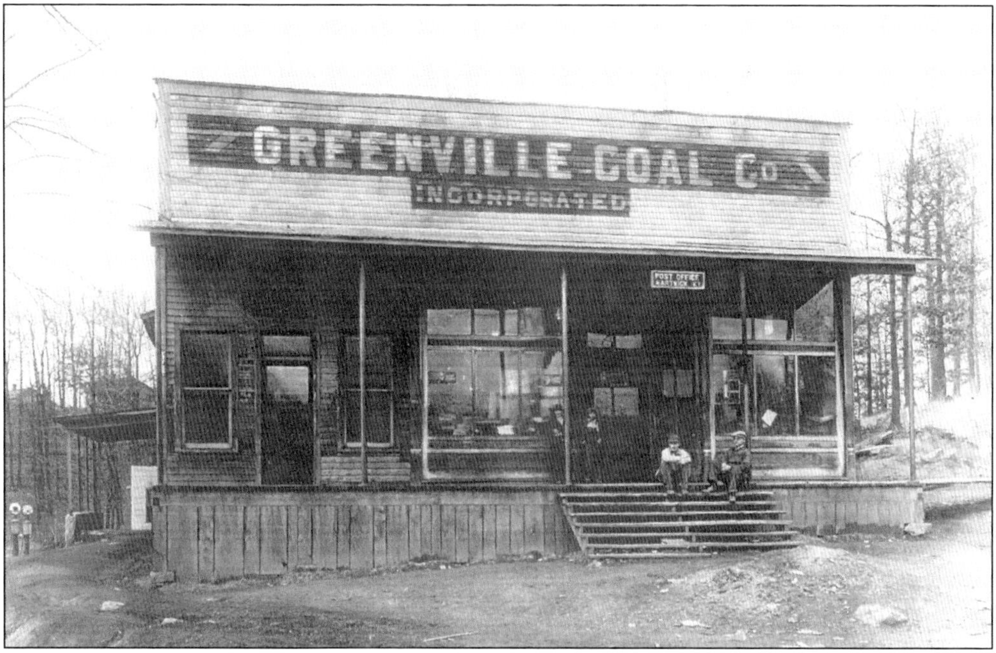

The Martwick Company Store, pictured around 1920, served the Martwick community and miners. The mine was developed in 1910 by Charles Martin and W. A. Wickliffe for the Greenville Coal Company. They named the company after themselves using the first syllables of their two last names. (William Raymer.)

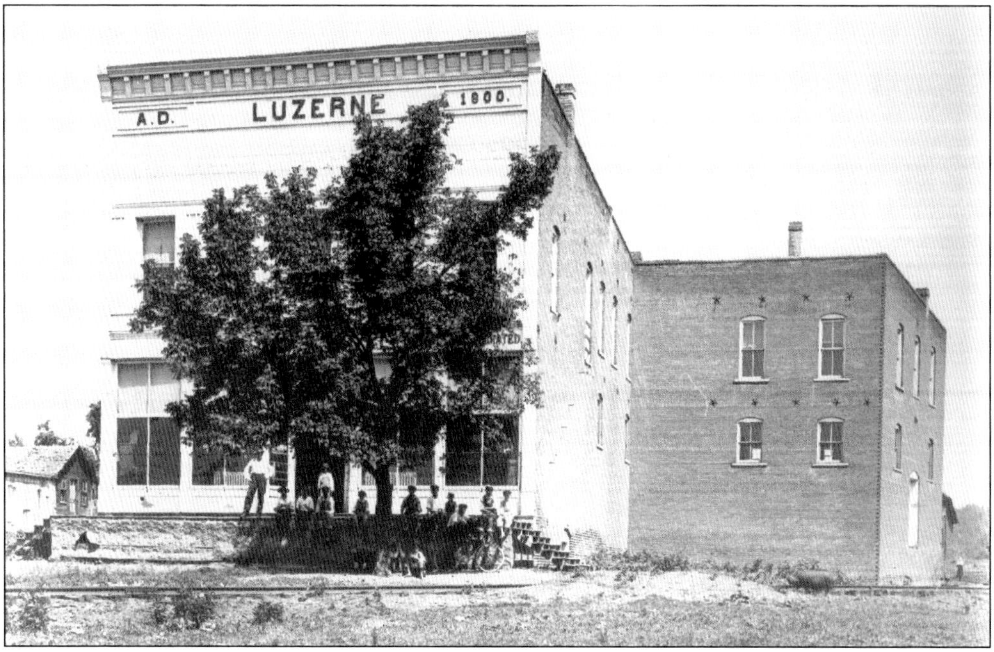

The Luzerne Mine was the first mine opened by W. G. Duncan in Muhlenberg County. The Luzerne Company Store opened around 1900. The company store carried everything a family could need, from coffee to coffins. Mattresses and beds were stacked to the ceilings, and porch swings and rocking chairs were always on display. (William Raymer.)

Flickers were multidenomination coinage bearing a coal mine's name that could be redeemed at the company store for food, clothing, furniture, and needed supplies. Some independent stores would take flickers in trade but never at full face value, for fear the mine would close and the storekeeper could not redeem the flickers. The flickers shown are from the Black Diamond Coal Company in Drakesboro around 1888. (Duncan Center.)

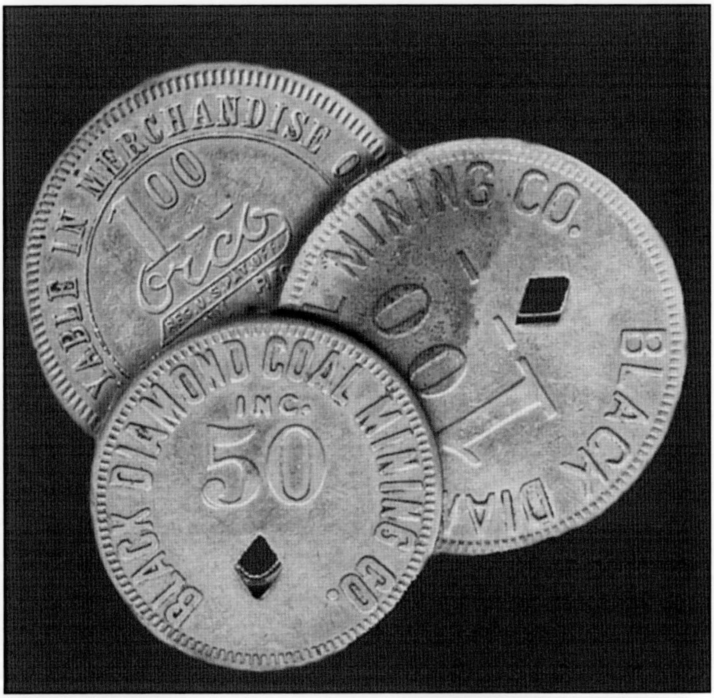

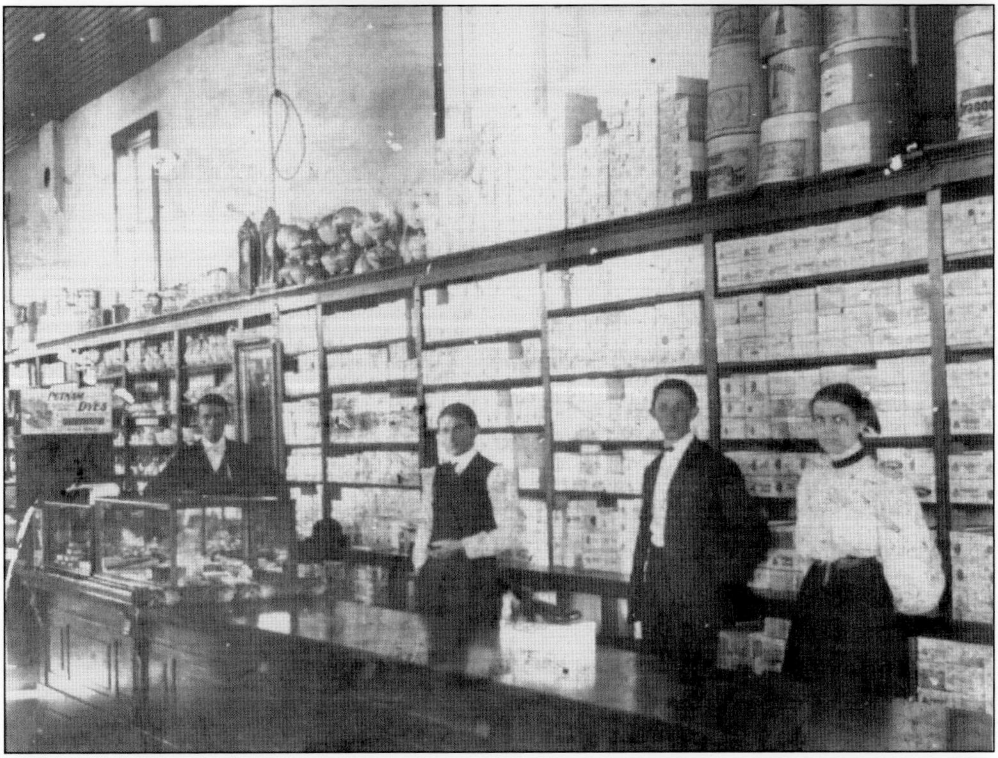

A partial view inside the W. G. Duncan Luzerne Company Store in 1900 demonstrates the vastness of the space available for the storage of merchandise in the cavernous two-story structure. (William Raymer.)

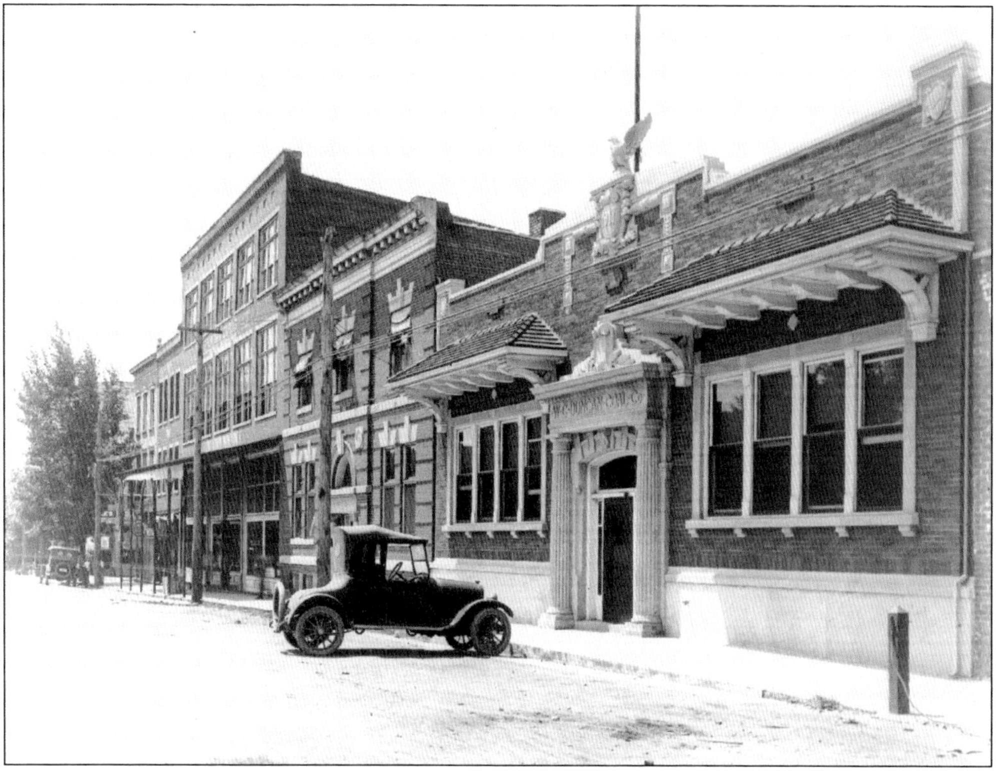

The W. G. Duncan Coal Company was incorporated on October 1, 1900, and opened the Luzerne Mine. Three years later, they opened mines at Graham and Skibo. Both of these mines operated from the same tipple but from slopes on opposite sides of a valley. The Duncan Company's main business office was located on East Main Street in Greenville. (Christine Hinsey.)

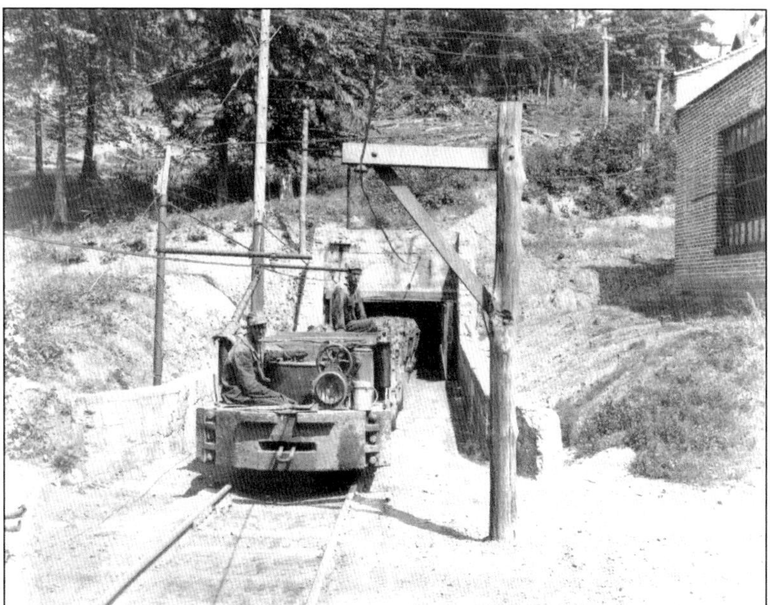

An electric mine cart heads into the mouth of the Jarvis opening in Graham around 1980. The locomotive operator on the cart is William Raymer, and the trip rider is Emery Vick. (William Raymer.)

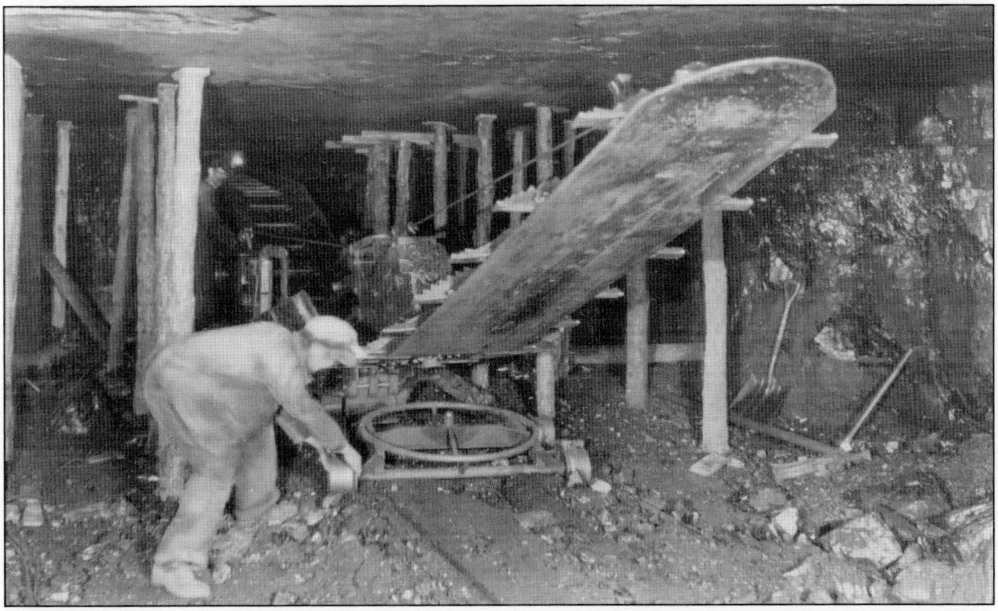

A miner is shown cutting coal from a seam in an underground mine around 1939. Prior to the introduction of these first continuous miners, picks and shovels were used to retrieve the coal deposits, and miners were often unable to stand upright as they worked. (William Raymer.)

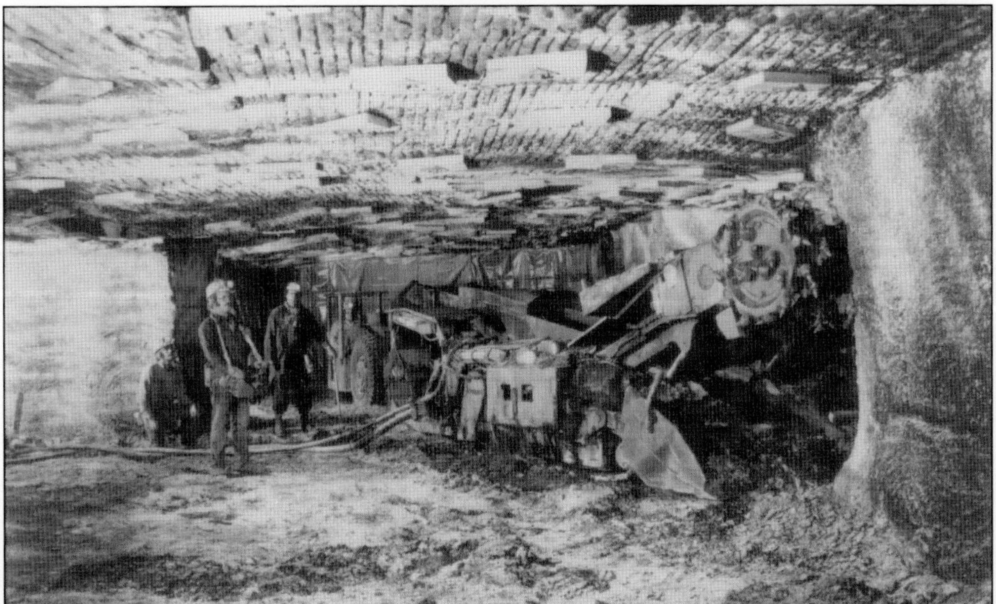

Miners are shown using a remote-control continuous miner in an underground mine around 1970. This newer version of the continuous miner enabled miners to extract coal at a rate of up to 38 tons a minute, depending upon the seam thickness. The remote control operation keeps the machine operator further away from the equipment. (William Raymer.)

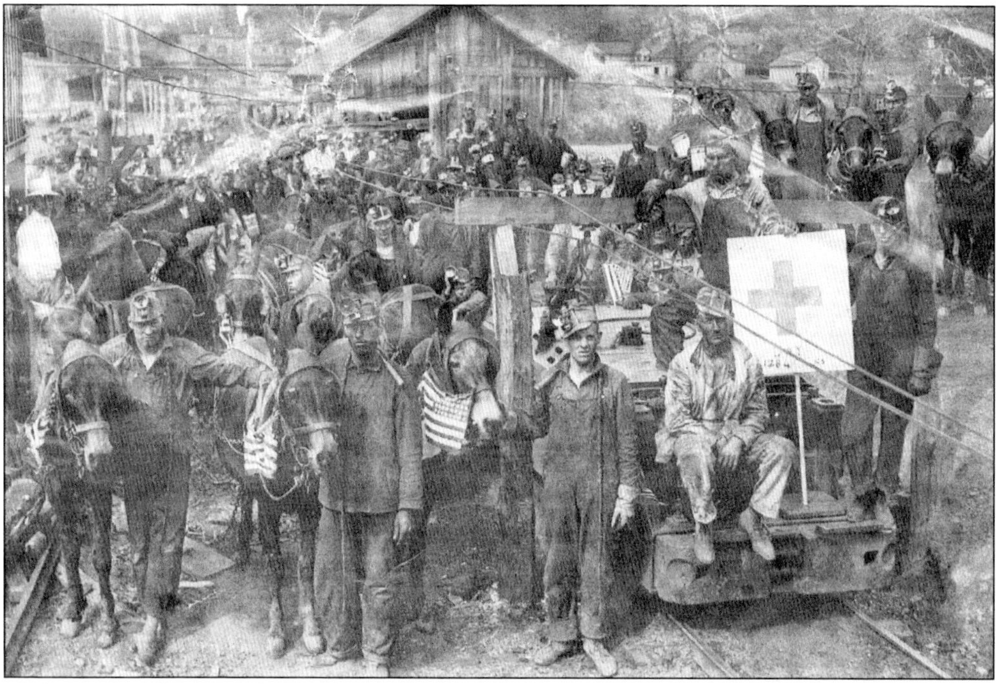

In the spring of 1918, with World War I in full force, the miners at the Bevier Mine of the Rogers Brothers Coal Company donated a full day's work to the war effort. Mine owner J. L. Rogers Sr., in the white suit on the left, gave the coal to the American Red Cross as his contribution to the war effort. (William Raymer.)

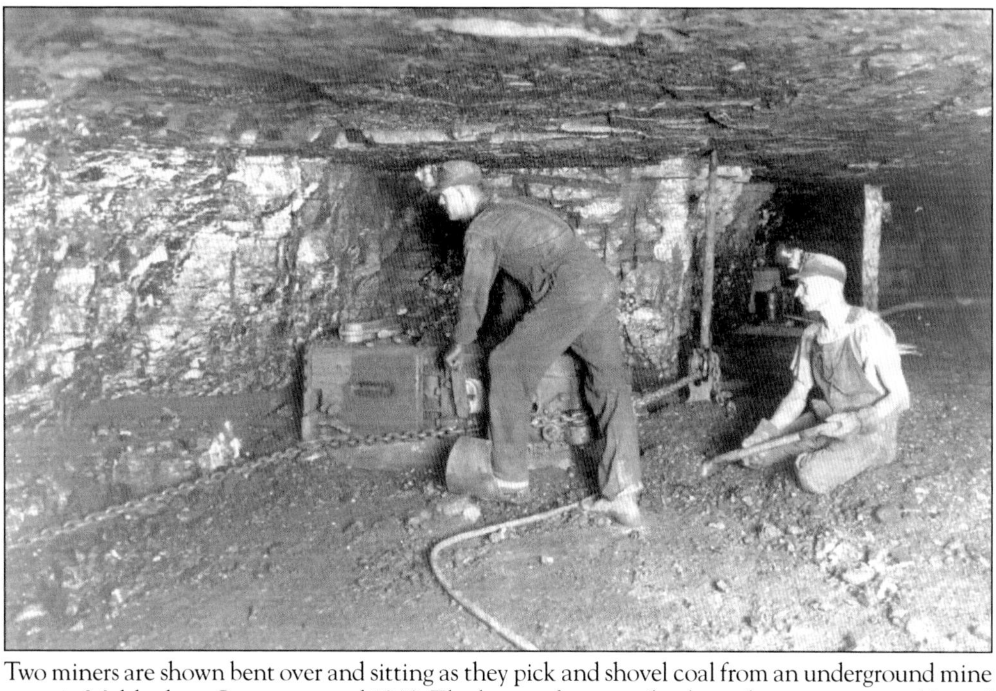

Two miners are shown bent over and sitting as they pick and shovel coal from an underground mine seam in Muhlenberg County around 1940. The low roofs required to keep the mine more stable and to prevent cave-ins caused unending back and leg discomfort for the miners. (William Raymer.)

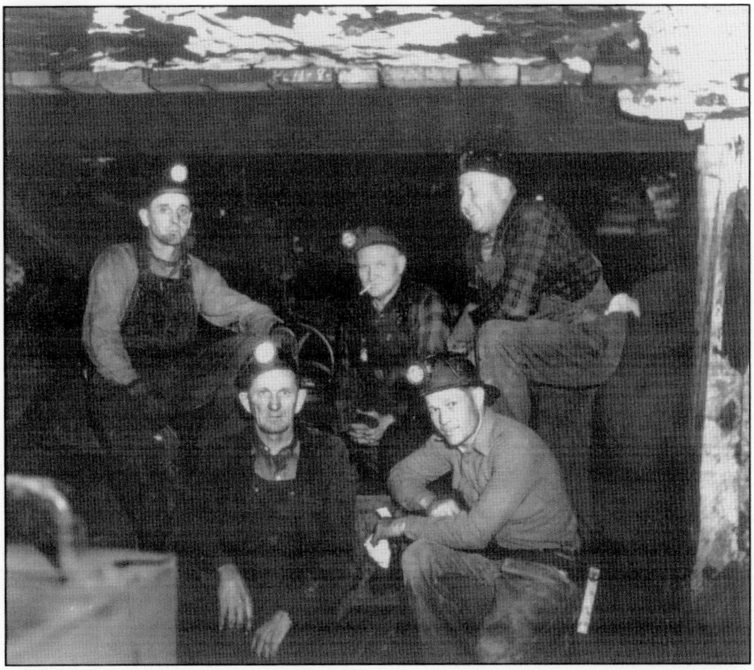

With the dark mouth of the mine waiting to close over them, five miners pause for a moment and glance backwards before starting to work. In the 1960s and 1970s, the county's coal production sometimes reached 20 million tons, making it the number-one coal-producing county in the United States. (William Raymer.)

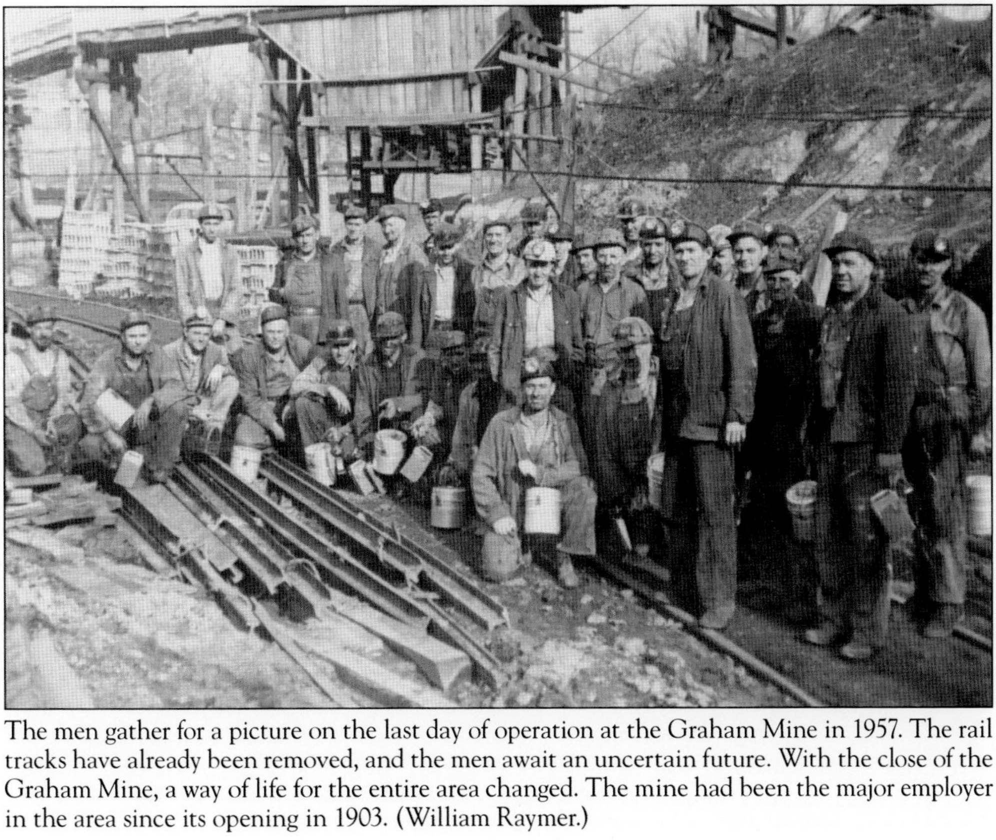

The men gather for a picture on the last day of operation at the Graham Mine in 1957. The rail tracks have already been removed, and the men await an uncertain future. With the close of the Graham Mine, a way of life for the entire area changed. The mine had been the major employer in the area since its opening in 1903. (William Raymer.)

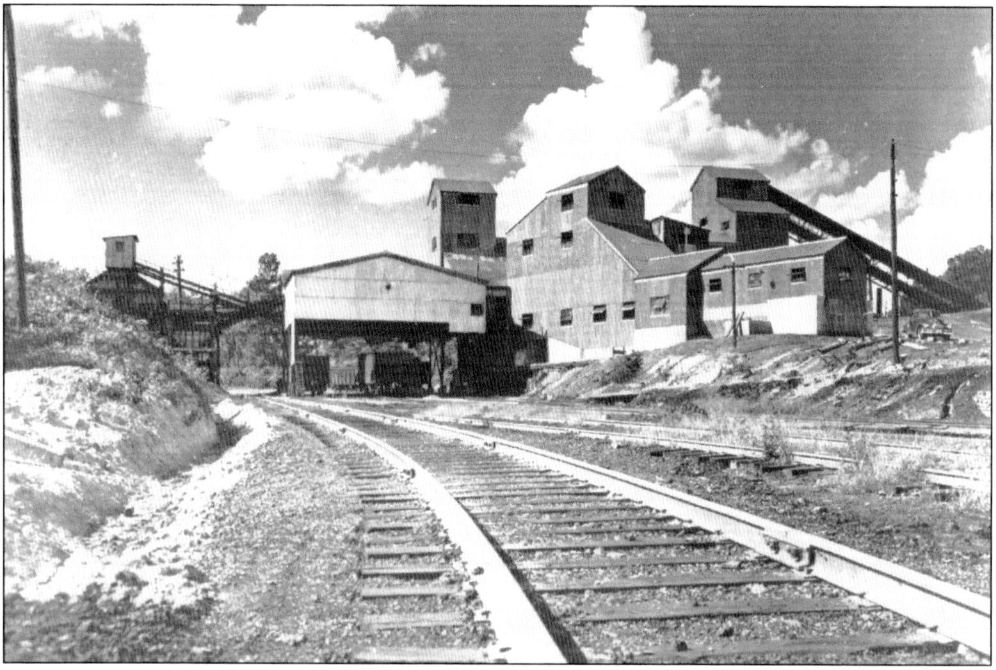

The last Luzerne coal tipple stands alone and lonely beneath a canopy of clouds in 1957. As the demand for coal with lower sulphur content increased, the markets for Western Kentucky coal decreased. Many men who had been coal miners like their fathers and grandfathers before them were now forced to consider other trades and vocations. (William Raymer.)

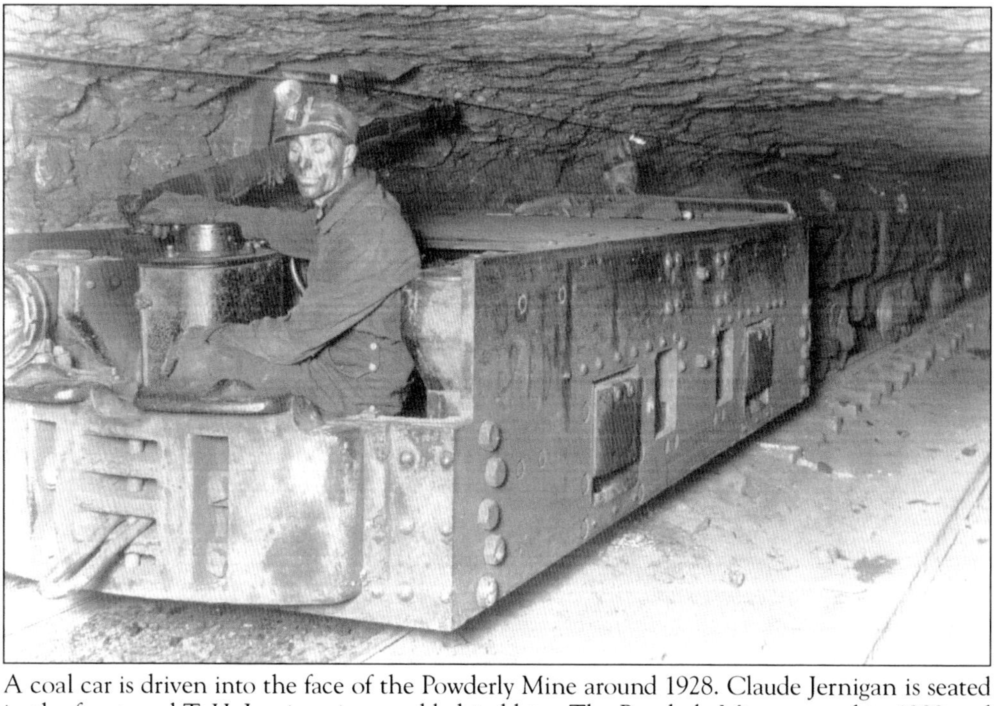

A coal car is driven into the face of the Powderly Mine around 1928. Claude Jernigan is seated in the front, and T. H. Jernigan is seated behind him. The Powderly Mine opened in 1888 and was sold to the Greenville Coal Company in 1890. (William Raymer.)

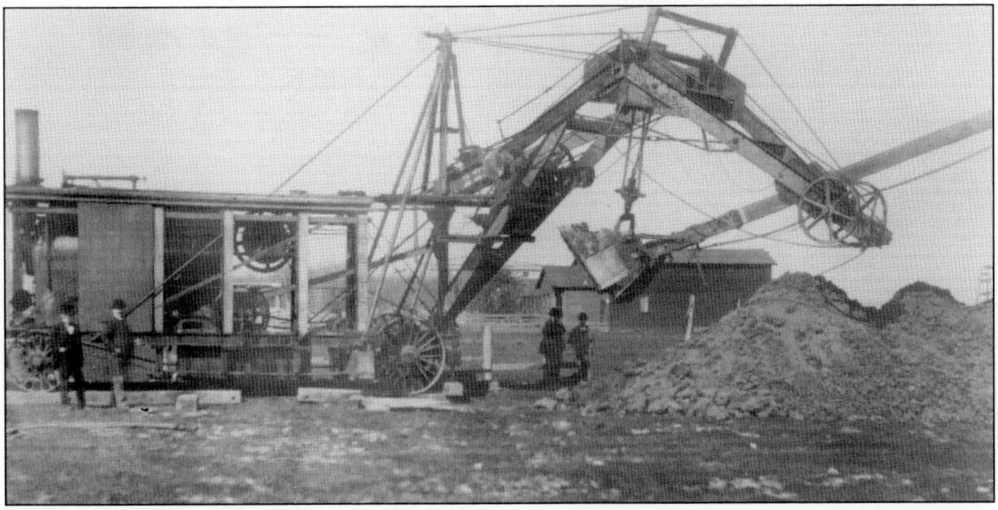

An early stripping machine is shown removing overburden from a coal seam in 1910. From 1890 through 1975, Muhlenberg County was the largest surface producer of coal in Kentucky at 300,987,395 tons. (William Raymer.)

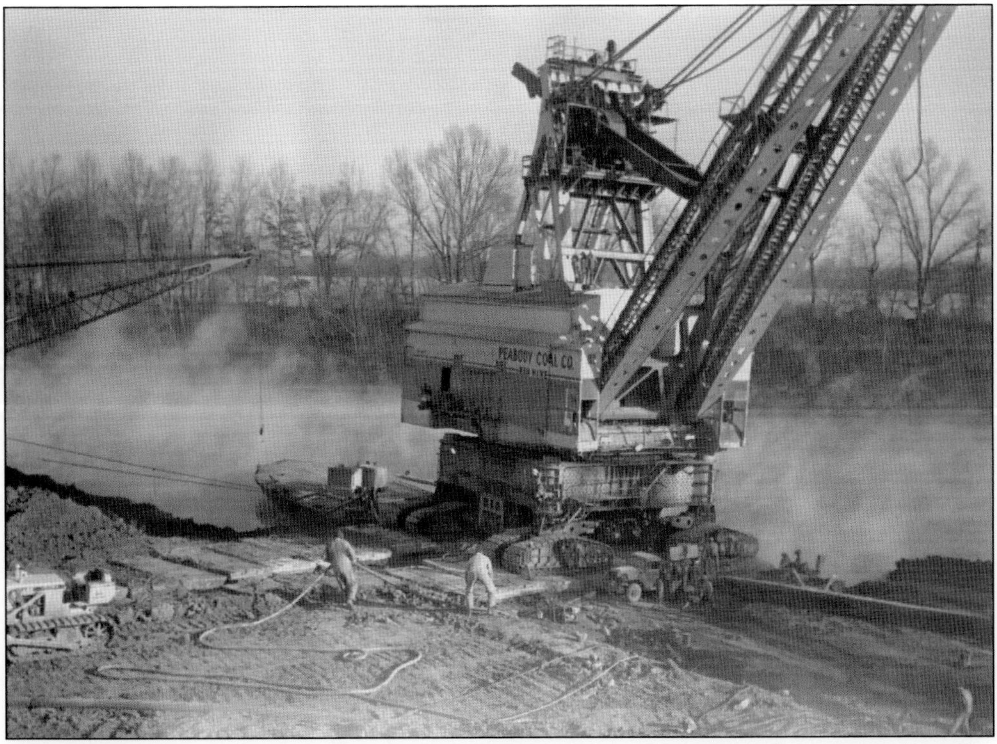

This 1,500-ton shovel was "walking tall" in 1976, when it took three days to crawl 3 miles from Homestead Mine in Ohio County to the Green River. At the river, it was loaded onto an oceangoing barge that took four days to reach the Sinclair Mine at Paradise. This 7-mile journey took the shovel and its entourage 10 days to complete. (William Raymer.)

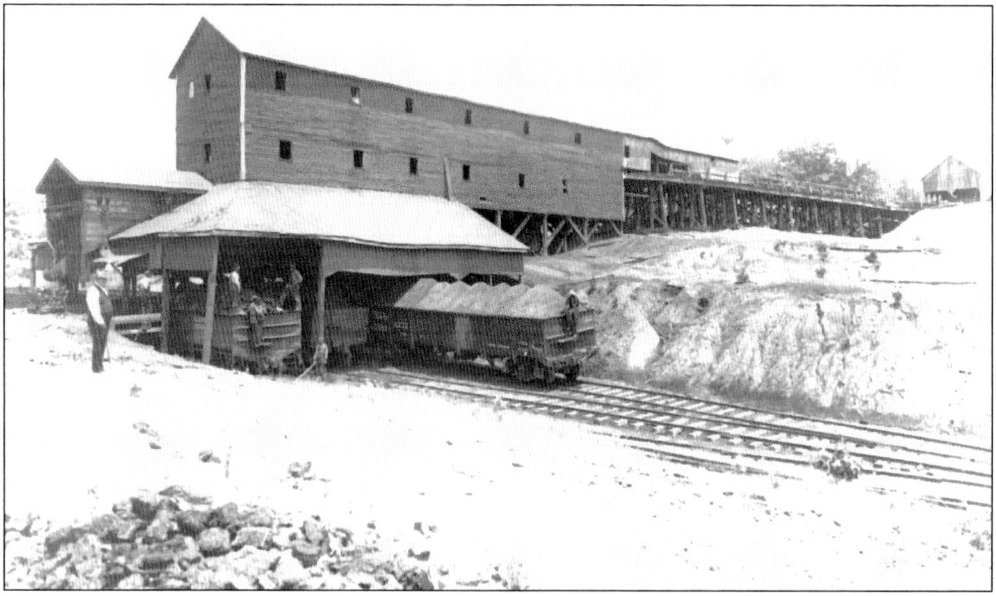

The first coal tipple in Luzerne is pictured around 1927. W. G. Duncan is pictured at left with his cane. The coal tipples, where raw coal was cleaned and sorted, were located near the mines. The coal ran over various-size screens with graduated openings from small to large. The different sizes of coal fell through the openings and were stored and loaded separately. (William Raymer.)

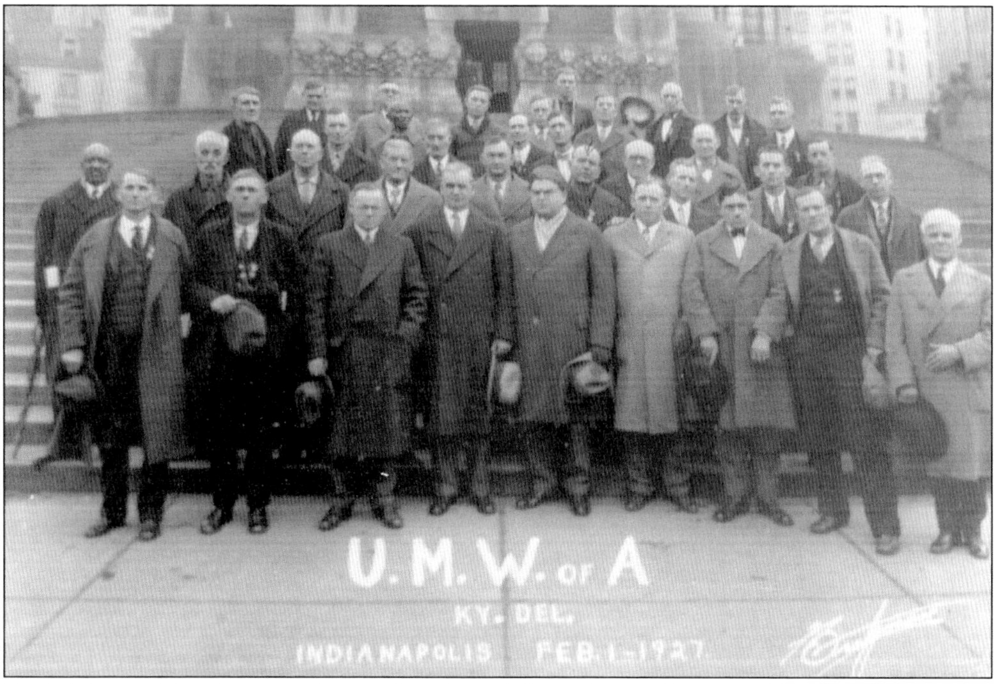

D. C. Morris of Graham stands directly behind John L. Lewis (first row, fifth from left) in this 1927 picture taken of the United Mine Workers of America (UMWA) meeting in Indianapolis. Morris was the first president of Local Union 1630 at the Luzerne Mine of the W. G. Duncan Coal Company. John L. Lewis, who organized the UMWA, used the nation's dependence on coal to improve the wages, benefits, and safety of miners. (William Raymer.)

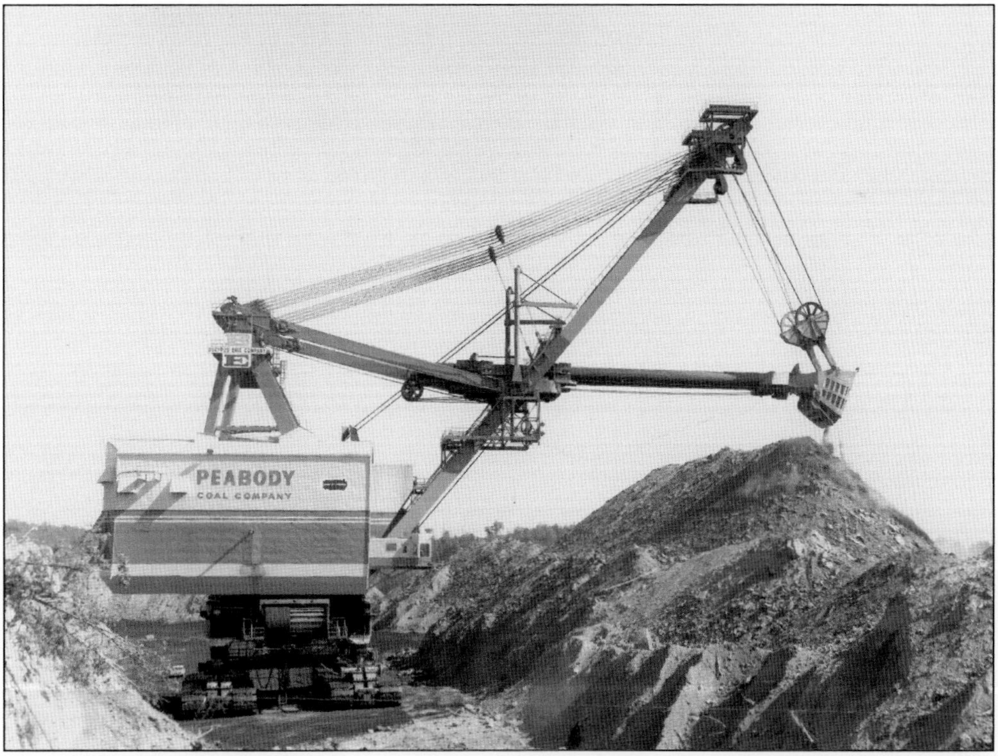

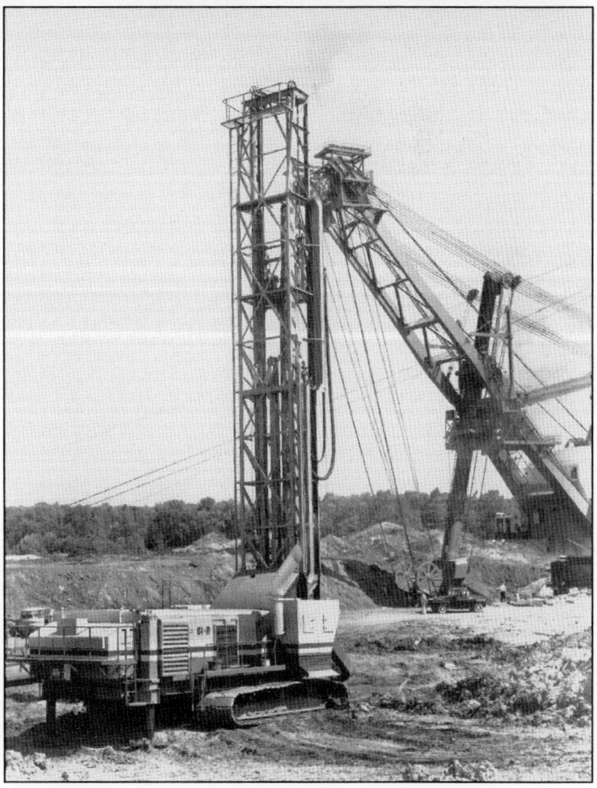

The largest stripping shovel in the world was put into service at Peabody's Sinclair Mine at Paradise in 1962. The operator's cab was five stories above ground and air-conditioned. With two hand controls and two foot pedals, the operator could accelerate a 200-ton dipper load of earth from 0 to 25 miles per hour in eight seconds and decelerate from top speed to stop in four seconds. The shovel stood 220 feet tall, 90 feet higher than the Statue of Liberty. It weighed 18 million pounds, scooped up 200 tons of rock and dirt per bite, and had 12,000 horsepower. The shovel's incoming voltage was 7,200 volts, and it removed 36 million cubic yards of earth annually. The Bucyrus-Erie drill at right could drill a 15-inch-diameter hole 150 feet deep through solid rock in 15 minutes. (William Raymer.)

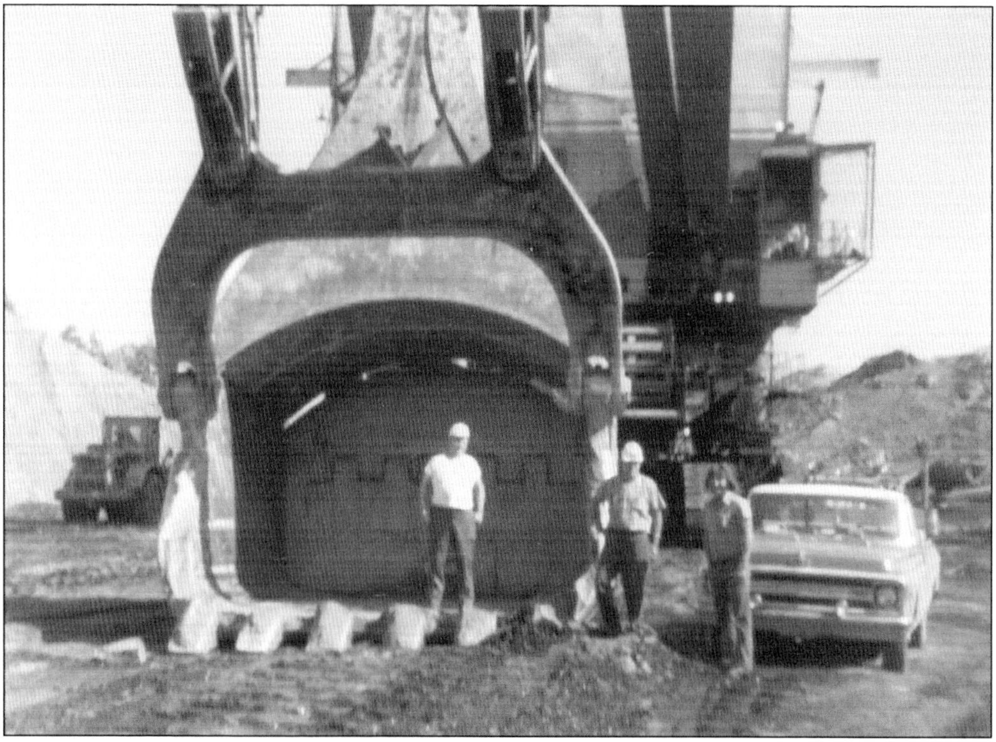

Bob Talley, standing in the bucket of the 5761 shovel at the Ayrgem Mine around 1970, looks to be lost in the kingdom of the giants. The large shovels like this one that arrived on the mining scene enabled the miners to increase their coal production to keep up with the fuel demands of an ever-increasingly industrialized world. Also shown in the picture are W. L. Raymer (center) and Terry Peterson (right). (William Raymer.)

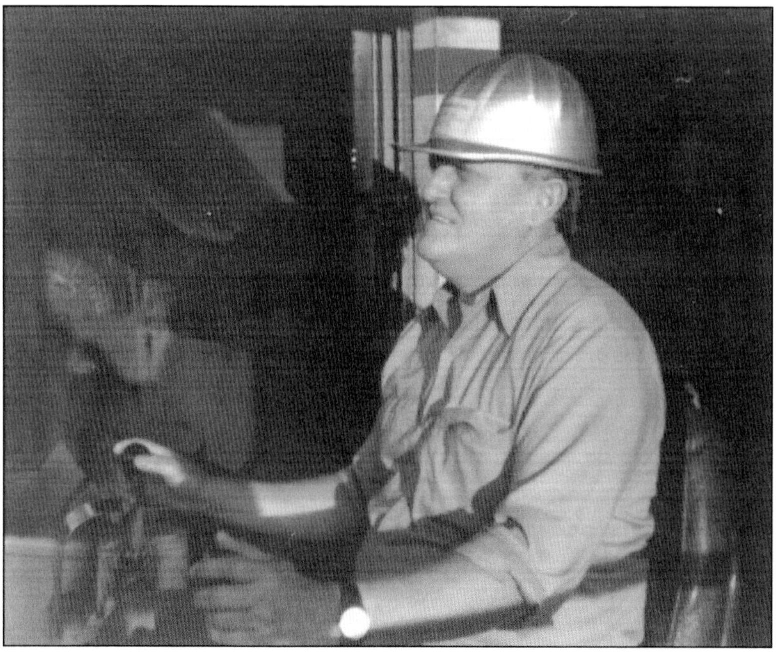

Following in his father's footsteps, William Raymer Jr. was a career coal miner. At right, he is shown operating the 5761 stripping shovel at Ayrgem Mine. His 45 years of mining were completed in 1993. (William Raymer.)

Nine

ARTS, MUSIC, AND ENTERTAINMENT

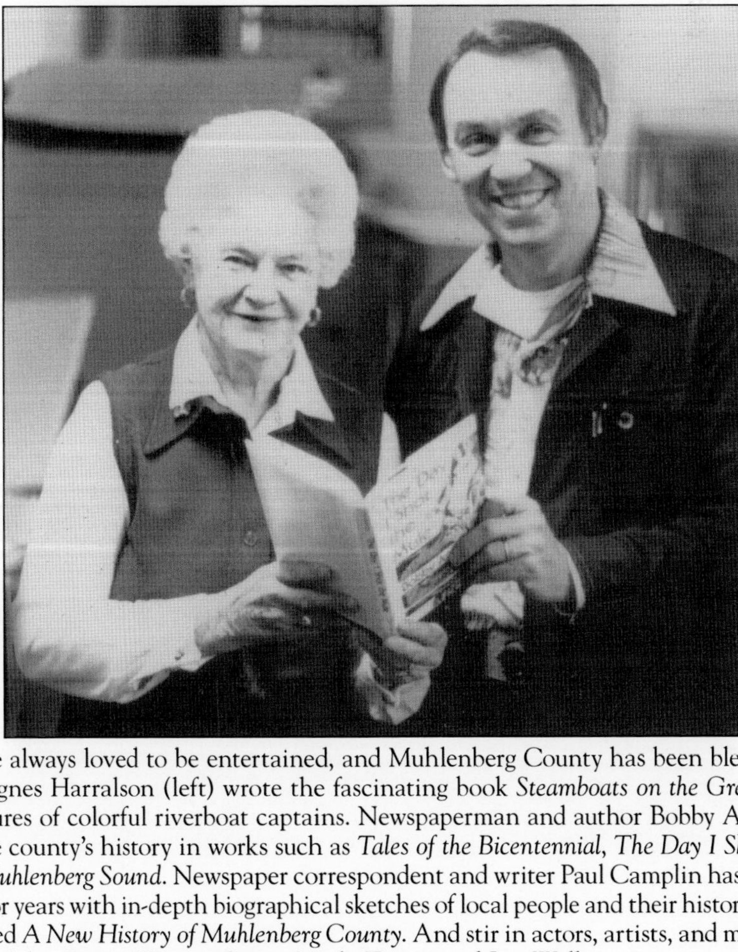

People have always loved to be entertained, and Muhlenberg County has been blessed to have the best. Agnes Harralson (left) wrote the fascinating book *Steamboats on the Green* detailing the adventures of colorful riverboat captains. Newspaperman and author Bobby Anderson has detailed the county's history in works such as *Tales of the Bicentennial*, *The Day I Shot the Mule*, and *That Muhlenberg Sound*. Newspaper correspondent and writer Paul Camplin has entertained audiences for years with in-depth biographical sketches of local people and their histories. Camplin also authored *A New History of Muhlenberg County*. And stir in actors, artists, and musicians like the Everlys, John Prine, Warren Oates, Merle Travis, and Jim Walker to sweeten the pot. The final result is unparalleled entertainment. (Christine Hinsey.)

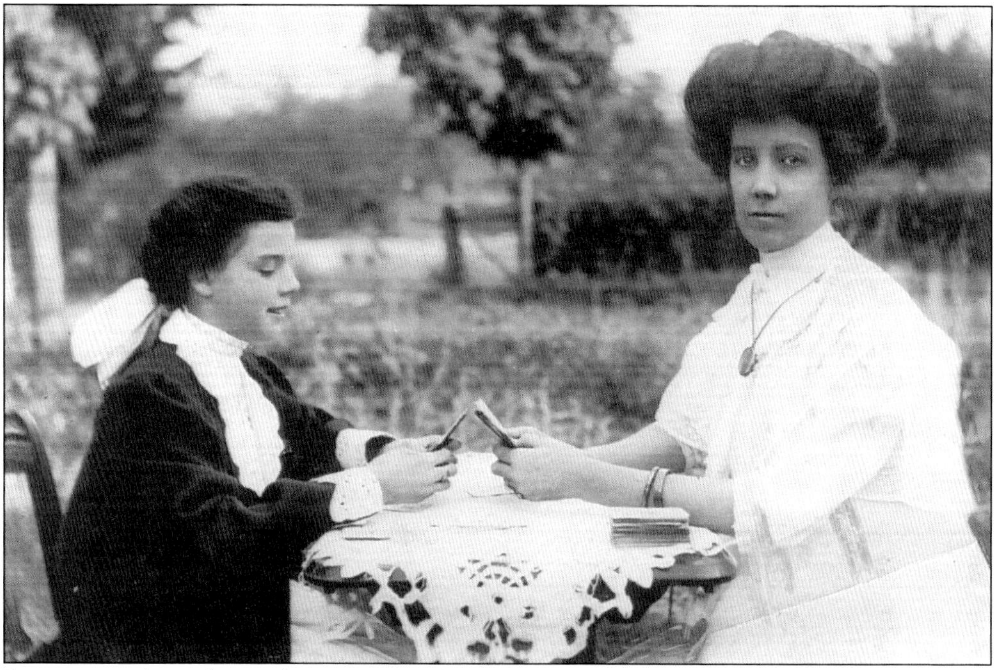

Entertaining themselves with a game of cards on a beautiful summer afternoon in South Carrollton in 1930 are Bessie (Ferguson) Gaynor and her daughter, Winifred. Bessie's husband was a professor at the South Carrollton College, and she was a sister of Dr. Jo Ferguson. (Molly Alward.)

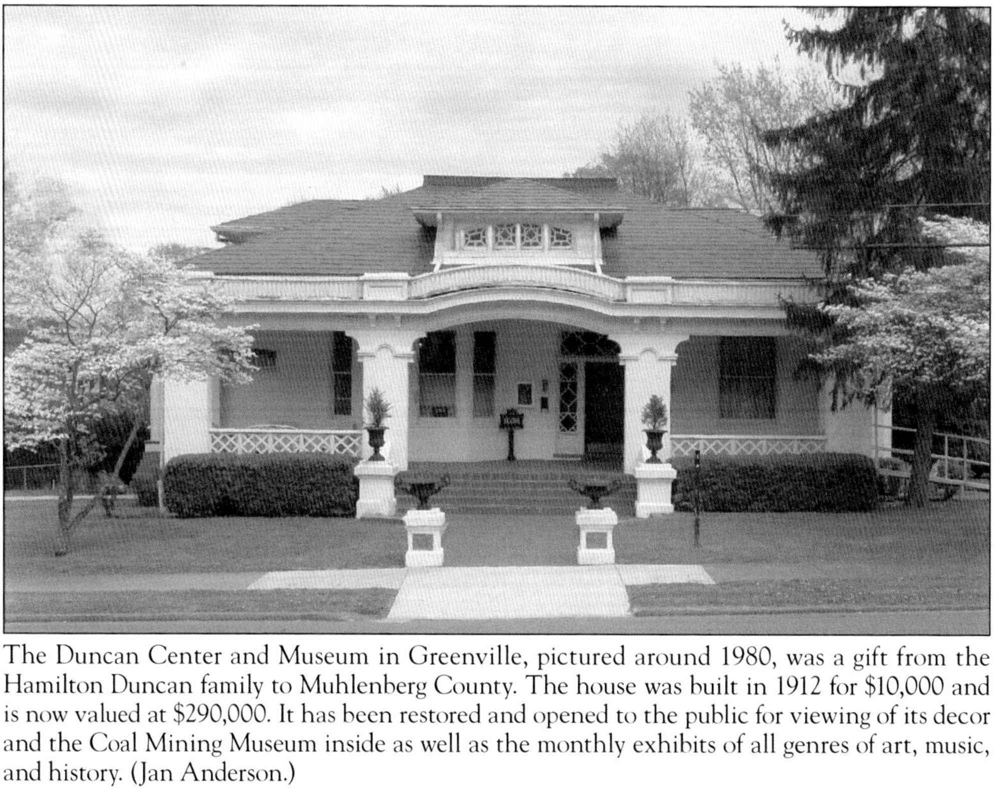

The Duncan Center and Museum in Greenville, pictured around 1980, was a gift from the Hamilton Duncan family to Muhlenberg County. The house was built in 1912 for $10,000 and is now valued at $290,000. It has been restored and opened to the public for viewing of its decor and the Coal Mining Museum inside as well as the monthly exhibits of all genres of art, music, and history. (Jan Anderson.)

J. E. Wood, the master of ceremonies for Muhlenberg County's sesquicentennial festivities, honors 104-year-old Columbus Martin for being the oldest citizen in the county in 1948. Christopher Columbus Martin was born into slavery in 1844 and died at the age of 112 in 1956. He endeared himself to everyone with his fiddle playing and folk songs. (Christine Hinsey.)

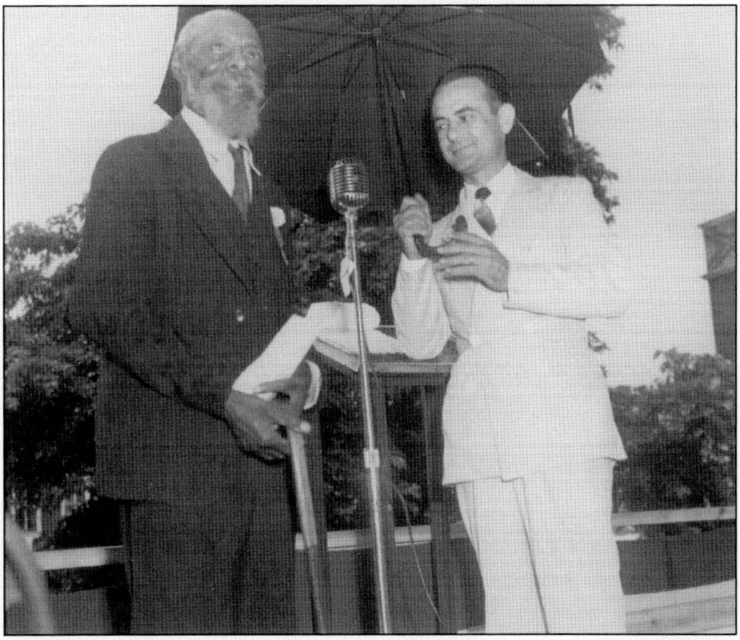

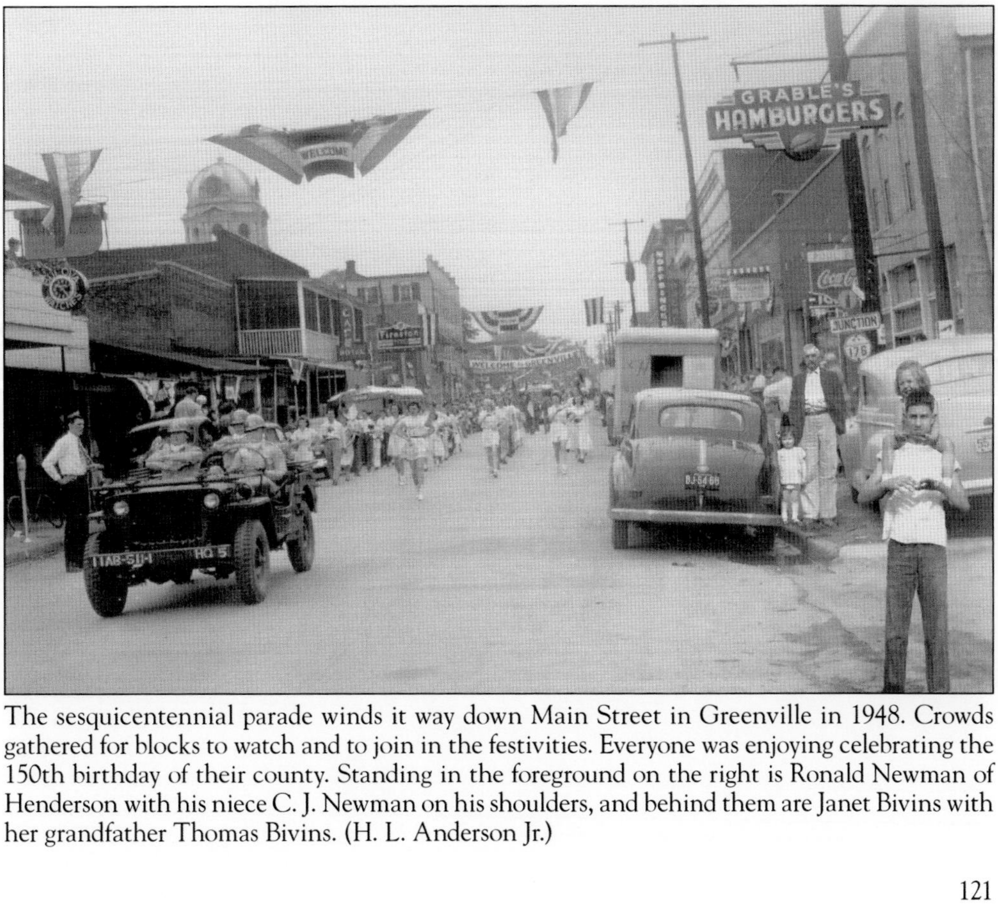

The sesquicentennial parade winds it way down Main Street in Greenville in 1948. Crowds gathered for blocks to watch and to join in the festivities. Everyone was enjoying celebrating the 150th birthday of their county. Standing in the foreground on the right is Ronald Newman of Henderson with his niece C. J. Newman on his shoulders, and behind them are Janet Bivins with her grandfather Thomas Bivins. (H. L. Anderson Jr.)

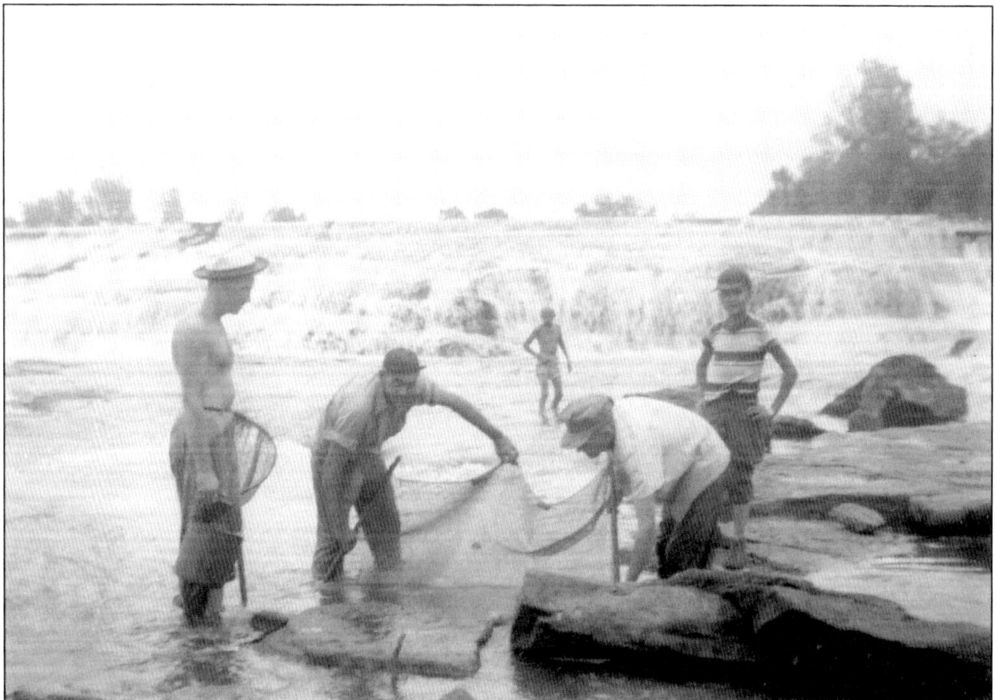

Enjoying net fishing below the Rochester Dam in 1956 are, from left to right, James T. Hale, R. E. Bivins, Bert Devine, and Kenneth Bivins. The person in the background is unidentified. General Buckner planned to blow up the dam on Green River during the Civil War, but Silas Brewer, a local merchant, convinced him to fill the lock with logs, depriving the enemy boats of navigational use. Buckner agreed, and the dam stood undamaged and useful for years. (Jan Anderson.)

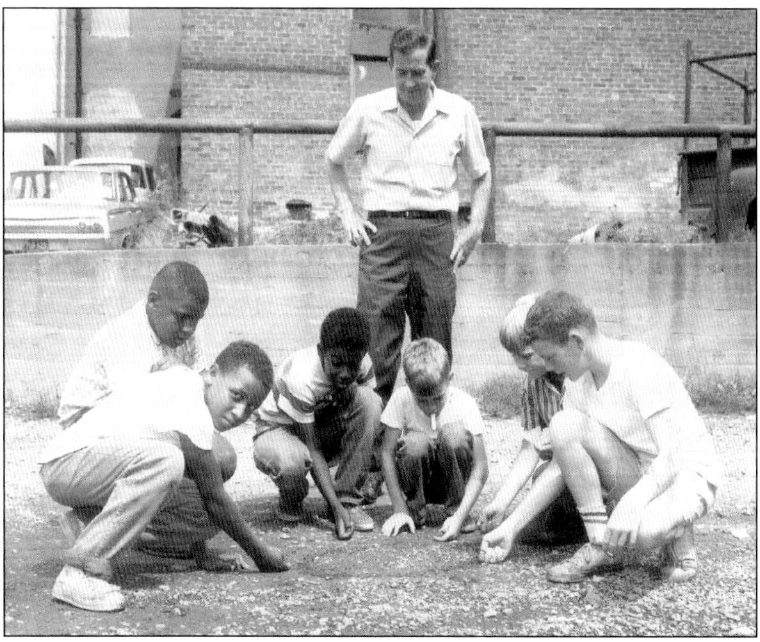

Muhlenberg County's 1931 national marble champion Johnny Jeffries instructs a group of local boys in some shooting techniques before the big game in 1960. The boys are, from left to right, James Shelton, James Hurt, Larry Boyd, Hugh Campbell, Mike Mulligan, and Wallace Landford. (Christine Hinsey.)

Merle Travis, a Rosewood native, shares the stage in Muhlenberg County with two star-struck fans and cowboy legend Gene Autry around 1957. Merle's father was a coal miner who inspired him to write the songs *Sixteen Tons* and *Dark as a Dungeon*, which revealed the exploitation of early coal miners. Merle was known for his guitar playing, which was inspired by Drakesboro's Kennedy Jones and Mose Rager. (Mark Stone.)

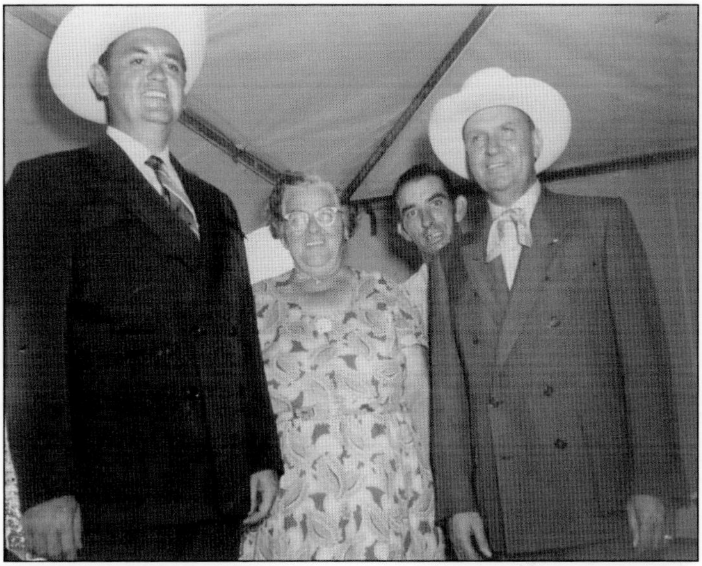

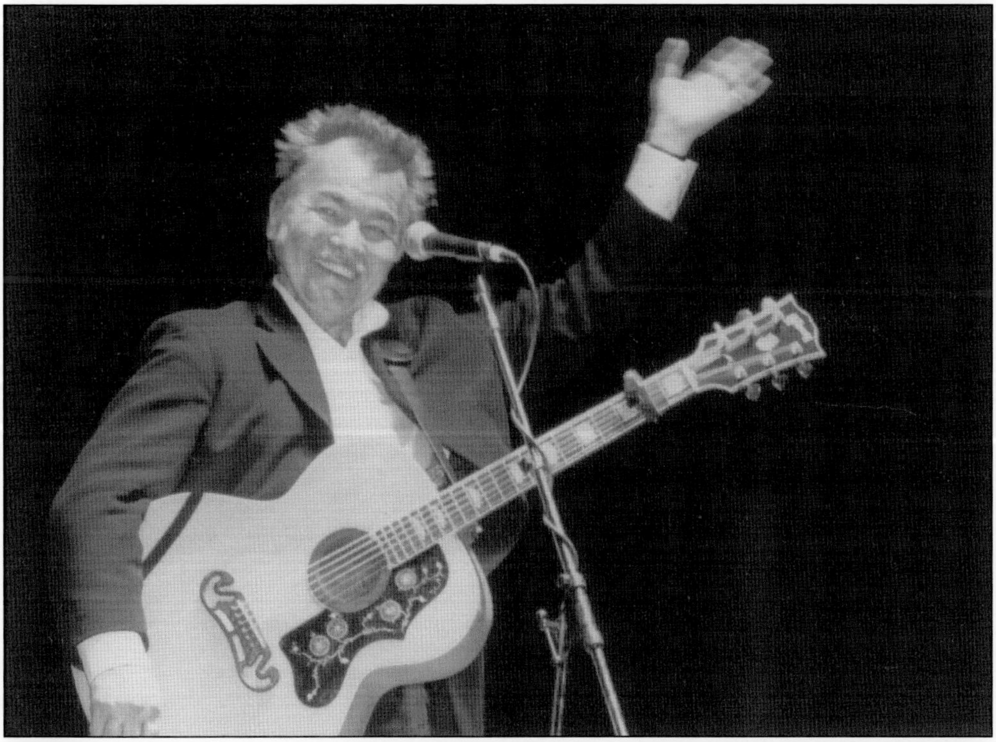

John Prine started playing the guitar at 14 but worked as a postman and joined the army before his career blossomed. His parents were Muhlenberg County natives and one of his famous songs, *Paradise*, in 1971 blamed the Peabody Coal Company for the demise of the town of Paradise. The line "Mr. Peabody's coal train done hauled it away" refers to the town's disappearance due to industrial demands. (Joe Ben Tucker.)

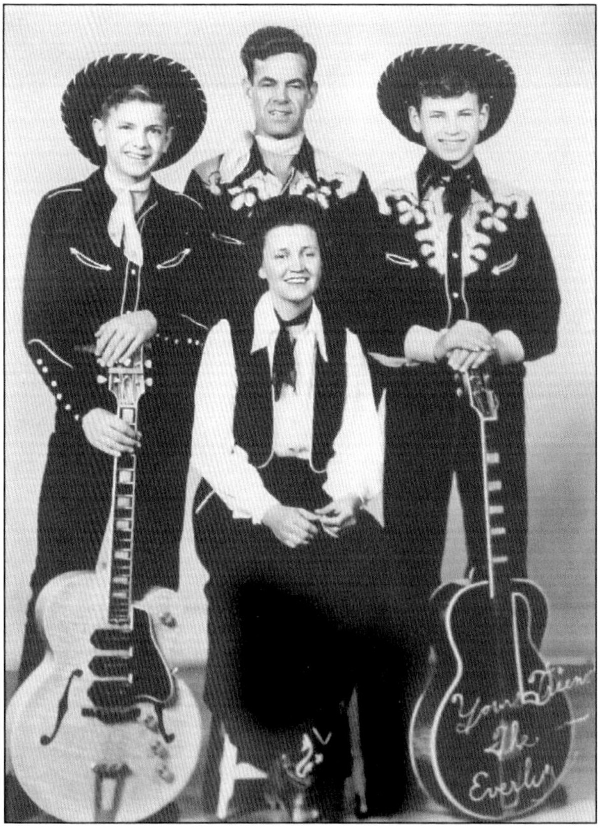

At left, the Everly family poses for a studio picture in the 1940s. Margaret is in front. Behind her are, from left to right, Phil, Ike, and Don. Don was born in the little town of Brownie near Drakesboro. Phil was born just a little later in the big town of Chicago. Ike had left work in the coal mines to try to make a living playing his music. Ike hated the mines and did not want his boys to end up there, so as they grew, he taught them to harmonize and play the guitar. The entire family began playing on radio shows to make money. On their visits to the county, they would sit on their grandparents' porch and play and sing for family and neighbors. Then they would go to the grocery store in Cleaton and play and sing for the miners. They made 50¢ for their efforts. The family moved to Nashville and got some breaks that eventually launched their career. Below, Phil (left) and Don (middle) are pictured with friend John Berry around 1980. (Tucker family.)

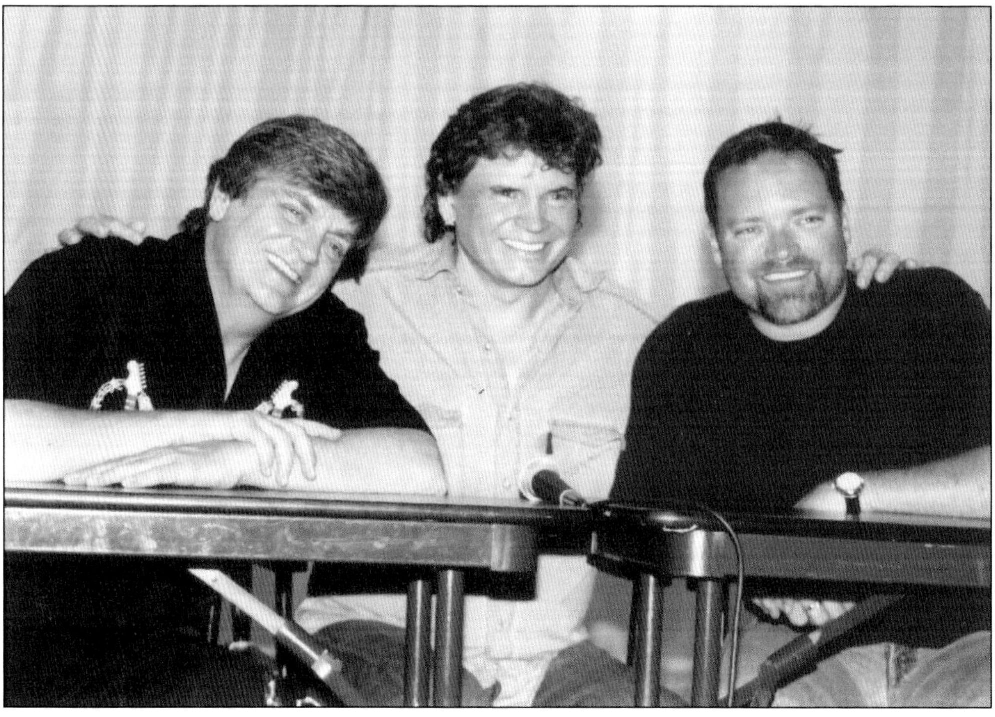

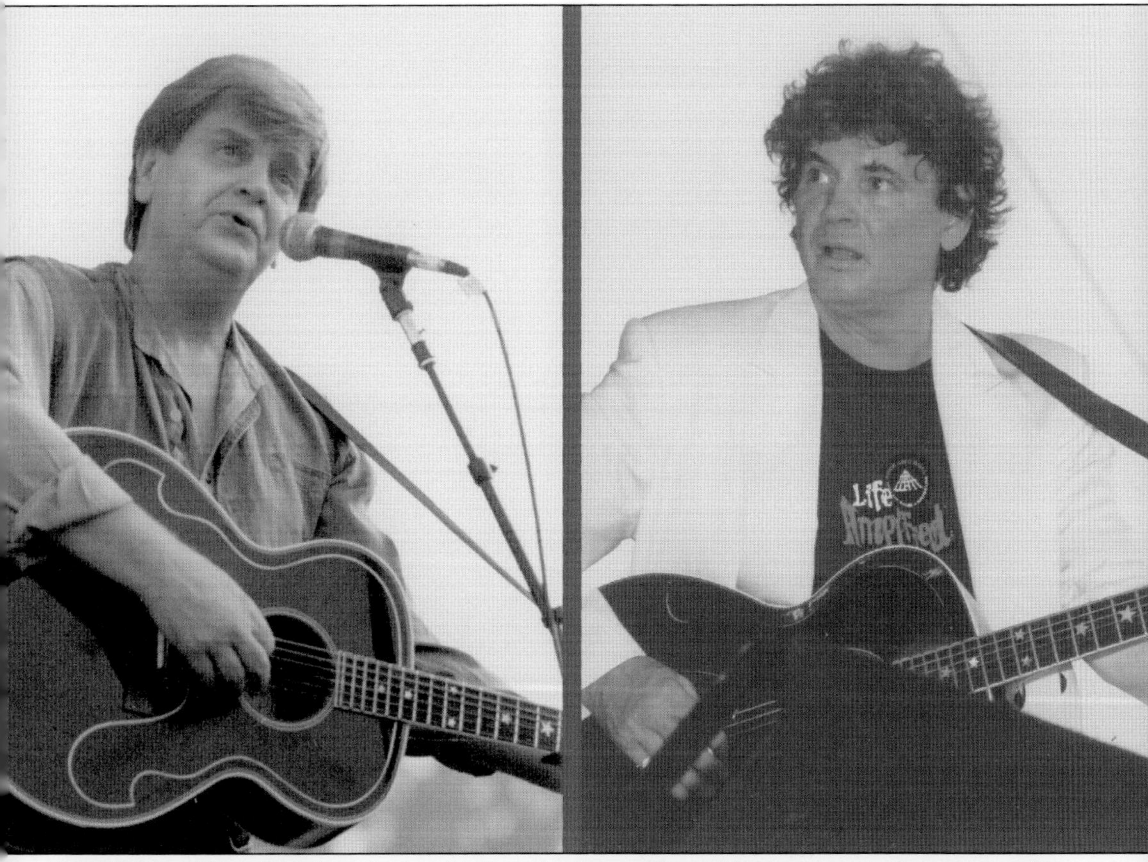

Phil (left) and Don (right) credit their hit *Bye, Bye Love* with establishing them in the music world in 1957. It had been rejected by 30 singers before they got their chance at it. The song shot to No. 1 on the country charts, crossed over to reach No. 2 on the pop charts, and then went to No. 5 on the rhythm and blues charts. That hit was followed by *Wake Up Little Susie* and *Dream*. The songwriting team of Felice and Boudleaux Bryant kept the songs coming for the Everlys. From 1957 through 1959, they had six top-10 songs on the country charts. Almost all of their singles sold over a million copies each. The Everly Brothers' unique talent and harmony have been cited by groups like the Beatles and the Rolling Stones for influencing their styles and sound. The two little boys with their roots deep in Muhlenberg County have made music that is heard and sung around the world. They were inducted into the Rock and Roll Hall of Fame in 1986. They are pictured here around 1980. (Joe Ben Tucker.)

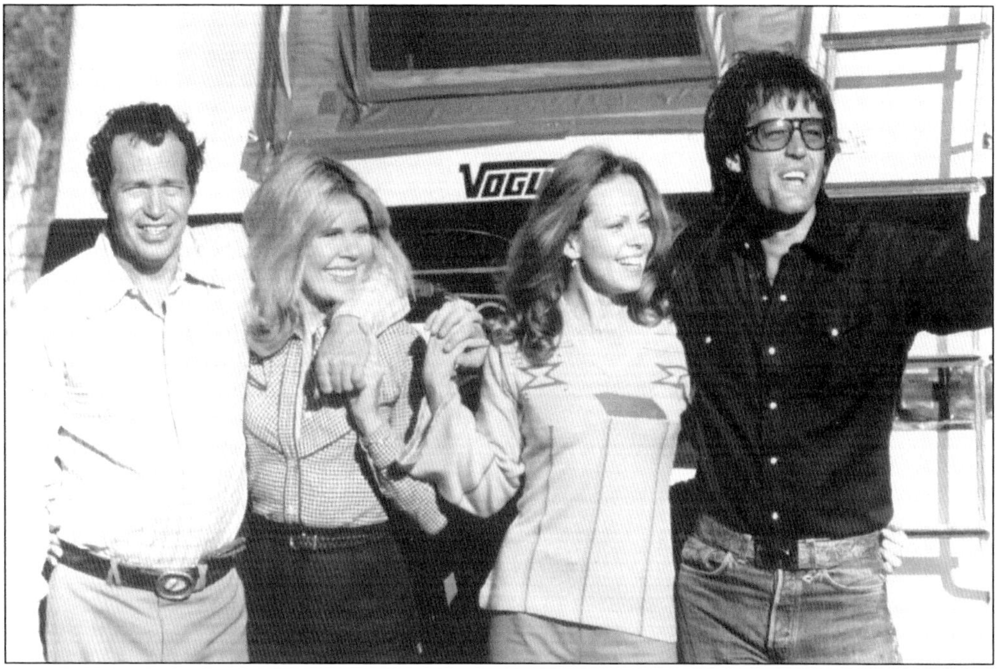

Warren Oates (1928–1967) was born in the town of Depoy, where his parents Sarah and Bayless owned a general store. He moved to Louisville and served in the marines before he began his acting career. His first starring role came with *In the Heat of the Night* in 1967. From left to right are Warren Oates, Loretta Swit, unidentified, and Peter Fonda around 1971. (Duncan Center.)

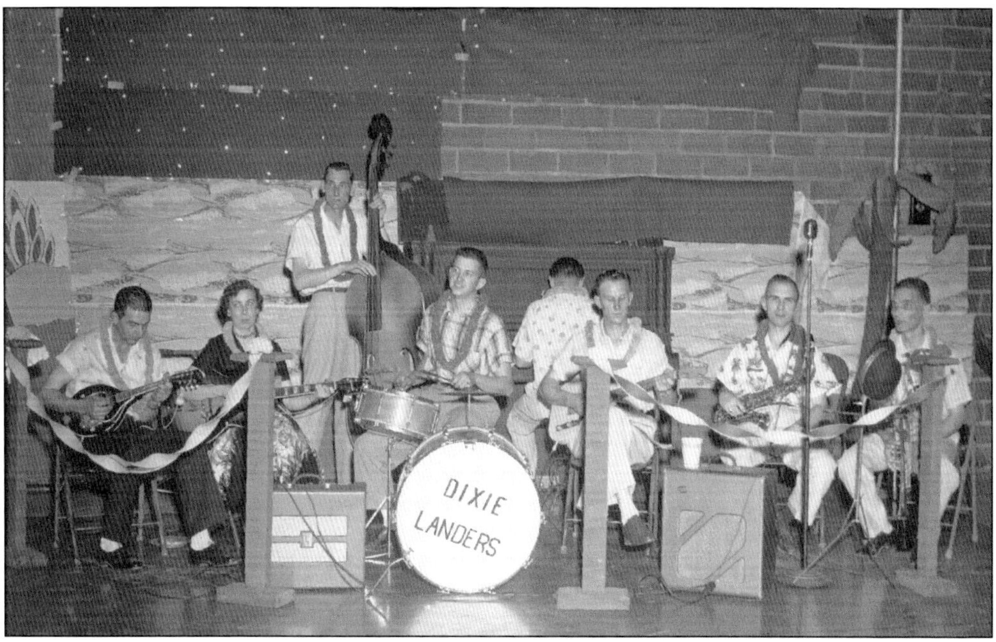

The Dixie Landers entertain a Muhlenberg crowd in 1960. The popular band was formed for fun and entertainment by Dr. William Bippus. From left to right are Wilson Parham, Imogene Parham, Charles Bethel, Harold Tudor, Marvin Davis, William Cornette, and Dr. Bippus, and on piano is Wilbur Buchanan. (Muhlenberg County Library Archives.)

Robert (Bob) Walker's band, the Four Sharps, play at an engagement in Central City in 1960. Bob (front center) was the band director at Central City High School until his retirement and is revered for instilling the knowledge and love of music in many students. (Jim Walker.)

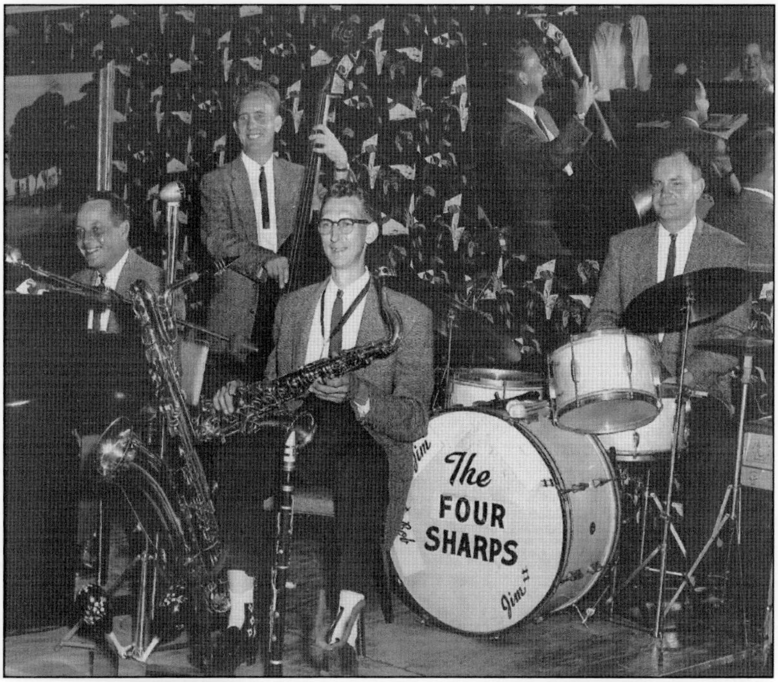

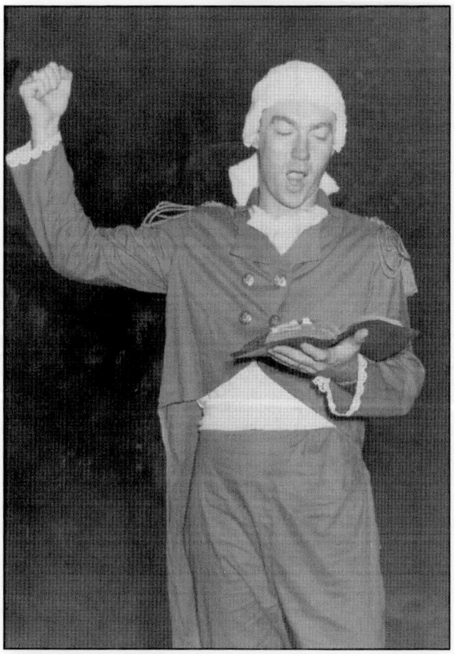

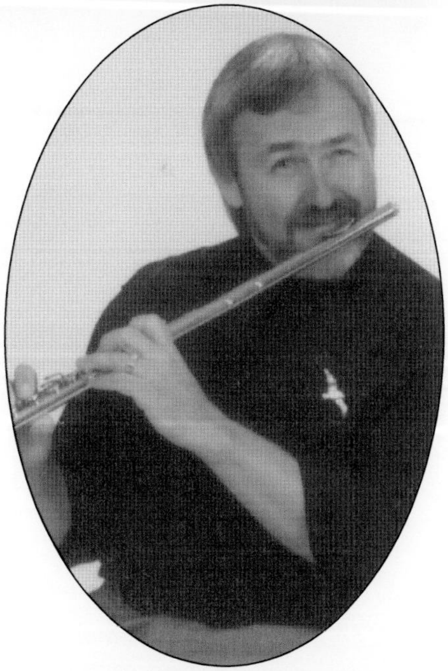

Above left, Ed Henry, a prominent Central City citizen and co-owner of Henry-Cisney Chevrolet, portrayed Gen. Peter Muhlenberg in the 1948–1949 county sesquicentennial celebration. Henry's portrayal paid tribute to the man for whom the county was named. Jim Walker (above right), the son of Robert and Barbara Walker, is a flutist who served as principal flute of the Los Angeles Philharmonic and founded a popular jazz quartet Free Flight. Jim's flute can be heard on movie soundtracks including *A Beautiful Mind*, *Memoirs of a Geisha*, *Ice Age*, *Titanic*, *Monsters Inc.*, *Far and Away*, and many others. (Left, Christine Hinsey; right, Jan Anderson.)

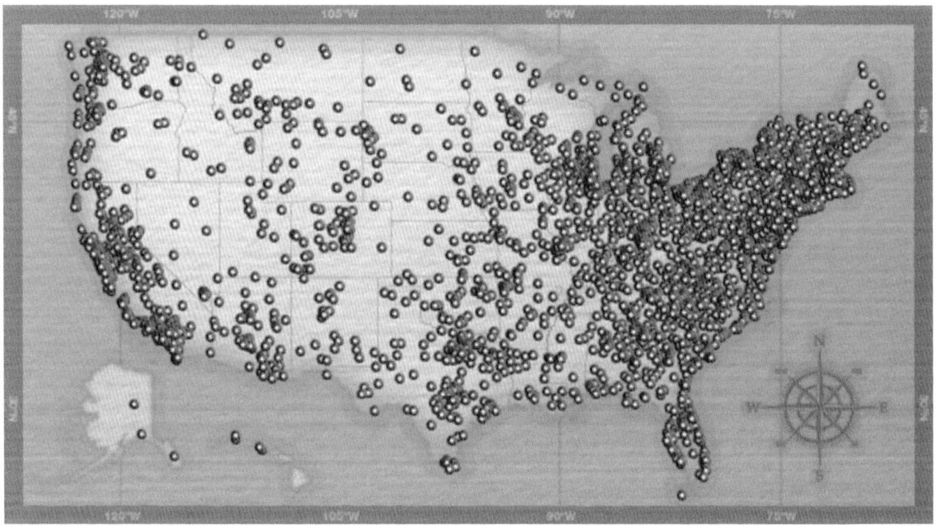